UNDERSTANDING TEACHING AND LEARNING

ST ANDREWS STUDIES
IN PHILOSOPHY AND PUBLIC AFFAIRS

Founding and General Editor:
John Haldane, University of St Andrews

Values, Education and the Human World
edited by John Haldane

Philosophy and its Public Role
edited by William Aiken and John Haldane

Relativism and the Foundations of Liberalism
by Graham Long

Human Life, Action and Ethics:
Essays by G.E.M. Anscombe
edited by Mary Geach and Luke Gormally

The Institution of Intellectual Values:
Realism and Idealism in Higher Education
by Gordon Graham

Life, Liberty and the Pursuit of Utility
by Anthony Kenny and Charles Kenny

Distributing Healthcare:
Principles, Practices and Politics
edited by Niall Maclean

Liberalism, Education and Schooling:
Essays by T.M. Mclaughlin
edited by David Carr, Mark Halstead and Richard Pring

The Landscape of Humanity: Art, Culture & Society
by Anthony O'Hear

Faith in a Hard Ground:
Essays on Religion, Philosophy and Ethics by G.E.M. Anscombe
edited by Mary Geach and Luke Gormally

Subjectivity and Being Somebody
by Grant Gillett

Understanding Faith:
Religious Belief and Its Place in Society
by Stephen R.L. Clark

Rethinking Business Management
edited by Samuel Gregg and James Stoner

Understanding Teaching & Learning

**Classic Texts on Education by
Augustine, Aquinas, Newman and Mill**

Edited by

T. Brian Mooney & Mark Nowacki

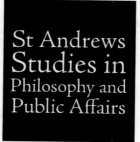

St Andrews
Studies in
Philosophy and
Public Affairs

IMPRINT ACADEMIC

Published in the UK by Imprint Academic
PO Box 200, Exeter EX5 5YX, UK

Published in the USA by Imprint Academic
Philosophy Documentation Center
PO Box 7147, Charlottesville, VA 22906-7147, USA

ISBN 9781845402419 (hbk)
ISBN 9781845402426 (pbk)

A CIP catalogue record for this book is available from the
British Library and US Library of Congress

Cover Photograph:
St Salvator's Quadrangle, St Andrews by Peter Adamson
from the University of St Andrews collection

Contents

Acknowledgments

Writing a book, even an edited one, takes its toll. As a result we would like to acknowledge the loving support of our families: Pat, Fionnuala, Thomas, Chuen, Dodge, Tippy, Callie, and Plato, who over the last year have put up with absentee fathers and husbands.

One of the great benefits of working at Singapore Management University is that we are supported in our research with funding for Research Assistants. We are grateful to Brian Sng who helped in the editing of the selections from John Henry Newman's *The Idea of a University* and John Stuart Mill's *Inaugural Address*. We are particularly grateful to Jared Poon for insightful and excellent editorial assistance with the text of Aquinas' *De Magistro*. We also would like to thank LogicMills for supporting Jared in his efforts. We thank Steven Burik who provided invaluable support in reading and editing the entire text.

We also thank John Haldane, Anthony Freeman, John Williams, Kirpal Singh, and the Wee Kim Wee Centre at the Singapore Management University. Without their encouragement and support this book may not have seen the light of day.

T. Brian Mooney
Mark Nowacki

Prologue

This book brings together four classic visions of the nature of liberal education and its perennial value. Augustine, the first of our authors, is temporally separated from Aquinas by 800 years, and Aquinas in turn is separated from the Victorian writers, Newman and Mill, by a further 600 years. Each author responds to issues in education particular to the historical and material conditions of his own time. Nonetheless, and despite major differences in their views, they are all united in the conviction that a good liberal education requires a mutually enriching relationship between teacher and student in which the teacher draws out the latent powers of the learner so that the learner is transformed as a person. Each of our four authors is united in the idea that the philosophy and practice of education is centrally related to persons, and thus they reflect deeply on the ways in which education can play a formative role in the self-transcendence of both teacher and pupil. The aim of this book is to re-present the four authors—Augustine, Aquinas, Newman and Mill—for contemporary readers in an accessible comparative format.

The title of our book is deliberately ambiguous, for we wish to take up issues dealing with how teaching, learning, and understanding mutually illuminate and constrain one another. In Chapter 1 we give an overview of some pivotal questions in the philosophy and practice of education. We concentrate on a fairly uncontroversial, common-sense encapsulation of what typically occurs in the teaching and learning context. We unpack a series of issues by dissecting the proposition 'X teaches Y to Z', using the conceptual tools of the analytic philosophy of education. The chapter is intended to act as a bridge between the sorts of issues, and manners of speaking about them, familiar to contemporary educationalists, and the ideas expressed by our four authors. Although the content of Chapter 1 represents the views and experiences of the editors of this book, it provides a useful framework for comparing and contrasting the works of Augustine, Aquinas, Newman and Mill, as well as insights into how the issues under discussion are applicable in contemporary educational contexts. We hope to move beyond those domains within the educational landscape that seem to be bogged down in interminable debates, thereby bringing out in a clear way where we all agree, and where we may choose to disagree, concerning what makes for good teaching, good learning, and successful understanding. It is our practice to do so without employing the conceptually loaded jargon that has come to characterise much recent writing on educational theory and practice. We focus on what is concretely done and what is concretely accomplished by teacher and pupil before drawing out the theoretical dimensions latent within practice. Thus our work occupies an intermediate position between pure theory and pure practice. It is our hope — and, we think, a distinctive contribution of this work — that we help readers move from theory to appropriate practices and also to find within practices the traces of pure theory.

When we explore the various dimensions of 'X teaches Y to Z', we find it useful to introduce a distinction concerning three different but mutually interpenetrating forms of knowing: know-that, know-how, and know-why. These three can be shown to be the hidden inspirations behind many apparently diverse educational models. So, both theoretically and in practice, understanding the sorts of knowing to be achieved in a given context will impact the range of potentially successful pedagogical practices and learning strategies. Moreover, we think that distinguishing and identifying these forms of knowing will help our readers to understand the unifying themes within our four authors.

Chapters 2 through 5 are arranged according to the same pattern. Each of our authors' texts is preceded by an introduction that provides brief biographical sketches as well as some context to the educational background, not just of the authors themselves, but to the times they lived in and the sorts of debates that informed their views. Each introduction also contains a discussion of the central positions adopted by the author. With Augustine and Aquinas these introductions are quite a bit longer and more detailed than for Newman and Mill. We justify this on the grounds that many readers of this volume may be unfamiliar with the language and thought categories of Augustine and Aquinas and because of the intrinsic difficulty of the texts themselves. As a result we anticipate many will find these longer expository essays helpful in achieving a richer understanding of those texts.

The text for Augustine is a new translation of his *De Magistro* based on the standard text reproduced in *Patrologia Latina*, vol. 32, edited by J.P. Migne, Paris, 1845. We have translated this work anew because we have not been satisfied with previous translations. The original Latin is extremely difficult to capture in translation and we hope that our new translation helps bring out the central ideas more clearly.

The text for Aquinas' *De Magistro* is based upon the translation by M. H. Mayer originally appearing in her *The Philosophy of Teaching of Saint Thomas Aquinas*, New York, Bruce Publishing Co., 1929. We have substantially modified this translation in two respects. First, we have corrected a number of infelicities in the light of more recent scholarship and with reference to the definitive Leonine Latin edition of *Quaestiones disputatae de veritate*, Volume 22. Second, we have rearranged the entire text into flowing paragraphs, thereby facilitating reading. While this decision was a difficult one to make for scholars, nonetheless we think it justified by the gain in comprehensibility for a modern audience that might not be as comfortable with the formal Scholastic presentation style of the original.

The selected text from Newman is excerpted from *The Idea of a University* in the 1899 impression published by Longmans, Green, and Company, from the commonly-regarded definitive edition of 1873. We have chosen Discourses 5 and 6 from this work because they contain the essence of his vision for education and, in particular, his elaboration of the value of liberal education.

The text from Mill, which is his *Inaugural Address Delivered to the University of St Andrews 1867*, is derived from *The Collected Works of John Stuart Mill*, volume 21, edited by J. M. Robson and introduced by S. Collini, Toronto, University of Toronto Press, 1984.

Finally, in Chapter 6, we elaborate a series of questions arising from the texts of our authors and own experience as educators. We hope to show by these reflections how the insights of our four authors can be relevant to contemporary issues in educational theory and practice.

CHAPTER 1

Understanding Teaching and Learning

Reflections on the Philosophy and Practice of Education

Introduction

Human beings are naturally curious. From our earliest days we encounter situations that evoke our wonder and interest. We seek to understand, often in the context of being taught and coming to learn, that which others have previously wondered about. We are all in some way teachers and learners, yet our understanding of what goes on in coming to understand or in teaching or in being taught or in learning are themselves objects of wonder.

Who among us has not been touched in deep and serious ways by a particularly excellent teacher? Or, from the perspective of a teacher, who has not experienced the joy of watching a student come to know and understand? For many professional teachers this is one of the most valuable elements in teaching, sustaining and enthusing teachers when either personal failures or political and bureaucratic obstacles contrive to make them lose heart.

It is fair to say that in those countries where teaching and learning have become the objects of institutionalisation, the systematised experiences of students play a massive role in the final shaping of both the individual and the polity to which he or she belongs. After all, most of us from a very young age spend more time in the institutional frameworks supporting teaching and learning than we do in any framework other than the immediate family setting. Given the dramatic impact of formalised education, and the many centuries of practice and theoretical understandings involved, it is nonetheless surprising that the entire field of philosophy of education remains highly contested.[1]

X teaches Y to Z

Although how we are able to successfully understand, teach, and learn becomes increasingly puzzling the closer we look, nonetheless the very fact that we are able to understand, teach, and learn is a common experience. As Socrates recommends, it is good practice to start from common, well-understood cases and to pay careful attention to what we say about those cases. Let us begin by reflecting on how we ordinarily speak about understanding, teaching, and learning.

Ordinary experience furnishes us with clear and straightforward examples of understanding, teaching, and learning. We come to understand, for example, mathematical theorems, how to play the piano, and why stealing food from babies is bad. All of these things which we understand are typically taught to us and learnt by us. More schematically, the various dimensions of understanding teaching and learning can be brought out by considering the following fairly uncontroversial locution:

(1)   X teaches Y to Z

This formulation has the disadvantage of privileging the *activity* of the teacher, and perhaps intimating the passivity or simple receptivity of the learner. An alternative formulation that reverses this could be:

(2)   Z learns Y from X

Taken conjointly, these formulations capture the active dimensions of both teacher and learner. Teaching is something that the teacher *does*, just as learning is something that the learner *does*. When it comes to understanding, there seems to be an overlap between the activities of teacher and learner. As we shall see presently, all four of our authors reject the view that pure passivity is a proper part of understanding, teaching, and learning. Even the most extreme of our authors, Augustine, holds a position that accords a key role to the active participation of the student, and he illustrates the relation between teacher and learner in the form of a dialogical partnership.

Our other authors accord an even more pronounced role to the active participation of the student, though there remains an impor-

---

[1]   For a survey see D.C. Phillips, 'Philosophy of Education', *Stanford Encyclopedia of Philosophy* 2008, http://plato.stanford.edu/entries/education-philosophy/.

tant dimension of receptivity, or even better, a well-formed *active passivity* on the part of the learner. Plato, who is a major influence on all four of our authors, also rejects the notion that learning is a passive reception of information, remarking in the *Symposium* that: 'How fine it would be ... if wisdom were a sort of thing that could flow out of the one of us who is fuller into him who is emptier, by our mere contact with each other, as water will flow through wool from the fuller cup into the emptier.'[2]

Given these cautionary remarks, we can concentrate on our first formulation (1), since we intend to unpack each part of the proposition and then deal with the various elements from a series of perspectives without privileging in advance any particular theoretical understanding. More simply, we will stick closely to common ways of speaking, taking these as a guide to what common sense has to say about the matter.

X (in 'X teaches Y to Z')

It may be fruitful to begin with a non-exhaustive catalogue of what 'X' might stand for. Of course, X will stand primarily for a *human* teacher — this is the most usual way of speaking and one that fits comfortably into institutional models of education in the contemporary world. However, we also commonly refer to other sorts of X as being teachers. We may say for example that *experience* teaches us. The school of hard knocks is admitted to be one of the most widely attended schools, and this brings home important lessons in a particularly effective and memorable way. In other words, by experiencing something we come to understand it. Who else but a lover could say that 'It is better to have loved and lost than never to have loved at all?' Only when we have loved do we understand the point the lover makes.

It is not unusual, either now or in the past, to say that *nature* teaches us, and indeed for Augustine and Aquinas this usage plays an important role in their overall accounts. Nature as teacher is a peculiarly pregnant notion with a long pedigree, stretching from the pre-Socratics through Plato, Aristotle, the Stoics and the Epicureans,

---

[2] Plato, *Lysis Symposium Gorgias*, trans. W.R.M. Lamb, Loeb Classical Library, Cambridge, Harvard University Press, 1991, 175d. As an aside, it is worth noting that the *de facto* approach adopted by many novice teachers runs aground on exactly this point. Teaching is more than transmission. Even the most passive of devices, a radio, needs to be both on and properly tuned to play the music broadcasted. When we say that someone is listening to a teacher, we have to assume that the listener is attuned and attending to what is said.

through the Middle Ages into the Enlightenment and from then into the modern period. It captures something of the distinction we make between *nature* and *nurture*. While experience seems to be more closely allied to our nurture, nature itself provides occasion for reflection on *the conditions of our teachability*.

At the deepest level, nature teaches us about what sort of beings we are and the sorts of things that beings like us are capable or incapable of either doing or being. Thus, in virtue of our possessing noses we can appreciate flowers and perfume, but the sorts of olfaction we are capable of processing differs markedly from dogs and bees. Excellence in olfaction belongs to dogs more than humans, and in this sense we come to appreciate the limits that nature imposes upon us; but by the same token there are many dimensions along which distinctively human excellences outstrip the capacities of other animals. Humans are moral animals, and some of our greatest teachers have been acknowledged for their excellence in this regard. Bees have no Jesus, no Plato, no Ghandi.

Reflecting is itself distinctive of our human nature. Reflection upon our fundamental natures reveals that we are not self-sufficient, that we require certain basic necessities to maintain our bodily existence, and that we, as social beings (unlike, say, great white sharks and sea turtles who do not nurture their offspring), require others to promote our flourishing in a variety of ways. If we are not cared for as infants we will simply die. By nature we need nurture—and our need for teachers is a clear example of this. Teaching normally begins in the family, continues through apprenticeship in crafts that answer to specific human wants and needs, and carries forward to those specialised forms of teaching that answer to our deepest yearnings and our desire to understand ourselves and our place in the cosmos.

Nature also sets limits to what can be taught and what can be learnt and understood at both the bodily and the intellectual levels. Human beings by nature cannot flap their arms and fly like birds, so it makes no sense to try teaching anyone to do so. Even within individuals sharing the same human nature there is much variation of capacity and talent. To mention a theme that we will pick up on later, appreciation for the *individual nature* of the student can and should influence choices about pedagogical methods as well as inform expectations about what potentialities for understanding are present.

We may also be taught by a series of *external resources* and by a range of *social teachers*. We learn from books, from libraries, and increasingly from the internet. We may be taught by overheard conversations, even gossip, as much as by the institutionalised forms of teaching with which we are so familiar, such as schools, universities, churches, temples, mosques, and synagogues. Moreover, though it appears to have dropped out of fashion, there is a very clear sense in which *lex est magister*, that is, 'Law is a teacher'. The laws that govern us in society inform much of what we internalise as appropriate modes of behaviour towards ourselves and others. The law is just one of a series of social teachers. Our political context also helps shape our relations with others and ourselves, and this is true of both good and bad polities. The Scholastic adage *corruptio optima pessima*, that 'the best are corrupted under the worst', captures the notion that a bad political order or institution corrupts even the best people. Insofar as we are prepared to admit that environment (nurture) influences who we are and what we learn, then the political system as well as social institutions generally must be acknowledged as teachers.

A crucial dimension of the ways in which our natural sociability opens us to broader features of our traditions and forms of culture, and shapes what we are and what we become, involves *narratives*. We are taught by the narratives we hear from childhood, by all the pressures of our social and cultural settings, including its folk-wisdom, and the advice of our elders and those whom society privileges in some way. Our parents, our guardians, our grandparents, our extended families are sources of learning and fonts of how we come to understand ourselves and our relations to others. There could be no feud between the Hatfields and the McCoys without family identity, nor could there be martyrs without identification with a cause. While the practical importance of narratives becomes clear upon reflection, the key next step in understanding the role of narratives must lie in their relation to *truth*. One of the great difficulties here is that the narratives that most deeply shape our selves and our communities may be darkened as much by propaganda and dubious ideology as they may be illuminated by the spark of truth. And yet, as many have noted, myths and fairy tales often contain profound layers of truth.

The *traditions* to which we belong, even the geographical topography to which we are accustomed, provide deep shape to the range of our sensibilities and what we find congenial or acceptable. The range of influences which shape the contours of our self-narratives, including many of which we are not consciously aware, are partially constituted by such factors. Why does one person prefer the mellifluous sounds of the piano, and another the tintinnabulations of West Indian steel drums? Our aesthetic appreciations are heavily impacted by our cultural deposits and this is at least one plausible reason for thinking that our preferences will be shaped by such contexts — not always or inescapably, but for the most part. It is also true that we can come to appreciate different art forms that are not central to our own traditions. Westerners can come to appreciate Eastern wood block prints, and Easterners can come to appreciate Mozart's symphonies. However, in both cases they usually do so with the aid of teachers who help make manifest the meanings of the experiences to which they are exposed. We need not be imprisoned by cultural vagaries.

While each of these elements in our experience acts as a teacher in varying ways and degrees, the paradigmatic form of the teacher in an institutional framework is undoubtedly a human being — a human being who is also shaped by all the forces we have just mentioned and no doubt by others that we have not. Among our authors, Augustine and Aquinas suspect that there may be significant limits to the possible impact of the human teacher. This is perhaps because Augustine and Aquinas would like to emphasise what they take to be a metaphysical truth, namely, that God is an active contributor to the processes of understanding, teaching, and learning. The divine contribution is conceived of in many ways: in Augustine the participation of the Divine is direct with respect to the interior illumination of the learner; in Aquinas a similar idea is explored, but the emphasis is instead placed on God as author of human nature.

To say 'teacher' is to say *agent who teaches*. Normally, when we talk about an agent, we take the example of someone who is successful at what they do. A batter is someone who hits the ball, not someone who misses, and a chef is someone who cooks a good dinner, not someone who burns it. So, following ordinary practice at this point, we take as our norm the *good teacher*. While we are here specifically addressing the nature of the agent X who teaches, the nature of X's agency requires both a subject matter, Y, namely that which is taught and a learner, Z, the student (or students) who in principle can learn. In other words, *teaching* involves a *relation* between a teacher and a pupil that is sustained by a *characteristic set of activities* that delimit the specific means of acting as well as the specific content that is taught.

Agency has another way of being understood, one that has dropped (perhaps significantly) out of contemporary discussions of teaching. Agency operates at the level of exemplification and imitation. The good teacher is an *exemplar* for students to emulate and model themselves upon. In this respect the good teacher may teach even when not engaged in a specific discipline. How the teacher approaches problems, how the teacher engages students in a manner that respects them, how the teacher corrects and where necessary admonishes, can all be explicit objects of student reflection and appropriation.

But perhaps we should ask a preliminary question. Should we not inquire into *why* a teacher teaches? This turns out to be a very complex question. After all, a person may well have a mastery over some area of expertise or knowledge yet have no desire to teach, subsequently refrain from teaching, and hence quite properly not be called a teacher. We might best approach a provisional answer by teasing out different aspects of the question. First, a teacher teaches because the teacher sees or assumes a *need* for what is taught. This appears to be as true of the teacher of car mechanics as of the teacher of metaphysics. Second, there is a *content* that fits the needs of a specific pupil or audience. These content-needs might be spelt out in a variety of ways. They may involve a perception that the teacher teaches so that the pupil or audience may get employment and money, or prestige, or some other pragmatic benefit; or that the pupil is just curious about the area that the teacher has some mastery over. In either range of cases the teacher seems to answer to genuine or perceived content-needs. Third, a good teacher prioritises the needs of the student both in respect to the content of what is to be known and also with respect to how, why, and when that content is to be broached. Thus the *ordering* of the curriculum is itself an important question for our authors, Newman and Mill in particular.

If these observations are correct, they call attention to several neglected aspects of what it is to be a teacher in the fullest sense. These aspects include the relationship of the teacher to the pupil, to the content taught, and to the proper motivations of the teacher qua agent. We often talk of an inspiring teacher and even of an inspired teacher. Sometimes we simply mean that the teacher's modes of delivery, personality, or approaches to the subject, inspires learners. The teacher enthuses the student about the subject matter being taught. But a teacher who inspires and enthuses may have an added characteristic—the inspired and inspiring teacher is often a focal point for the generation of a set of questions or problems that tease out or educe the students' own powers of understanding and learning. Not that long ago it was commonly believed that teaching was a *vocation*—a calling not unlike a vocation to holy orders. The gravity and intrinsic nobility of the teacher as someone who answers and fulfils one of the most distinctive of human needs helps us understand why this way of looking at the teacher is appropriate. We will have cause to return to this thought later.

So we may say that as a corollary of the needs to which the teacher responds there is evidence in our authors of specific motivations associated with teachers. This might be put as follows: the good teacher teaches because the teacher answers needs, and does so both because the subject matter is cared about and because the teacher cares about (Augustine says 'loves') the learner. This notion of love that characterises to some extent the motivation of the good teacher also implies a personal commitment to truth as embodied in the subject matter to be taught as well as to the personal cultivation of those *virtues* necessary for truth's attainment. For example, the good teacher is humble before the truth, is committed to an ever-deepening understanding of both subject matter taught and modes of pedagogical presentation, and is willing to revise both claims and practices in the light of new personal discovery. This means that the good teacher is necessarily a life-long learner.

The good teacher is not motivated primarily by extrinsic concerns such as the desire for popularity or power or prestige or even money. The good teacher loves both who and what are taught for their own sakes. This seems to be a dimension of the nature of the teacher that has received scant attention in recent discussions in the philosophy of education.[3] Yet among our authors the role of love appears to be a defining characteristic of liberal education and what in part distinguishes teaching from transmission or training.

Much of the work in the philosophy and practice of education has, for a long time, centred upon the technical dimensions of teaching: the classroom setting, the psychology of student and teacher, administrative feedback mechanisms such as the omnipresent portfolio—with a corresponding neglect of the vocational dimension of

---

[3]   The great exceptions here are the Leo Strauss-inspired philosophers such as Alan Bloom. See for example A. Bloom, *The Closing of the American Mind*, New York, Simon & Schuster, 1987.

teaching which was previously considered central to understanding the craft and calling of the teacher. While these remarks might seem abstract, idealistic, and even anachronistic, we are all witnesses to the practical effects of the absence of this vocational dimension. How often do parents voice concern that teachers don't seem to care? Or that teachers do not know details of students' lives that would have been considered commonplace in an earlier day? Why did a teacher not spot the warning signs of a difficulty so apparent in hindsight? Or overlook manifest talent?

One way in which we can focus upon the qualities and motivations of the good teacher is by reflecting on how and why a teacher can *fail as a teacher*. The ensuing discussion is designed to highlight what is good by calling attention to that which is easier to spot, namely how things can go awry. To begin, consider that one of the basic ways in which a teacher teaches is by presenting *experiences* to the learner and then guiding the learner in drawing out appropriate meanings from those experiences. For instance, a teacher might wish to show a student that one's individual good can only be realised within the context of the common good. A simple way to achieve this would be to have the student work through the problem of the Tragedy of the Commons.[4] Thus, the teacher might have students in a class imagine that they are all fisher-folk who make their living by fishing in a lake next to their village. The more successful fishers will be those who catch more fish. However, if everyone maximises the amount of fish that they catch, the fish stocks will be depleted and everyone, including those individuals who maximised their catches, will starve. How then, the teacher may ask, can the villagers simultaneously satisfy their basic needs—for there must be enough fish caught to sustain the village—and their private ambitions, without causing the system to collapse? Private good is thus realizable only within the context of sustaining the common good. But a bad teacher might pull out the wrong lesson, seeing this as fundamentally a problem about maximising private benefits. Or the bad teacher might place inappropriate *a priori* constraints on good solutions, for instance allowing only radical egalitarian solutions in which everyone takes precisely the same number of fish independent of other important factors, such as size of family. Teachers fail when employing experiential learning techniques by closing off possibilities for

---

[4]   While noted by earlier authors, the classic discussion by Hardin crystallised the contemporary understanding of the problem. See G. Hardin, 'The Tragedy of the Commons', *Science* 162:3859, 1968, pp. 1243-48.

discussion and consideration. They can also fail at the levels of selection, definition, and presentation of the proper experience as vehicle for student learning, for not every thought experiment is equally suited to illuminating the Tragedy of the Commons.

When considering teaching at the level of *nature*, difficulties can arise in various ways. First, problems may occur when there is a failure to recognise appropriate limits for a given audience: most kindergarten students should not be expected to learn differential calculus. Second, there can be imposition of inappropriate limits: were we to follow Piaget, the learning potential of students would be seriously underestimated, for very young students are demonstrably capable of expert ratiocination and philosophical discussion.[5] Third, there are natural limits to the teacher's personal and professional development that condition how the teacher realises his or her vocation. As was well said, when you first begin teaching you teach more than you know; in the middle of your career you teach as much as you know; and at the end of your career you teach far less than you know.[6] Fourth, the vocational aspect of teaching may have bearing on the adequacy of given temperaments for teaching. Someone who cannot learn to care either about the subject being taught or the learners entrusted to his or her care is likely to fail as a teacher, thus marking a failure to recognise limitations in the teacher's own nature.

Someone may also fall short due to a lack of *reflection* upon the subject matter, its appropriate modes of presentation, and the qualities of one's pupils. We have all met experienced teachers who use the same lecture notes year in and year out, whose content and method of delivery have ossified. A key feature of the good teacher is an openness to discovery qua life-long learner. A degree of reflectiveness is required to sustain such openness, to instil enthusiasm, and to maintain the requisite care for and interest in one's students and one's craft.

Our *social teachers*, be they *laws*, *narratives*, or *traditions* and *cultures*, can be in good or poor order. Any given teacher is ineluctably shaped by these environing forces, and can be an active contributor to them as conduit, innovator, or critic. Some of the ways in which teachers can fail with respect to their own social teachers are by not taking them seriously enough or by allowing them to achieve the sta-

---

[5]   See for example G. Matthews, *The Philosophy of Childhood*, Cambridge, Harvard University Press, 1996. Matthews also has an extended engagement with and references to Piaget.

[6]   This observation is due to James F. Ross.

tus of monolithic bodies of received truths closed off to questioning. One of a teacher's most challenging tasks is to mediate between proper respect and appreciation for the depth and resources of one's social teachers and, at the same time, to foster openness to evaluating, developing, and critiquing of those social teachers. In all this, the teacher's one sure guide is an adherence to the standard of truth and those virtuous qualities of character that support truth's attainment.

While our own era is not unique in presenting difficulties with respect to social teachers, education has increasingly become regimented by a business-inspired utilitarianism that has far-reaching effects. No teacher is immune to this broader cultural trend. In a period marked by an input/output model of efficiency drawn from neo-classical economics, teacher and pupil are institutionalised and depersonalised, a trend which negatively impacts some of the crucial relational aspects of teaching envisaged by our four authors.[7] They would see such a model as inimical to the goals of what is best in education since personal flourishing is difficult to realise under such conditions. When we view students primarily as units to be produced for society's general consumption, formative dimensions of the teacher/pupil relation are inevitably attenuated.

The business-inspired approach to education also impacts what gets taught. Not only do we have a profusion of professional disciplines being taught at universities and other schools, but the prioritisation by our social teachers of these very disciplines effects the choices made by those who want to become teachers, thus shaping their priorities and their interests, perhaps to the detriment of natural talent. At the secondary school level it is often prudent for apprentice teachers to gravitate towards those subjects that are presently in vogue to the detriment of certain more traditional subjects which are deemed to lack market prestige, and this results in business studies and accounting replacing classics and literature. At university level the best paying jobs and the ones that are most secure are generally either in or associated with business schools. Even in comprehensive universities classics are often no longer taught.

Moreover, teachers are now largely evaluated by criteria that have their sources external to the concrete teaching relation. Success in teaching, and success in knowledge acquisition by students, are judged according to bureaucratic, largely quantitative, measures.

---

[7]   It is with both sadness and resignation that we have witnessed educational environments in which students are referred to as 'clients' and learning marketed as a 'commodity' (with a graduated price tag) all in the service of the 'business of education'.

The emphasis on quantitative assessment is understandable, insofar as such measures are far easier to implement than more qualitative (though still objective) standards. However, emphasis on quantitative metrics has a profound impact on what gets taught and how teaching is carried out. A shift toward quantitative assessment brings in its train a shift towards *know-that*, that is, knowledge of facts, instead of *know-how* (skills) or *know-why* (theoretical understanding).[8]

It is normal for teachers to internalise markers imposed by bureaucracies, and thus measure themselves as teachers against those extrinsic standards. This can have consequences for how teachers view not only their students but also their own modes of content delivery. If purely factual content is privileged, then modes of delivery suited to imparting such content will be adopted, often to the detriment of other modes of teaching that are better adapted to teaching things like skills. Experienced teachers familiar with a traditional lecture style are sometimes unable to recognise when a class conducted using experiential learning methods is successful simply because they are unable to see the value or understand the teaching objectives of this alternative approach.

Our social teachers also influence the prestige and desirability of becoming a certain kind of teacher. Conformists to bureaucracies are rewarded (with *inter alia* stable employment and promotion), while innovators or those who adhere to older dialectical styles are both financially and socially discouraged. For instance, a dialectical approach, which might in certain disciplines be the optimal delivery mode, can be hamstrung by the imposition of larger class sizes due to economic priorities. This negatively impacts not just the students, who are precluded from experiencing what is acknowledged as best practice, but ultimately damages the discipline being taught with respect to its inter-generational transmission and development. It may also seriously damage the morale of the teacher.

Most importantly, and potentially most damagingly, a teacher can fail in respect to *truth*, and this in a number of ways. First, there is *truth within disciplines* conceived of as bodies of knowledge. Ignorance can be culpable for teachers, for in all genuine disciplines there are bodies of fact that all expert practitioners are expected to know. Teachers who are overly casual with respect to the truths they are

---

[8]   We explain these epistemological distinctions more fully below. Interestingly, this shift towards know-that is often accompanied by an official rhetoric alleging that such changes will foster greater student know-how and deepen student engagement at the level of know-why.

expected to teach can systematically misinform students. Moreover, teachers must hold onto truth as something attainable and normatively sought within their discipline. One may err by claiming less than one should as well as by claiming more than one should: facts are to be presented as facts, not opinions; and if one does not know, then it is most proper to truthfully say that one does not know. Of course, there are many things that are considered to be settled facts that are nonetheless open to question; but there is no charge to be laid against teachers who teach what they have diligently investigated and have reason to think true, though they might be mistaken. If something is true, then it is simply true and not merely half-true; but our understanding of truth is not simple, it admits of degrees and differing levels of certitude.

The teacher may also fail in being *true to the discipline* taught. This can occur when a teacher does not follow the proper order, structure, and methods of the discipline. So, even though a teacher may have a firm professional grasp of the truths within a discipline, it is still possible to misconstrue a discipline's intrinsic goals and the various practices that support attainment of those goals. For example, impatient and anxious teachers may rest content when students are able to reproduce a method without understanding either the method or the solution obtained. This is often justified by saying that the students will obtain better results on various tests and assessments. A mathematics teacher might dogmatically insist that a particular method is the only correct approach to solving a problem, even when other methods may be equally reliable. To be true to the discipline of mathematics, an answer must be reliably obtained and understood. The nature of a given mathematical problem determines the range of appropriate methods; it is a perversion of mathematics to permit methods, which are ultimately instruments, to predetermine the range of acceptable solutions.[9] Students are not pocket calculators, though they can certainly be trained to imitate them.

Perhaps one of the deepest failures that may afflict a teacher is the least discussed of all, namely the relationship between the *character* of a teacher and his or her relation to truth. There are *truth-directed virtues* that a teacher needs to cultivate, first, for their own sake, second, in respect to the relationship between teacher and pupil, and

---

[9]   *Ceteris paribus*, of course, for there are legitimate questions in mathematics that ask about which results can be obtained with, say, a restricted range of assumptions, as when proofs are given in set theory without use of the axiom of choice.

third, in respect to the integrity of the teacher as a person. Some of the failures in this regard arise in the context of seeking the truth, others in the context of holding on to the truth, and still others in the context of sharing what is true.

It seems uncontroversial to note that intellectual virtues are important for their own sake because truth is a good thing.[10] Truth is the good of the intellect, just as health is the good of the body. There are several virtues necessary for the successful acquisition of truth, many of which obtain not only for the teacher as teacher, but also for the teacher qua life-long learner. Among these are intellectual humility, intellectual courage, and most particularly, intellectual curiosity. One of the cardinal facets of a good teacher is the delight taken in inquiry and questioning. Indeed it would seem that these are also key features that operate at the level of the *teacher as exemplar*, who in embodying and manifesting these traits elicits a similar existential resonance in students. Truth-directed virtues may be taken up by the student in an unreflective way, at least initially. (This feature they share with all moral virtues, which are acquired first by imitation, consolidated by habit, and finally possessed in full by reflective appropriation.) Teachers who do not embody truth-directed virtues may well elicit habits and resonances in their students that become stumbling blocks for the students' growth as learners. Just as the good teach virtue to the potentially good, so too do the bad teach vice to the potentially bad. Such teachers typically will have no love of questioning and even less fondness for students as inquirers, thereby vitiating the proper relationship between teacher and pupil.

A dismissive attitude, a complacency with what one thinks one knows, and a resolute refusal to connect up what one knows with other things that one knows: these spell the death of the inquiring mind. A failure to admit one is wrong, an incapacity to change one's mind, and a wilful and sometimes articulate adherence to falsity: these are the marks of the truncated self, a self caught in amber, fossilised in static rejection of self-transcendence.

Failure to cultivate truth-directed virtues can lead to an attitude of complacency in respect to our social teachers. Lack of intellectual courage can lead to tolerance of error and acquiescence in contested areas where commitment to the truth is important. (It is far easier to

[10] To use language presupposes an interest in and commitment to truth. See Aristotle *Meta.* IV, 3-6, and his classic definition of truth at 1011b25: 'To say that what *is*, is not; or that what *is not*, is, is *false*; but to say that what *is*, is, and what *is not*, is not, is *true*'.

say that there is no truth, or that all truth is relative, than to seek a truth to hold in a thicket of confusion and error.) Moreover, this lack breeds a psychological contempt for those who take principled stands against the social forces of their community. Standard fallacies in reasoning attend the intellectually vicious because lack of commitment to truth has the psychological effect of confounding ideas with persons and persons with ideas, with all the accompanying unpleasantness. Ideas do not need our tolerance and respect, people do. To respect an idea and not respect a person is a category mistake. A good teacher does not love error, but should love the one who errs.

Yet another way in which a teacher may fall short involves improper *motivation*. There are goods internal to teaching that are realised by keeping one's focus on the good of the student, one's chosen discipline, and the proper relations that obtain among teacher, student, and subject matter. These are the relations in-which and through-which a teacher realises personal flourishing and psychic self-integration. Pursuit of goods extrinsic to these relations to the detriment of understanding, teaching, and learning, results in failure as a teacher. To be sure, some extrinsic motivations are compatible with, or even supportive of, the internal goods of the teacher and teaching. Having good work conditions, or being engaged with one's community of fellow teachers, and indeed being compensated appropriately, are all motivations that can sit comfortably with the motivations internal to the teaching vocation.

Nonetheless, it seems likely that if compensation, for instance, were a teacher's primary motivation, then this may detract from one's capacity to be a good teacher. Job security is fine, but the motivation for mere job security does not make a good teacher. Conscientious teachers will, precisely because they are conscientious teachers, sometimes give up teaching when some or all of the goods internal to teaching are impossible to obtain. This once again emphasises a feature we find in all four of our authors; namely, that the teaching art is intimately connected with love—love for what one teaches and for those whom one teaches.

There are serious issues at stake here for the teacher as a self. A teacher who fails in respect to love of subject matter or students often descends to soul-deadening psittacism, on the one hand, and contempt or indifference towards students, and ultimately oneself on the other. Over the past three decades, as teachers, we have witnessed the demoralising effects of a mixture of social and institutional factors that have combined to frustrate the attainment of the goods internal to teaching. A human consequence of this has been the systematic detachment of many of our former colleagues from the very goals and motivations that brought them into teaching in the first place. When these internal goods are suppressed, there is a danger of good teachers stopping teaching. The painful outcome is often expressed in the fragmentation and psychic disintegration of such teachers. By way of contrast, we have also seen how good mentoring, good environments, genuine social esteem, and supportive institutional structures can enhance the internal integration and flourishing of teachers who find fulfilment in living out their vocation.

Teaches ... To (in 'X teaches Y to Z')

Let us return to our formulation, *X teaches Y to Z*, and now focus on the phrasal verb 'teaches ... to'. The Latin word *educare* used by Augustine and Aquinas is etymologically linked to an *activity of drawing out*, and is the root of our words *education* and *educe*. This insight about education as involving a drawing-forth pervades the approaches to liberal education advocated by all our authors. The teacher in teaching acts as a *catalyst* for the internal powers of the learner, drawing out potentialities into their active realisations. Thus, our etymological elucidation suggests a worthwhile distinction. While it is probably the case that every form, mode, or activity employed in teaching will be closely allied to a form of transmission (Latin *transmissio*, 'sending across', thus emphasising the activity of the teacher rather than the active receptivity of the student), not every form of transmission will count as teaching. Many forms of transmission, including training and instruction, will involve teaching. But teaching as understood by our authors entails more than transmission, training, and instruction. It implies a *relation* between teacher and learner in which the end of the teacher's teaching is not just some skill or body of knowledge but rather *the awakening and quickening of the powers latent in the learner*.

When we emphasise the term 'teaches' in *X teaches Y to Z*, we commonly think of a *characteristic set of activities* which include modes of presentation and forms of questioning and inquiry. These activities are dependent to some extent on what is being taught, when it is taught, to whom, and why. The university lecture or tutorial format would be inappropriate for a kindergarten classroom setting, and the whistle usefully employed by a coach on a soccer pitch probably should not find its way into a secondary school French class.

Some standard, and again, non-exhaustive cataloguing of such activities, modes, and forms of inquiry includes: lecturing, tutoring, demonstrating, displaying, explaining, repeating, drilling, revising, reviewing, manifesting, pointing out, indicating, acting, modelling, and so on. These are among the canonical ways of operationalising teaching. The activities of teaching are situated in different environments, ranging from the traditional classroom to the football field, immersive learning environments (as when students are brought to another land to learn a language), the library, and the armchair, to mention just a few. Teaching as an activity is more or less successful depending on the qualities of teachers and learners, their relations to one another, and their respective environmental contexts (as when a tutor delivers an on-line lesson which is viewed at home by a student).

Many of the characteristic activities of teaching are embedded in the relationship between teacher and student. (We have already discussed how the character of the teacher as an exemplar overflows into the student's learning.) Teaching also embraces forms of eliciting by means of emulation, copying, imitation and attentiveness. The pupil is a dynamic part of the relation, participating, reflecting, and refracting the teacher in these respects, often subconsciously.

There are numerous ways in which the activities involved in 'teaching ... to' can go awry. Some characteristic ways include environmental problems such as poor acoustics, lack of funding and equipment, and personal difficulties on the part of teachers and learners, such as illness. Broadly considered, there are intrinsic and extrinsic factors that impact teaching activities. Some are within the control of the participants in the teaching relation, some are not. For example, a teacher who chooses to deliver in an inaudible, mumbling fashion fails intrinsically, while a class being conducted next to a construction site can fail extrinsically.

The activities involved in 'teaching ... to' are of course intimately connected to what is taught. Which approach, why, when, and what activities are selected by the teacher, are inevitably tied up with their suitability for the particular subject content. Methodology, which tells us about how to select, organise, refine, shape, and evaluate our teaching activities, cannot help but be sensitive to, and dependent upon, both the discipline and specific content within the discipline. It is for these reasons of interconnectivity that deeper exploration of the activities involved in teaching are deferred to the next subsection.

Y (in 'X teaches Y to Z')

When we focus on 'Y' in *X teaches Y to Z*, we seem to be pointing at the content of what is taught. We may say Fionnuala teaches literature, law, traditional music, gardening, dancing, football, and so on. In each, Y designates the content expressed by literature, law, etc. The content of each subject domain will involve the acquisition of a range of skills, information, facts, heuristics, and almost certainly some supporting virtues. Whatever Y is in particular cases, it will not be independent of the other parts of the teacher/student relation. It will also call forth questions about how, when, where, why, and to whom we teach, for clearly many elements of content (considered widely) can be appropriated in degrees.

To begin, let us take the case of a student being taught how to paint. Painting involves many objects: paints, paintbrushes, canvasses, pencils, crayons, and so on. These are the materials of painting. But someone learning to paint must also come to appreciate the qualitative aspects of their materials: paints come in different hues, saturations, and consistencies (water colours versus oils). There are also the questions of how to use these materials and why the painter would choose one method instead of another to better realise the composition. So clearly we need to *know how* to utilise the material elements used in painting, *know that* the materials possess the qualities that they do, and in addressing questions of composition we want to *know why* we should care about painting in the first place. In what follows we will analyse these three ways of characterising our understanding of content.

At first glance, teaching *know-how* seems very straightforward. It involves a teacher teaching a learner how to do or be something: philosophy, Ancient Greek, car maintenance, laying bricks, knitting, a good person, and so on. Somewhat surprisingly, in the context of the classroom and formal teaching, our common-sense understanding of how we, as individual learners, come to learn how to do things is often neglected. Take for example learning how to swim. We learn to swim by swimming, just as we learn to ride a bike by riding one, and learn to speak a language by speaking it. Much of the art in teaching these forms of know-how comes in selecting and structuring those experiences that occasion the development of the desired skills. For instance, a swimming teacher encourages students not only to get into the water, but also to practise (and thereby learn) certain elements of swimming before others. We typically learn how to kick before how to do arm strokes. The swimming teacher has the student practise all of the necessary elements in sequence until the student is able to experience, from the inside, what it feels like to be engaged in successful practice. Finally, the student leaves the shallow end of the pool and reproduces all of these elements, and the result is swimming. Skill in swimming would thus involve consolidated know-how. Excellent swimmers, who are very skilled at swimming, practise more, and more often, than those who are less skilled.

But it is common for teachers, who know at the personal level what is required for learning know-how, to forget these insights when they enter the classroom. Know-how can only be acquired through experience, but instead students are frequently addressed using pedagogical methods better suited to the imparting of facts, that is, *know-that*. It is as if we asked our students to read a swimming textbook, have them pass a multiple-choice exam, and then expect them to be swimmers.

While all know-how involves experiential learning, the variety of ways we can teach know-how is as diverse and wide-ranging as the sorts of experiences that can embody and operationalise the concepts and skills to be mastered. The ways we can teach someone how to think philosophically differ from the ways we can teach someone how to knit or indeed how to be a good person. This is because the sorts of experiences involved are themselves diverse.

There may be some forms of know-how that are extremely difficult to teach, such as chicken sexing, because of the nature of the content. (It is very difficult to tell one chick from another.)[11] Other forms of know-how might be relatively easy to impart (like how to peel an orange), while yet others may be extremely difficult dependent upon factors pertaining to a particular learner. Perhaps there are some who lack the necessary capacity or aptness for certain forms of know-how. A colour-blind individual may lack the capacity to distinguish red and green in the visual field. But even if someone has the requisite capacity, they may still lack an aptness for skilful execution. Someone might earnestly desire to paint but never learn how to paint well.

We have said that know-how often admits of degrees. We may know how to ride a bicycle but not many of us can do so as well as

---

[11]   See R. Horsey, 'The Art of Chicken Sexing', University College London, *UCL Working Papers in Linguistics*, 14. 2002.

Lance Armstrong. Nonetheless the successful and habitual practice of various forms of know-how will often result in know-how becoming skills. Some of these skills in turn will be the reflectively appropriated forms of know-how we call virtues, which help us flourish as individuals and as social beings.

Moreover, the successful appropriation of know-how is often, perhaps always, dependent on forms of *know-that*. Know-how and know-that interpenetrate. I may know how to drive a car, having learnt how to do so in Ireland, but if I do not know that it would be extremely dangerous to drive on the left-hand-side of the road in the USA, then my know-how is seriously impaired. Know-how thus seems to require know-that.

While know-how clearly requires experiential learning, know-that has an experiential dimension as well, though we would usually characterise the sort of experience needed as one of acquaintance. For me to know that this cake is sweet, it is likely that I need to be acquainted with its taste. But direct acquaintance is not always required: I know that Caesar crossed the Rubicon in 49 BC. Know-that, then, appears to involve knowledge of both facts and experiences. However know-that is not exhausted by facts or experiences. It will involve propositional knowledge but also conditional forms of knowing, such as: If I drive on the left-hand-side of the road in the USA, then it will be very dangerous. Know-that also includes what we have appropriated from all the aspects of our traditions and social teachers. Thus, I know that it is good for me to brush my teeth every day. Know-that embraces modes of deliberation and the exercise of the imaginative faculty. Take, for example, empathy. To know that someone's grief on the passing of a beloved is especially painful, I need to be able to imagine that I am in that situation or, to put it somewhat differently, know that I am imaginatively acquainted with what it would be like to be in that situation.

There is good reason to think that both know-how and know-that are hierarchically related to *know-why*. A concern with know-why unites our four authors, and it is when we talk of know-why that we most easily talk of genuine understanding. Such understanding moves well beyond knowing-how or knowing-that. Know-why is concerned with uncovering causes, ends, and goals; with identifying that for the sake of which something is done, undertaken or pursued, or holds true. All our authors point out the ways in which our various fields of study and inquiry illuminate each other. In many arenas of life know-how and know-that can be enough—I can know that this particular mushroom is poisonous and how to distinguish this kind of poisonous mushroom from non-poisonous ones, but I need not inquire into why it is poisonous — this may be an object of study for a chemist or botanist.

The desire to know-why, as Aristotle intimates, is a fundamental dimension of the human condition — as evidenced by our sense of wonder and our attempts to formulate and reformulate questions and answers that open and deepen our understanding.[12] We are naturally curious. Even as infants, the desire to understand and experience the world around us is exhibited in sensuous corporeal gropings, putting anything to hand into one's mouth. Know-why responds to an aspect of our being. Or, to say the same thing in different words, human beings are naturally inclined towards knowing and find their fulfilment at least partially constituted by coming to know why things are as they are. By reflecting on this fundamental orientation of our nature as encountered in our social settings, we can collaboratively extend our questioning to everything in our collective range of experience that can be experienced as questionable. Knowing-why (as understanding) also comes in degrees, not just in respect to the marvellous diaphaneity of the objects and branches of knowledge, but also in respect to their appropriation by given temperaments and persons. Not everyone can be a Plato or an Aristotle, but everyone seeks meaning and understanding, and is hence a metaphysician.

The answers to our questions and how we understand these answers are themselves expressions of a deeper attachment to getting things right, in a word, to truth. The very possibility of sustained sociability, of understanding and being understood, implies a tacit commitment to truth and therefore to the standards and appropriate methods by which we can reasonably attain truth.[13] Indeed, we adapt our methods of seeking truth in response to the sort of truth we are trying to obtain. For instance, if we are confused by the meaning of a word, we might consult a dictionary, but if we are curious about the features of the moon, we have recourse to a telescope.

Commitment to truth entails existential commitments by both teachers and learners: first, to veracity as a virtue, enabling meanings to be reliably drawn from discourse with others; and second, to

[12] See Aristotle's opening sentence of the *Metaphysics*.

[13] MacIntyre has argued that a commitment to truth is a necessary condition of sociability on numerous occasions. See for example A. MacIntyre, *The Tasks of Philosophy*, vol. 1, Cambridge, Cambridge University Press, 2006, essays 3, 8, 9, and 10.

the canons of reasonable argumentation. These specific canons may be demanded by the rules that govern the conditions of our being. Our curiosity would be undirected, and hence unsatisfied, without commitment to ontological and logical principles such as the principle of non-contradiction. This is a logical principle because the conjunction '*p & not-p*' is always false. This logical principle, however, also reflects the ontological commonplace that the same thing cannot both be and not be at the same time and in the same respect: Eunice cannot both be *and* not be a human being at the same time; she either is human or not.[14]

In our division of knowledge into know-that, know-how, and know-why, it is know-why that drives the theoretical concern of our four authors. They privilege know-why because there is an abiding relation and deep connection between the activity of questioning and the selves that question. Questioning is how humans manifest their natural wonder, and the most satisfying answers to the best questions are inevitably concerned with know-why. The self that questions is defined (at least partially) by the questions asked and the sorts of answers arrived at. This is why education in its broadest sense, as conceived by our authors, involves self-making or self-realisation. To draw out the powers of the student is to help the student be more than what he or she was before; hence, successful education entails *self-transcendence*. All of the relations captured by X *teaches* Y *to* Z are transformed in the activities associated with education: teacher, student, and appropriated understanding are altered as teaching and learning illuminate their subjects.

In consequence, our authors are especially concerned with the process of inquiry or questioning. It is interesting to note that teaching the art of inquiry or questioning extends, at least in Augustine and Aquinas, to the literary form in which their ideas are presented. Augustine's *De Magistro* is a *dialogue* in which master and pupil work cooperatively. They find something within their shared experience open to question, and interrogate their experience in each other's presence, arriving at answers which in turn generate new questions. Aquinas' *De Magistro* explicitly embodies the so-called Scholastic Method. This method involves a formal distillation of communal inquiry in which a question is posed and perhaps followed by a series of subsidiary questions which, when taken together, illuminate the root problem. In answering these questions a range of possible answers, including the best answers offered thus far by one's

---

[14] Also see note 33, pp. 115–116 below.

opponents, are canvassed. Disagreement is taken very seriously, for all interlocutors are treated as serious seekers of truth, and as such worthy of profound respect. This method is deliberately adopted with the intention of gathering the best answers available while, at least in some arenas, allowing for the possibility of revision in the light of new experience.

With Newman and Mill there remains a deep attachment to the awakening of wonder and nurturing of the powers of questioning in learners, but both are no longer attached to questioning in the literary form of their writings. By the 19th century the institutionalised lecture or address had become *de rigeur*—though, as we will see, Newman was a staunch advocate, contrary to some major currents of his time, of the small or individual tutorial system in which a bond between teacher and pupil is preserved and joint questioning and deliberation can occur.

Mill, on the other hand, seems to have conducted most of his teaching in the forms of treatises, pamphlets, addresses and open letters, while still holding that an openness to questioning is central to the education of a learner. In one of his best-known works, *On Liberty*, questioning is a vital dimension of public inquiry and a requirement for effective democratic citizenship.[15] However, Mill's own education was more closely allied to earlier models in that he was educated largely by his father and personal tutors.

The leitmotif of the value of questioning involves above all an existentially appropriated attitude of a *self* concerned with truth, typically in a shared exploration (that is manifested either interpersonally or culturally). This existential dimension of *being a questioner*, of being concerned with and taught to be inquiring, preoccupies our authors partly because they see the questioning attitude as preserving a sense of wonder, but also because they are concerned with the limitations of our abilities to arrive at adequate answers. A teacher who fosters a questioning attitude encourages crucial virtues within the learner such as intellectual humility and love of truth. This is another way in which teaching goes beyond transmission, instruction, and training, because it promotes a qualitatively different set of concerns—ones not primarily directed towards skill acquisition or a body of knowledge, but rather towards actualising the self of the learner. The good teacher's teaching has a qualitative, non-neutral dimension in educing the powers of the

---

[15] See J.S. Mill, *On Liberty*, Buffalo, Prometheus Books, 1986.

learner. A good teacher is not neutral about realising the good of the learner.

The cultivation of a questioning attitude opens a further meditation central to our authors, namely, the ways in which the various branches of knowledge are mutually interrelated. This is a key theme in Newman, who explicitly argues for the unity of knowledge. The driving idea is that a systematic unpacking of know-why will reveal how questions in one domain impact what is known in another and thereby fertilise new investigations. Our understanding is enhanced by seeing that there are mediate and immediate connections among the diverse branches of human knowing.

Are there characteristic methodologies for pursuing truth in various disciplines? The pursuit of know-why raises questions about the ordering of one discipline to another as well as about how objects of knowledge within a discipline are to be ordered. Given that the object of teaching is to educe the powers of the learner, how is this drawing forth best achieved? What skills can teachers foster in their students to better equip them for the life-long task of questioning?

While not explicitly formulated by our authors in the manner we suggest here, we think that they are implicitly committed to something like the following. A good teacher will help a student be guided by this principle: *Accepting or rejecting presupposes understanding*. That is, before a student can meaningfully *accept* a claim as true, or *reject* a claim as false, the student must first *understand* what it is that is being claimed. To realise this goal, two sets of skills need to be cultivated within the learner.

First, the learner must acquire concepts and skills related to *clarification*. In an obvious way, clarity is improved when vagueness and ambiguity are lessened. Thus, imagine a student who hears the claim: 'I saw a large crane by the pond.' Is the crane in question a bird, a mechanical crane, or even an origami paper crane? Clarity is also improved by paying attention to the logical forms of claims. For instance, it is worth calling attention to the fact that there are two types of opposites: contraries and contradictories. Contradictories are pairs like living/dead and on/off: when one is not the case then the other term necessarily applies. So if one is not dead then one is living. On the other hand, contraries come in pairs like hot/cold and short/tall. While still opposites, there are intermediate values, so that a claim to the effect that this water is not hot does not entail that it is cold, for it might be lukewarm. But any means of clarifying one's environment fits into this basket of skills. Thus, for example, cost/benefit analysis clarifies matters from a certain perspective, and is important in accountancy, finance, and economics.

Once a claim has been clarified, it is still not fully understood. For genuine understanding, a second basket of skills may be brought into play, namely, concepts and skills of reliable *judgement*. Clarified claims must be brought into relation with other claims that one already either accepts or rejects. It is also important to see what follows from accepting or rejecting the clarified claim. To accept that Pat wears earrings entails that she wears jewellery. Again, suppose a minister claims that 'All of our unemployed people are unskilled, so we should help them develop the skills they need to re-enter the workforce.' While the social programme advocated may be good and noble, the justification given is poor because the claim regarding the unemployed is simply false. This is because the claim 'all unemployed people are unskilled' is logically equivalent to the claim that 'all skilled people are employed', which is falsified by the many skilled parents who choose to stay home to take care of their children. Skills in both inductive and deductive reasoning are therefore important to the inquiring self. Our authors' commitment to the essential unity of knowledge implies a version of this insight.

Once the relevant skill sets have been identified there remain important questions concerning the subject matters to be taught and the pedagogical methods to be employed in their teaching. We here defer consideration of which disciplines and subject matters should be taught, as these are examined in varying degrees of detail by our authors. What we will dwell upon, however, are broad characterisations of the sorts of pedagogical approaches and methods of presentation appropriate for each of the three types of knowledge that we have distinguished. Naturally, given the interpenetration and mutual dependence of know-how, know-that, and know-why, there is no one-size-fits-all solution for all disciplines and subject matters. But there are a number of general considerations that may prove fruitful for reflection and possibly useful as starting points for teachers thinking about their craft.

The most familiar place to start is with know-that. The pedagogic tools of know-that are generally well-accepted. They include textbooks, note-taking, formal lectures, and in short, whatever enables the student to appropriate relevant facts and information in an orderly way. Knowledge of facts is often seen as the primary marker of successful learning on the part of the student. Thus, a student coming to learn zoology must master a mass of facts the significance of many of which might not be understood until the student is more advanced in his or her studies. It is only after becoming acquainted with facts about kangaroos, panthers, and platypuses that a student can come to understand the traditional taxonomic division of mammals into marsupials, placentals, and monotremes. Given the nature of the discipline of zoology as a branch of biology, an orderly presentation of facts to students via a lecture can be an effective way of fostering genuine understanding, which can in turn provide a foundation for a more abstract inductive account of the general structures of living organisms. Thus, understanding Darwin's theory of natural selection requires wider appreciation of biological facts than mammalian zoology.

The orderly and systematic cultivation of know-how presents different challenges. To return to our earlier example of teaching swimming, it would not be sensible to rely exclusively upon pedagogical methods better suited to teaching know-that. Furnishing students with examples, which is characteristic of teaching know-that, is different from guiding students through appropriately chosen experiences, which is characteristic of teaching know-how.

What would a classroom lesson that uses experiential learning to teach know-how be like? One approach is to divide the lesson into four distinct parts. First, the teacher briefly introduces the concept or skill the students will be learning. Second, the teacher begins an activity which is selected precisely because it embodies the specific concept or skill being taught.[16] Third, upon completing the activity, the teacher asks the students where and when in the activity they used the target concept or skill. Fourth, the teacher asks the students where else in their lives they might use that concept or skill. These four distinct stages are captured by the *I-ACE* framework: *Introduction*, *Activity*, *Consolidation*, and *Extension*. A more detailed example is developed below.[17]

During the *introduction* stage, the central point of the lesson is shared with the students. Let us work with the following example: suppose we wish to teach students what a *heuristic* is. Coming to

[16]   Activities like the one developed below should occupy approximately 75% of the total class time.

[17]   While our language here is prescriptive, this is because as educators we have found this framework particularly useful for the sorts of things that we teach. Despite the prescriptive language we have no intention of suggesting that this is the only framework or always the best framework for teaching know-how. It might be noted, though, that the I-ACE framework can be modified to suit different teaching scenarios. For instance, a soccer coach could use something like this.

understand and appreciate heuristics involves know-how. Ultimately we want our students to be able to use, generate, test, and refine heuristics for themselves. So, the teacher begins by asking the students about their past experiences with, and present understanding of, heuristics. Some students might have heard the word 'heuristics' in a mathematics class.[18] But while students may have heard of heuristics, they might not have a general understanding of what heuristics are and why they are useful. Even less are students likely to be aware that they can generate new heuristics by reflecting on their own experiences, and that doing so is very much worth their while. So, after gathering the students' opinions, the teacher may draw out common elements and then propose a provisional definition. In this case, heuristics are *rules of thumb*, that is, action-guiding principles or ways of performing tasks that make us more effective.

After the introduction, the students engage in an *activity* that involves clear and repeated application of the skill or concept being learnt. Directed practice is central to the acquisition of know-how. As mentioned before, we cannot teach students how to swim by giving them examples of swimming; rather, they need to get into the water and practise swimming for themselves.

Imagine then that our students are presented with a game, for instance, *Blokus*.[19] This is a tessellation game in which four players take turns placing pieces on a board. The *Blokus* pieces are of different sizes, and there are rules governing their placement. One rule is that every piece placed must touch one of that player's previous pieces. The winner of the game is the player who manages to cover the most area of the board. Space is at a premium and it is not possible for all four players to get all of their pieces on the board. Given this experiential learning context, the heuristics generated by students will take the form of advice that they would give a friend on how to play *Blokus* well.

After playing the game once, students are invited to reflect on their experiences. For instance, the teacher could direct the students' attention to the pieces that they were unable to place. How would the students describe these pieces? What common features do the problematic pieces share? Invariably, the students notice that their leftover pieces tend to be much larger than the other pieces. They also note that the reason why they were unable to place these pieces

[18] For instance, the teacher might suggest that the students use the heuristic of estimating answers before solving a problem in detail.
[19] *Blokus* was invented by Bernard Tavitian and first released in 2000. For more information on the game itself check http://www.blokus.com/

is that they ran out of space to do so as the game progressed. For students, transforming these observations into a useful heuristic is straightforward: 'We should tell our friend to play large pieces before smaller ones.' Students typically suggest two other heuristics, namely that players should head towards the centre and that they should play pieces with more corners near the centre.

After clarifying the three heuristics generated by the students, the teacher then invites the students to play the game again. This time, though, the students will play a speed round and will be given a maximum of 10 seconds for each move. Just before playing '*Speed Blokus*', the teacher makes a series of predictions. First, most of the students in the class will do better than they did in the previous round even though they have much less time to think. Second, students who use all three heuristics will do better than students who employ two or only one. After being reminded once more of the heuristics that they have generated for themselves, the students launch into the game.

The *consolidation* phase of an experiential learning lesson occurs both at specific junctures during the activity and also immediately after the activity has been completed. Throughout the activity the teacher will, of course, be moving among the students, asking questions about what the students are doing and planning—basically, encouraging the students to be reflective. For the *Blokus* lesson, formal consolidation occurs immediately after the first game, when students are encouraged to generate heuristics for themselves, and again after the second game, when they are asked to evaluate whether the various players used the three heuristics and whether the teacher's predictions about improved performance came true. At this point the students might point out how the various heuristics helped them and then make suggestions about how the heuristics could be improved. Students are thereby furnished with immediate feedback showing how a bit of reflection on their own experiences can have a practical pay off, thereby motivating them to become more reflective learners. Furthermore, having operationalised the target concept, the students have little difficulty recalling specific examples of heuristics as well as a deeper understanding of what is meant by saying that a heuristic is an action-guiding principle or rule of thumb.

In the final *extension* stage of the lesson, students transfer their understanding of the concept or skill and deliberately explore other areas of their lives in which its application is possible. Adaptations and alterations are considered as students stretch their imaginative faculties, hooking the target concept into other operational contexts. For instance, after consolidating the students' understanding of heuristics, a teacher might ask the students to identify where else in their lives they encounter heuristics. At this point students are likely to reiterate the examples they mentioned during the introduction stage. This is entirely appropriate, for it indicates that the students are now better able to contextualise and correctly recognise their own examples and prior experiences. But then the teacher may ask: 'Where else do you find heuristics?', and then there is likely to be silence. The silence is not, however, due to confusion but to increased conceptual clarity and the difficulty of searching for new applications, a need which was not felt before. This is one reason why some level of befuddlement, even angst, is not a bad thing in the learning relation. With patience some student invariably takes the next step: 'Perhaps I use a heuristic when I cross the street? I always look both ways before crossing.' Then the students see that heuristics are everywhere. They are in games: in soccer one kicks the ball with the side or top of one's foot, not with the toes. They are in school and in all subjects: 'i before e except after c', 'a preposition is a terrible thing to end a sentence with', 'when taking a multiple choice exam and two of the answers are the same, cross them out'. The students give meaning and structure to their own experiences, thus integrating what previously appeared disparate and unconnected.

One advantage of following an I-ACE framework to teach know-how is that there is a narrative thread available that will help students make their experiences both more coherent and more memorable. In addition, students become more responsible for their own learning, in the sense that they are actively encouraged to try to formulate questions and find answers before immediately asking the teacher for the correct answer. Students are given a lot of heuristic advice in their daily lives, but whether they choose to follow those heuristics or not is often a function of whether they understand what the advice means and how following it can actually help them. Without understanding, students are likely to not follow the good advice that they are given, but with understanding, they are more likely to be on the lookout for opportunities to apply the useful heuristics that they have learnt.

The interpenetration of know-that and know-how is especially clear in the example of teaching heuristics. Consider the introduction stage of the *Blokus* lesson: the teacher draws out a provisional definition and presents it as a specimen of know-that. This know-that will structure the meanings that the students come to glean from their experience. During the consolidation phase know-that is also important, for while a rich experience is open to a multiplicity of interpretations, it is by selecting and focusing attention upon a particular meaning or range of meanings that the experience becomes a learning opportunity. This makes the know-that, as well as its associated know-how, more memorable for the student and thus easier to recall and apply in appropriate analogous situations.

However, note what typically happens when heuristics are successfully appropriated by a learner. The student may now be said not just to know how to play the game and to play it well, but also to see the point in playing the game and playing it well. Moreover, the capable student will have extrapolated the heuristics involved and be capable of applying them in analogous circumstances. This entails that the student is able to *recognise salience* insofar as the student is moving from a knowledge of particulars to generalities and perhaps even universals. It is at this point that the student may become increasingly questioning about ends, purposes, principles, and causes at higher levels of abstraction. This is the domain of *know-why*.

To return to our classroom example, heuristics are action-guiding principles. But not all action-guiding principles are of a technical sort, like those involved in *Blokus*. This is why educators need to be deeply concerned with the order of education broadly considered. Quite simply, some arenas of study are deeper and more important than others. Agrostography (the art of writing about grass) is not as important as political science. Architectonic arts structure purposes and are in a position to judge the adequacy of subordinate arts. For instance, the art of medicine is architectonic with respect to cosmetic surgery, for the ends and purposes of medicine are more comprehensive, and if ever a proposed cosmetic surgical procedure were to trespass the limits of what medicine deems appropriate, then that surgery would not be licit.

Many of the most important heuristics are intimately bound up with the realisation of those human potentialities that conduce to our flourishing as persons. Take the heuristic: 'You should be respectful to strangers.' First, a student must clarify what is meant by the terms 'strangers' and 'respect' and the moral force of 'should'. Then, the student must know how to manifest respect, something that we are typically habituated into by our social teachers.[20] Successful appropriation of the habits of know-how in terms of respectfulness to strangers may be generalised and extrapolated in a wide variety of ways. It could end up embracing members of one's immediate community, one's fellow citizens, all the way up to the notion of global citizenship. Only when we push to higher levels of abstraction can we see that different social teachers are aiming at the same goal even though they may prescribe different actions.

We might go on to ask: What is the relationship between respect and distinctive other-directed forms of relation such as love and friendship? These sorts of questions lead us into the realm of moral philosophy. But what we have remarked about how heuristics can be generalised in respect to the simple game of *Blokus*, and in turn elaborated in the direction of moral philosophy, find parallel expression in all deep forms of human inquiry.

The characteristic form of teaching in respect to know-why is *dialectic*. This usually involves Socratic questioning, embodying a communal pursuit of understanding and truth that unites all participants and transforms the participants as selves. Nonetheless, we need to be sensitive to the idea that not all forms of questioning are Socratic. What characterises truly Socratic questioning is the openness of the *teacher* to the *discovery* of new answers. When the teacher asks a question that must be answered with a patterned response already known by the teacher, such as: 'What is the sum of 34 and 42?', this is not Socratic.

Nor do questions that close off important ranges of possibly relevant lines of inquiry or answers on the part of the student count as Socratic questioning. Thus, the question: 'How should we execute persons deemed worthy of capital punishment?' would presuppose, in an objectionable way, the question as to whether capital punishment should be socially accepted. Socratic questioning opens *conversations* that in principle can be deepened and extended without limit.[21] The Socratic question: 'Why be good?' is an example. Teaching know-why, viewed as a structured activity involving question-

---

[20] It is interesting to note that different social teachers habituate us into showing respect in different ways even though it is a common interest in showing respect that motivates those varying expressions. Belching after a meal is a sign of approval in some cultures whereas in others it may be deemed rude.

[21] This is decidedly not to say that when questioning is open-ended then nothing is achieved by it. Socratic questioning rightly moves on when truth has been discovered. The fundamental purpose of the new questions and new dialogue that emerge is to consolidate and deepen our understanding of those truths we have uncovered and the ways those truths relate to other truths. We must not fall

ing and dialectic, more closely resembles the *order of discovery* than the *order of teaching*. For example, we may come to know why being kind to strangers is a good thing, and then consider how we concretely do so, but when we are teaching our children, we first teach them concretely how to behave (say 'please' and 'thank you') before we teach them why they should behave that way. Furthermore, for Augustine, Aquinas, and Newman, there is a deep structure and ordering of our know-why, for there is a single goal or *telos* towards which wonder is ultimately directed, namely, God as cause and end of existence.

Some of the ways in which Socratic questioning may be evinced will involve practical considerations about length of time, immediacy of engagement among participants, number of interlocutors, as well as appropriate environmental settings (symposia are a good idea and wine often helps). Not all four of our authors, at least in terms of the formal presentation of their ideas within the texts selected, display Socratic techniques. Augustine and Aquinas certainly do internalise the movement of question and answer characteristic of dialectic. They are addressing students in their works, however advanced those students might be. Newman and Mill, on the other hand, are engaged at the level of rhetorical persuasion. They are not primarily addressing students but rather are pitching their views to university professors and to an intellectual and social elite. Nonetheless, all four are committed to questioning as the central activity at the heart of education.

Mention of the order of teaching prompts questions about the *order of teaching teaching*. The order of presentation and mode of presentation should vary for teaching teachers. This is especially clear when a teacher who has been accustomed to traditional lecture-style methods is introduced to experiential learning. There is no short-cut through experiential learning, and so teachers who would teach using experiential methods would benefit from participating in the very activities they would use in the classroom. Doing so builds a bridge between teacher and student, and the teacher can empathise more readily with what the student is experiencing during the lesson. Furthermore, any teacher who is tasked with presenting a new lesson will naturally focus on the mechanics of what is to be done in the classroom. This is prompted by a concern to know the answer to the very practical question: 'What is it I need to do in the classroom?'

---

into the trap of valorising a mere method, Socratic questioning, over the end which it is intended to serve, the discovery of truth.

As such, those who would engage in teaching teachers often vary the order in which they present the content of the classes taught from the I-ACE framework mentioned above.[22] Thus, one might wish to expose those who will have to teach the new lesson to the concrete activities first and only afterwards have those trainee teachers observe a sample experiential learning class using that activity. This has the benefit of allowing the teachers to worry less about distracting peripheral matters, like game rules or how to run the particular activity, and focus instead on what is really being taught.

Failures in the teaching of know-why can occur by supposing that the order of teaching is the same as the order of teaching teaching. A disordered approach to know-why can preclude successful appropriation of know-how. For example, this can occur when teachers focus on learning the rules of a game like *Blokus* instead of attending to the concept that the activity is intended to serve.

It is in the interrelationships among know-that, know-how, and know-why that much of education and teaching stumbles. The ways in which this can happen are legion, and we can only draw attention to some of the more dramatic instances here. Failures within one type of knowledge infect others. In particular, failures in know-that will negatively impact know-how, and failures in know-how will negatively impact know-why.

One genus of failing is characterised by confusing one sort of knowledge for another. It is only when we move from know-that to the experiential forms of knowing-how and knowing-why that we really come to discover the connections among and the meanings of what we know. Teachers accustomed to a lecture style of presentation may treat an experiential learning class as a case of know-that. A teacher could hijack the *Blokus* lesson by telling the students up front what the three heuristics are. This would block the students from having the experience of discovering the heuristics for themselves. This is as undesirable as the teacher making all of the moves for the student, thereby preventing any personal operationalisation of the desired concepts by the students themselves.

At the level of the interrelation between know-how and know-why, failure may arise because the teacher neglects to provide the context within which the particular know-how finds its justification. It is possible to pass a language examination by memorising model answers, and thereby know how to answer the questions,

---

[22] These remarks also apply analogously to coaches of coaches and trainers of trainers.

without ever knowing why those responses constitute good answers to the questions posed.

Focus upon one type of knowledge at the expense of the others can also lead to failures in teaching and learning. A mind occupied with know-that may be likened to the magpie that collects whatever items strike its fancy without thought of the coherence or meaning of the collection. Focus on know-how can degenerate into an unreflective valorisation of technique over substance. And an exclusive focus on know-why can lead to disastrous ineffectiveness in practical affairs.

Failures may occur within the individual domains of knowing. Let us begin with failures in know-that. We have already discussed some of these in the context of the X who teaches. The teacher must guard against failures in respect to truth, and be vigilant in the pursuit, retention, and presentation of what is true. This is to say that at the simplest level the teacher must get the facts straight and at the personal level exhibit the virtue of diligence. Moreover, teachers can also fall short by assuming that knowledge of facts is sufficient for knowledge by acquaintance. For example, one might read all of the books and see all of the movies about love, but until one has experienced love, one does not understand love. To have command of the know-that of love, one must be acquainted with the experience of what it is to be a lover and a beloved.

The know-that of love requires the know-how of the lover. The teacher of know-how might err in choosing the wrong experiential vehicle for instruction (not all games are as well suited to teaching heuristics as *Blokus*). The teacher might draw out the wrong meaning from an experience, or focus attention upon a confusing subsidiary aspect of the experience. *Blokus*, for example, could be used to teach the methods of deductive reasoning, because game rules are expressible as propositions and one may draw out inferences from them, but this would be to emphasise a dimension that is not experientially privileged in *Blokus*.

Again, a teacher may fail to sufficiently focus the student's learning experience. Any rich activity is open to a multiplicity of meanings, but only one key meaning or range of meanings should be selected. Otherwise confusion is likely to arise in the student, and the useful and memorable specificity of the experience is lost. A student who temporarily forgets what the word 'heuristic' means will recall what is meant in detail by being reminded of the game that was used to teach the concept. Finally, a teacher can fail in respect to teaching know-how by not using sufficiently varied experiences and techniques. If the same technique is always used — for instance, a student is taught to draw a diagram for every word problem in mathematics the same way — then the student may become confused about important nuances and thus the utility of the method will be undercut. Different experiences and models should be chosen to reflect and illuminate the diversity of what is being taught.

Failure in respect to know-why can also involve failures with respect to truth and the truth-seeking virtues. Einstein is reported as saying that when the theory doesn't fit the facts, change the facts. Someone as insightful as Einstein can apply this tongue-in-cheek advice with aplomb, but in many cases it is the theory that is blinkered and needs adjusting. An overly-doctrinaire approach to teaching know-why is deadly to the spirit of open inquiry. The notion that teaching know-why is the transmission of ready-made explanations that capture the whole story is inimical to know-why. Often the failing of philosophers — and all educationists are philosophers — involves elevating a genuine insight and partial truth to the status of the whole truth. For instance, it is true that behaving ethically involves both good intentions and good results, but to emphasise one dimension at the expense of the other can lead to a doctrinally motivated rejection of the evidence of common sense and experience. Another way of putting the same point is to highlight the failure as a lack of due intellectual humility. Here the truth-seeking virtues are closed off either by a refusal to be seriously engaged in the questioning process or by an intransigence which fails to take seriously plausible alternatives. We have noted that there is a self-transformative dimension on the part of teacher and pupil within a genuine dialectic. One warning sign that self-transformation on the part of the teacher is not present occurs when a teacher does not sufficiently take on board the insights of the pupil. Surprise is a mark of dialogue, and a Socratic teacher should be able to note instances in which the teacher has learnt from the pupil.

Z (in 'X teaches Y to Z')

In analysing the 'Z' component of *X teaches Y to Z*, the paradigm case will surely be the *student* or *pupil*. However, under the conditions of advanced modernity it is increasingly rare for a student to be a sole learner. Most institutionalised settings of education demand a group or *community of learners and inquirers,* whether it be in the setting of the school, university, or some other such organised framework. A recognition of this is found in sentences in which we say that the teacher teaches a subject to the class. This emphasises the class-room as a social environment and nuances the sort of experiences that one may expect students to have. Again the paradigm case is not exhaustive. We can in some sense teach animals. However, this is not the sense of teaching pre-eminent in our four authors. A clear indication of this is that our authors are much occupied with the concept of know-why, and as such leave the notion of training, which at best is technique-driven, behind.

It might also be said that we teach *society at large*, as when the Civil Rights Movement, which was initially a small group of activists, taught the larger society around them about the systemic brutalisation and victimisation of minorities in the USA; or again in the time of Newman and Mill, when the Suffragettes began the process of changing wider society's views of women. Similarly in so far as we can talk of a business as a *corporate person*, certain individuals or groups can help shape, and thus teach, the corporation to be, for example, either more ethical or more ruthless. The notion of a 'learning organisation' finds its root here.

Z may also refer to more elusive categories, as when we say that Socrates, by his example of accepting the unjust imposition of the death penalty, taught *posterity* something about the meaning of courage and commitment to ideals. This is the level at which pivotal figures in history, be they political (Alexander the Great, Charlemagne, Nelson Mandela), religious (Jesus, Buddha, Mohammed), or otherwise (Aristotle, Newton) operate.

These examples of Z as representing society or posterity are important because they emphasise once again the crucial connections that understanding, teaching, and learning have to communities of inquirers and thus to the social context within which all education is elaborated. It is worth mentioning again the idea that when we say X *teaches* Y *to* Z we are pointing to a relation, one that embraces in diverse modes the teacher and student (since at least in many cases the education process is reciprocal — the student learns from the teacher but the teacher in turn learns from the student). The mutuality of teaching and learning extends to the community of fellow inquirers and the social context within which all are inter-related.

Even when we focus on the paradigm case of Z as student, the student is not immune to issues of temporality, temperament, and circumstance. Plato and Aristotle thought that certain fields of inquiry are better deferred until a student is middle-aged. They suggested that moral philosophy requires a long experience of life before it can be broached. Clearly we cannot treat the primary school pupil and the doctoral student in the same way for they are different kinds of Z's even though they are both apprentices.[23] Moreover temperaments and capacities differ widely, so that much of education will be devoted to know-how and know-that while proportionately less will be expended on know-why. Both Newman and Mill are very concerned that higher level education should be expressly occupied with knowing why, and this helps contextualise their focus on the specific content of a liberal education.

These reflections raise a further important question since they are related to the nature of the learner. So we should ask: In virtue of *what* is it that the learner qua learner can learn? One answer has already been discussed: we are by nature all learners because we are curious and because the world around us is such that we wonder about it and our place within it. In this respect we are all learners from infancy until we draw our last breath. But given the wide range of aptitudes and capacities in individuals, there are different motivations among learners and these motivations are shaped by many varied and sometimes competing forces.

As philosophy professors, we often come across capable, even gifted, students, who become energised and excited (like the initial moments in a love affair) when taking their first philosophy courses, but who refuse to major in philosophy because of family pressures (what can you do with a philosophy degree?), and those pressures are themselves often shaped by broader trends in society. The profusion of MBAs is a direct consequence of the perceived needs of contemporary economics and the privileged status of business in advanced capitalism.

The corollary of this is a diminishment in the status of the humanities within the university and even in pre-university curricula. In many parts of the world there is a corresponding diminishment in the status of the teacher both at school and university levels. The loss of social status of teachers is often tied up with social and political factors. In highly egalitarian societies where direct participation in school budgeting occurs, there is typically a strong current against increasing teacher salaries or expanding teacher recruitment. This is because many citizens are uncomfortable with what the teacher does

---

[23] The notion of an apprentice clearly applies to know-how and know-why; analogous usage covers know-that, insofar as even when we learn for ourselves, the realities themselves, as prompts of our learning, are the masters that teach us.

from a societal perspective. Teachers are, at least historically, required to be the enforcers of a meritocratic system wherein individual students are assessed and judged.

These forces have a profound impact on the learner, for basic material conditions of the teacher/student relation are partially determined by these wider social concerns. Liberal educational ideals are difficult to justify at the political level when they are subject to the judgment of a voting populace that is widely innocent of them and whose concerns are primarily attached to the practical demands of the marketplace. Professional training is immediately comprehensible and desirable within such a context, whereas the longer-range implications of education in the liberal arts are more difficult to appreciate.

This challenge also faces the university system in general, for a certain pragmatic view would suggest that students be exposed only to trades and those aspects of disciplines that are directly useful in the student's future working life. (Indeed, this is precisely the debate which concerned Newman and Mill.) These political positions neglect the reality that all practical disciplines are examples of applied theory, and without theory and the articulation of theory there can be no application and no progress. But since progress of at least a technological sort does occur within society at large, students trained only in explicit procedures run the risk of becoming economically irrelevant and hence sidelined by the very market forces they were supposed to serve.

Thus far we have considered the learner Z in the context of wider social relations. We would now like to emphasise two features particular to the learner qua learner. First, it would seem to be the case that a certain level of *receptivity* is required by the learner concerning what is to be taught. When we use the term receptivity, it may well be thought to designate a form of passivity on the part of a learner. But while certainly there is a dimension of passivity in being receptive to learning, it is not a purely passive phenomenon. Our ability to be receptive of learning, though markedly different among individuals, nonetheless requires some form of interest or questioning attitude in respect to the subject matter of the teaching. In the absence of such interest or questioning it would be hard to see how receptivity would even be possible, and this seems to be true even for cases in which our interest in the subject matter is entirely extrinsic, pragmatic, or utilitarian. In other words, the learner may be motivated in two ways. Firstly, the learner may have a genuine desire or need to know about the subject, in which case the interest is intrinsic. Secondly, the learner may desire or need to know something for the sake of some other concern, such as making a livelihood, in which case it is extrinsic. In both cases there is an *active receptivity* on the part of the learner.

The second feature of the learner qua learner is closely related to the first, but perhaps is more deeply related to individual capacities. It would seem that along with receptivity we need, in many instances, to talk of *aptness*, which is closely aligned with *aptitude*. Different temperaments are drawn to different objects of learning. Some people are, as it were, naturally inclined and show an early aptitude for mathematics, athletics, dancing, building, and so on. Others may be interested in painting, and as pointed out earlier, may have an earnest desire to be a painter, but lack the requisite aptness and aptitudes to realise their desire. Of course aptitudes can be developed, and the virtue of tenacity is an important one in such development, but sometimes, even often, the summoning of all the resources of desire and tenacity will not result in successful appropriation of the object of knowledge. Not everyone can be a ballerina; some people love music, but are tone deaf when it comes to performing.

As custodians of their own active receptivity, *learners are responsible for their own learning*. As such, they too can be prone to fail as learners. They can fail with respect to truth and the truth-seeking virtues. Stubborn mulishness, sloth, indifference, cynicism and rampant scepticism, lack of openness, docility, are only some of the ways in which the learner can fail. But each of these vices comes with a contrasting vice: overweening enthusiasm, frenetic activity, blind attachment, uncritical acceptance, close-mindedness, lack of attachment to truth, and fear of questioning. Many of these may be traced to two sources: pride and lack of love.

X teaches Y to Z

When our proposition is taken as a whole it indicates just how complex the processes and relations in understanding teaching and learning are. We have only touched on some of the central concerns because many of these issues are explored in the four texts collected in this work. However, a fuller treatment would need to look at the rapidly expanding social science literature (much of it quantitative and empirical, backed by qualitative consideration) on education. Of particular importance will be questions addressing the psychology of both the teacher and the learner at different stages, studies of classroom dynamics, spatial organisation, and the various modes of learning and teaching. We could learn much from sociology: the classroom is a social setting, and as such comes with its own characteristic power relations, group dynamics, and interactions inside classrooms, between classes, and at the whole school level. These relations in turn will be impacted by broader social and institutional questions and how these shape and are shaped by both desired and actual practices and outcomes. From political science we can learn much about how political structures, public policy decision making, and ideologies impact education. And from economics we can learn how resource allocation conditions what can and should be done, for the economic notion of an opportunity cost becomes value-laden once realised in concrete institutional structures. These are just a few of the host of questions and challenges facing educators from these perspectives.

Our four authors, Augustine, Aquinas, Newman, and Mill, and the texts presented in this volume bear witness to abiding controversies in the philosophy and practice of education. Each author addresses perennial problems that we have attempted to illuminate in our discussion of *X teaches Y to Z*. Each does so in provocative and engaging ways, but in different contexts, with different nuances, and as a result of different polemics arising from their social contexts. There is much they agree on but also much that divides them. In what follows we will provide some context and brief overviews of the central arguments and concerns of our authors. They are noteworthy exemplars not only as fine flowerings of the human intellect, but as embodying the truth-seeking virtues that all educators strive to cultivate. What they have to say is not dated, for they preserve an attachment to open-ended questioning regarding issues of know-that, know-how, and especially know-why that are very much with us today. Their arguments are open to refutation and to containing truth of contemporary import. Indeed, it is our hope that the readers of this volume will reflectively engage our four authors from a contemporary perspective. This is entirely fair to our authors because they are self-aware participants in a community of reflection and inquiry dispersed over space and time yet cohesive in its common vision and commitment to uncovering what is true and good.

CHAPTER 2.1

Augustine: Commentary

Augustine

Aurelius Augustinus Hipponensis (henceforth Augustine) was born in 354 AD in the *municipium* of Thagaste (modern day Souk Ahras, Algeria, close to the border with Tunisia). He died in 430, as the Arian[1] Vandals besieged the city of Hippo where he was bishop, marking another stage in the demise of the Roman Empire. Rome had already been sacked in 410 by Alaric the Visigoth, but the slow decline of Roman grandeur took place over a period of about 320 years which culminated in 476 when Romulus Augustus, the last Emperor of the Western Roman Empire, was deposed by Odoacer, a Germanic chieftain. Augustine thus lived at a time which heralded the death knell of the ancient world and the beginnings of mediaeval western European Christendom.[2] Augustine's great legacy to western civilization is that intellectually he united both worlds in drawing from the ancient thought of Greece and Rome and providing a Christian understanding of the intellectual achievements of the ancients. His new synthesis is a remarkable achievement even today and for those of us, who remain Christians in the West, our debates, agreements and disagreements are still pursued in Augustine's shadow.[3]

---

[1] Arianism was a schismatic sect of Christianity that held the view that the Second Person of the Trinity, Christ, is created and thus does not exist eternally with the Father.

[2] See J. M. Rist's magnificent *Augustine: Ancient Thought Baptized*, Cambridge, Cambridge University Press, 2003. Rist notes that, 'Despite his lack of resources he managed to sit in judgment on ancient philosophy and ancient culture.' p. 1.

[3] He was canonised by popular recognition before official procedures were ratified. In 1298 he was recognised as one of the great Doctors of the Church.

Augustine's educational background reflects not just the preoccupations of his era but their lived existential facticity. His father, Patricius, was a polytheist[4] while his mother, Monica, was a Christian. So Augustine must have been aware from a very young age of one of the central problems of his era — the conflict between the polytheism of much of the ancient world and the new monotheistic religion, Christianity. In what follows we present some of the key features of Augustine's life and times that have particular bearing on his views on education and in particular on the *De Magistro*.

The formal education Augustine received was very much that of anyone who held Roman citizenship, an education that had changed little from its origins in ancient Greece.[5] Children went to primary school when they were about seven years old, then to a *grammaticus* (a professional teacher of poetry and literature) from the age of 11 or 12, and finally to the *rhetor* (an orator and teacher of rhetoric) at about 15 until the student reached 20.[6] It was as a result largely a literary education concentrating on the great classical authors Vergil, Sallust, Terrence, and Cicero,[7] with little attention paid to philosophy, science and history.[8] The goal of such an education was to produce orators capable of persuading people — a political art with a pedigree originating with the professional teachers (Sophists) in ancient Greece.[9]

Augustine's elementary education was conducted in his home town of Thagaste and nearby at Madaura, but his father recognised

---

(*Doctor Gratiae*, Doctor of Grace) under Pope Boniface VIII. He is the patron saint of brewers, theologians, printers, and sore eyes.

[4]   We prefer the term polytheist to the more usual 'pagan' because of the latter's (contested) etymological link to 'country bumpkin', and certainly in this sense it is not applicable to someone as sophisticated as Porphyry, a determined critic of Christianity.

[5]   Marrou suggests that 'It was not even a case of imitating; it was on the whole a pure and simple transfer.' H.I. Marrou, *A History of Education in Antiquity*, New York, Sheed and Ward, 1956, p. 265. For an accessible treatment of the development of educational theory and practice relevant for Augustine, see David Knowles, *The Evolution of Medieval Thought*, Hong Kong, Longman, 1962.

[6]   See A. Stock, 'Chiastic Awareness and Education In Antiquity,' *Biblical Theology Bulletin*, 1984, 14: 23, p. 25.

[7]   See S. Harrison, 'Augustinian Learning', in A. O. Rorty (ed.), *Philosophers on Education: Historical Perspectives*, London and New York, Routledge, 1998, p.67.

[8]   See, P. Brown's peerless biography, *Augustine of Hippo: A Biography*, Berkeley, University of California Press, 2000, p. 24.

[9]   See for example G.B. Kerferd, *The Sophistic Movement*, Cambridge, Cambridge University Press, 1981.

his precocious intelligence and, despite financial hardship, Augustine was sent to the provincial capital, Carthage, to continue his studies with the *rhetors*. So aged 17 he arrived in Carthage, a young man from the country open to the allures of a big city. At Carthage he discovered theatre, found like-minded friends who indulged in sensual delights, took a concubine and fathered a son, Adeodatus, who is his interlocutor in the *De Magistro*.

Augustine's life may well be seen in terms of a series of conversions (seven are mentioned in his *Confessions*), the first of which occurs in Carthage. In 386, while reading a copy of Cicero's *Hortensius*,[10] he is first converted to philosophy. For the ancients there does not appear to have been a strict dichotomy between philosophy and religion. Indeed, philosophy was conceived of as a way of life that has much in common with religious conversion and vocation.[11] The *Hortensius* provided Augustine with arguments rejecting his dissolute libertinism and advocating a life of reason and contemplation. But it was only one of the major sources of influence on the shaping of his philosophical character.

Before his conversion to philosophy Augustine was attracted to the teachings of the Manichaeans. Manichaeism was a mystical cult that exemplified the relation between philosophy and religion because it embraced both a way of life — a method of living — and a doctrine concerning ultimate reality. Manichaeism was based on the doctrines of the Zoroastrian-inspired Mani (AD 216–276), who articulated a cosmology involving the struggle between a good, spiritual world of light, and an evil, material world of darkness.[12] It may be speculated that what excited Augustine and led to him joining this group (apart from their proposed solution to the problem of evil, which he later rejects) was their appeal to a form of gnosticism. Gnosticism in its non-dogmatic formulations asserted a direct illu-

---

[10] Cicero's *Hortensius* is an encomium to the philosophical life of reason and overcoming passions. Despite its popularity in the ancient world it is no longer extant. A reconstruction of the Aristotelian work upon which Cicero based his *Hortensius* has been attempted. See Aristotle's *Protrepticus, An Attempt at Reconstruction*. I. Düring, Göteborg, Studia graeca et latina Gothoburgensia, 1961; translated by A. H. Chroust, South Bend, University of Notre Dame Press, 1964.

[11] The clearest articulation of this symmetry of religion and philosophy in the ancient world is still P. Hadot's ground-breaking study *Philosophy as a Way of Life: Spiritual Exercises from Socrates to Foucault*, ed. A.I. Davidson, trans. M. Chase, Oxford, Blackwell, 1995.

[12] For a recent treatment of Manichaeism see J. BeDuhn, *The Manichaen Body: In Discipline and Ritual*, Baltimore, The Johns Hopkins University Press, 2000.

mination of the soul by God and this viewpoint was to be of enormous influence on Augustine's epistemology and, in particular, on his theory of illumination which appears in the *De Magistro*.[13] Augustine was profoundly sensitive to the symbolic (one might say sacramental) dimensions of reality, and the symbolic aspects of light, illumination, and the relations and distinctions between God's Word (*Verbum*) and human speech provide much of the raw material discussed in the *De Magistro*.

Perhaps the most important intellectual influence on Augustine's milieu was that of Platonism.[14] It was his discovery of the books of the Platonists that led first to his rejection of Manichaeism and subsequently to his rejection of the scepticism and materialism of the New Academy and its leading figure Cicero.[15] Augustine was attracted to two key features in Platonism. First, its account of Truth and certainty, and second its characteristic concern with non-material reality. Just as Aquinas is widely held to have synthesised Aristotelian and Christian thought, so Augustine (who in some measure always remains a Platonist) synthesises Christianity and Platonism.[16] Augustine's conversion to Platonism represents another step in his spiritual understanding of man's relation to the divine.

The ancient world, conceiving of philosophy as a way of life, not merely an academic pursuit, had maintained a fascination with small communities of like-minded persons living together apart

[13] For more on gnosticism see B. A. Pearson, *Ancient Gnosticism: Traditions And Literature*, Minneapolis, Fortress Press, 2007.

[14] Augustine's understanding of 'the Platonic books' is largely drawn from just a few books of Plotinus, a little of the Platonic corpus, and commentators of Plato in Latin.

[15] The Academy was founded by Plato around 387 BC. Scholars generally distinguish three phases of the Academy beginning with Plato, then the Middle Academy of 266 BC led by Arcesilaus, and finally the New Academy beginning under the leadership of Carneades in 155 BC. It was to the latter that Cicero's philosophical scepticism appeals. Ancient scepticism held the view that knowledge of things is impossible, and so a proper response is one of withdrawal and impassivity. For an overview of the Platonic Academy, see W. K. C. Guthrie, *A History of Greek Philosophy*, Vol. 5, Cambridge, Cambridge University Press, 1978. On Cicero, see E. Rawson, *Cicero: A Portrait*, London, Duckworth, 2009.

[16] We should, however, be aware of Aquinas' debt to Platonism, much of which is due to Augustine's influence. See, for example, the classic discussion of C. Fabro, *Participation et Causalité selon S. Tomas d'Aquin*, Louvain, Université Catholique de Louvain, 1961.

from society.[17] It was with this whole-hearted conversion to philosophy as a way of life that Augustine founds a commune of friends, including Monica and Adeodatus, at Cassiciacum, where communally they pursue their philosophical studies.[18] However, the Platonism he embraces is complemented by yet another conversion he undergoes while pursuing an academic career as *rhetor* in Milan (384), one which, in his view, unites true philosophy and true religion.

While in Milan Augustine came under the influence of many Christians, most notably Bishop Ambrose, who provides Augustine with a concern that helps shape much of his thinking. Ambrose's use of Biblical exegesis is brought to bear in debates against the Manichaeans and is allied to a forthright espousal of the immateriality of both the soul and God (*Confessions* 6.5.7-8). These views raised for Augustine a powerful set of questions centred around the nature of belief and certainty. While Platonism had converted Augustine at an intellectual level, he now begins to wonder whether believing is a necessary component of some kinds of knowing and understanding. Such belief requires more than intellectual assent. It requires a re-orientation of the whole person, mind, will, body and spirit. Augustine comes to think that some truths can only be understood when complemented by faith. Moreover, this marks a breach with the philosophy of the Platonists because an ideal of the ancient world (going back to Homer) was the notion of human self-sufficiency.[19] Augustine was beginning to think that human beings need both faith and God's grace to ascend towards, let alone attain, certitude of truth.

---

[17] This renunciation of wider society has its origins in the Pythagorean brotherhoods or *synedria* who held all things in common. A Christian form of ascetic renunciation of wider social life was known to Augustine through his reading of the monks of Egypt and particularly St. Anthony. See Brown, *op. cit.*, p. 99, and Augustine, *Confessions* VIII, vi, 15.

[18] Brown, *op. cit.*, writes: 'The Ideal of philosophical retirement was as stringent as any call to monastic life.' p. 99.

[19] The Greek ideal of self-sufficiency, which was originally part of the aristocratic warrior code found in the Homeric epics, later took on a more philosophical tint. Essentially it came to signify the capacity of an individual to attain knowledge of the divine and perfection of virtue in the self without *requiring* others or supernatural help. It is thus an extreme view of self-actualisation. This ancient notion was subsequently transferred to the retirement of philosophers in a community that was relatively self-sufficient and able to provide for those necessary accompaniments of self-actualisation such as friendship among community members. On the Greek ideal, see A.W.H. Adkins, '"Friendship" and "Self-Sufficiency" in Homer and Aristotle,' *The Classical Quarterly* (New Series) 13, 1963, pp. 30-45.

While in a garden in Milan Augustine's movement towards embracing Christianity achieves a dramatic break-through when he receives what he takes to be a mystical epiphany. He hears a child repeatedly chanting the phrase *Tolle lege! Tolle lege!* ('take it and read'). Opening the nearest book he reads St. Paul's *Letter to the Romans* and his conversion to Christianity is sealed, though he is not formally baptised until late July 386.[20] A second mystical experience befalls Augustine together with his mother in Ostia—a mystical vision of God—but by this time Augustine has fully embraced Christianity and is about to embark on his life-time mission, as priest and later bishop, showing that true philosophy and true religion are one and the same.

Understanding Augustine's *De Magistro*

In his *Retractiones* (I, x, ii), written towards the end of his life, Augustine briefly reviews his *De Magistro*, highlighting the intellectual capacities of his son, Adeodatus, and the latter's contribution to the ideas explored in that work. It is significant that Augustine explicitly recalls that the *De Magistro* was written around the same time as *De Genesi contra Manichaeos* (388-89). Augustine returns time and again over his long life to the first book of the Bible. The uncompleted *De Genesi contra Manichaeos* is followed by *De Genesi ad litteram* (393-94), and again in an extended discussion at the end of the *Confessions* (401). A longer commentary is penned in 402, and in the 11th and 12th books of *De civitate Dei* he provides further reflections. The significance of Augustine's abiding concerns with *Genesis* together with the fact that the *De Magistro* was written around the same time as *De Genesi contra Manichaeos* provide cause for speculating that the *De Magistro* exemplifies themes that are deeply connected to his understanding of God's creative agency in *Genesis*.[21] Indeed, Augustine explicitly heralds the connection between teaching and God's creative agency in *Confessions* (II.8). He also points to the crucial connections at a symbolic level between God's Word (*Verbum*), human speaking, language, and illumination, all of which are central foci of his discussion of teaching, learning, and understanding in the *De Magistro*.

---

[20] Brown, *op. cit.*, p. 97.

[21] This line of thought is suggested by D. Chidester, 'The Symbolism of Learning in St. Augustine,' *The Harvard Theological Review* 76:1, 1983, pp. 73-90. We are indebted to Chidester in what follows, though it should be pointed out that Chidester's interpretation implicitly draws upon the work of Hadot, *op cit.*

The Gospel of St. John begins *In principio erat verbum...* ('In the beginning was the Word...'). All creation comes to be out of God's Word. This Word is identified as divine Wisdom — the perfection of understanding and certitude, a role accorded to the interior teacher in the *De Magistro*. Augustine writes: 'In this Beginning, O God, hast thou made heaven and earth, namely, in thy Word, in thy Son, in thy Power, in thy Wisdom, in thy Truth; after a wonderful manner speaking, and after a wonderful manner making.'[22] Wisdom is experienced as a super-sensory light directly attributable to, and manifesting, God's creative agency — *Fiat lux* ('Let there be light'). It is this light that illuminates the soul of the learner by means of the interior teacher in the *De Magistro (xi.38)*. As Chidester puts it: 'Every act of learning symbolically recapitulates the primordial creation in this convergence of word and light ... Augustine's learning theory is a religious statement based on a correspondence between the intrinsic process of human learning and the primordial creative event.'[23]

The parallels between God's creative agency and the processes involved in teaching, learning, and understanding are too close to be accidental. When God's Word creates, it does so with wisdom and light, and heaven and earth come to be. For Augustine, Heaven designates the spiritual order which is perfect and beautiful.[24] Earth, on the other hand, is at first an unformed bodily substance.[25] Later Scholastic philosophers would refer to earth in this sense as a substratum, pure potency, or universal substance.[26] Augustine describes earth as 'a formless depth also lacking light'.[27] In order to have form something must receive light. Light is bestowed upon earth by God's participative agency by means of his eternal Word. This Word which is Wisdom breathes form into the formless. The divine Word brings all realities into being by enlightening them.

A central distinction in Augustine's *De Magistro* is between the exterior teacher (a human being) and the interior teacher, who is Christ, the Word of God illuminating the human soul. The first two kinds of teaching broached in the *De Magistro* are associated with the

---

[22]   *Confessions* 11.9. *St. Augustine's Confessions*, trans. W. Watts, Cambridge, Harvard University Press, 1988, pp. 227 & 229.

[23]   *Op. cit.*, pp. 75-76.

[24]   *De Genesi ad litteram* I.3.

[25]   *Ibid.*

[26]   See, for example, Aquinas, *De Principiis Naturæ*.

[27]   *De Genesi imperfecta*, 14. *On Genesis*, trans. E. Hill, ed. J. E. Rotelle, New York, New City Press, 2002, p. 121.

exterior teacher — teaching as reminding and teaching as presentation. Both of these forms of teaching (which we discuss in more detail presently) are somewhat inadequate since the knowledge imparted by such forms of teaching lack the level of certitude Augustine thinks is necessary for proper understanding. The third kind of teaching discussed in the *De Magistro* — discovering truth within — parallels God's creative activity in *Genesis*. Human teaching begins by using words (signs), but words are open to multiple senses and misinterpretation. Even indicating, as in teaching as presentation, involves ambiguities and possible failures of interpretation. By indicating realities in themselves, instead of merely their signs, teaching as presentation constitutes a higher form of teaching, learning, and understanding than that afforded by teaching as reminding which relies on audible signs or, in the case of the written word, visible signs of signs.

Teaching as reminding directs the learner by audible signs towards the realities that the signs point to. But teaching as presentation involves grasping realities in themselves by directing our vision towards realities. However, teaching as discovering truth within provides secure and firm certitude in respect to reality because it moves beyond the changeable sensible world to embrace the intelligible world. Here learning is a process of illumination — a direct vision of the soul much like Augustine's mystical vision in Ostia. God, or rather Christ as Word, directly and mysteriously illuminates the soul. It is then the Word of God that illuminates the soul as interior teacher just as God's creative Word breathes form into formless potential matter.[28]

---

[28] As Chidester aptly summarises:
'Augustine understands learning as a reflection of a deeper symbolic process, based on the paradigm of creation, in which the word initiates an action and the light gives it intelligible form and order... Therefore, based on the pattern of creation, it is possible to conclude that the word, as the *interior magister*, initiates the process of learning by generating ideas in the human mind. But the word, as in the creation of the primary *informis materia*, generates ideas without form or light. In other words, it may be the case that the activity of the word, as the inner teacher, is to be understood as the motive force which generates ideas within the human mind *in potentia*. The activity of the word is a kind of living potential for knowledge, as yet unformed and unrealised, which must be completed by illumination....Word and light come to life simultaneously in the act of learning; the distinction between them merely clarifies two dimensions of the process, the agency of the word and the formative influence of light, which Augustine understands to occur simultaneously as Christ teaches within the soul in every act of learning.' (*Op. cit.*, p. 89)

Before we turn to providing a more detailed exegesis of the arguments we need to briefly say a few words about Augustine's idiosyncratic account of memory, as his views on memory are likely to present an obstacle to contemporary readers of the *De Magistro*. Human beings, in common with other animals, have a perceptive faculty that gathers information from the material world and forms images corresponding to these realities. Augustine thinks that it is in the memory that these images are stored and operated upon. Memory recalls the past, considers the present, and projects into the future. (*Confessions* XI.20.) Thus, Augustine's discussion of memory brings together what we would nowadays call imagination as well as memory. Indeed, Augustine's account of memory makes of it a kind of storehouse of all possible representations of experience and possible experiences. We might be temped to simply say that for Augustine memory is mind, though that would distort his thought somewhat, since he accepts that there are non-representational forms of thinking that go beyond the necessarily representational operations of memory. When reading the *De Magistro*, it may be useful to think of memory as a storehouse of images, and when one encounters locutions that sound very peculiar to the modern ear, such as the notion of memory of the present, this may be thought of simply as the collection of sensory representations brought to our immediate awareness.

Augustine's *De Magistro* is a work of great subtlety and complexity. Of all the works collected in this volume it is the most difficult for the contemporary reader. One of the central reasons for this is that no translation can adequately capture the nuances of Augustine's Latin nor the technical specificity of the language used in advancing each stage of the inquiry. Perhaps unusually for Augustine there is also quite a bit of joking in the *De Magistro*, much of which trades on intricacies of language, and this too, is very difficult to capture in translation. As shown by the difficulties in translating French *jeux de mots* and puns, any translation must fail utterly to capture jokes that are tied to ordinary language and trade on multiple meanings of words and indeed pronunciation.

One example of how difficult it is to adequately translate the Latin of the *De Magistro* is apparent in the following passage. At v.13, Augustine deals with the grammatical feature of conjunction. Augustine asks Adeodatus for several examples of conjunction. Adeodatus replies citing the Latin words *et*, *que*, *at*, and *atque*, corresponding respectively to the English conjunctions 'and', 'but' (which appears as a copulative particle affixed to the word it connects), 'even', and 'and even'. Augustine then goes on to force the point he is arguing for, namely that all words are ultimately noun-like, by linguistically grouping the four conjunctions and referring to them by means of a pronoun (*haec omnia*) 'all these', which he earlier had argued functions as a quasi-noun. Adeodatus' inspired reply rejects Augustine's use of the pronoun as a quasi-noun when he says, referring to 'all these', 'not all' (*non omino*), thus referring to them without use of a pronoun. The complexity of this passage continues beyond this point but it is sufficient to show the difficulties of translation and the subtleties involved in the arguments. As a result we will need to spend more time and space interpreting Augustine's *De Magistro* to help make sense of these sorts of difficulties.

Like Aquinas in his *De Magistro*, Augustine's approach is dialectical. But whereas Aquinas' dialectic is presented in the Scholastic form of questions, replies, and responses, and in a third person, impersonal style, Augustine's *De Magistro* is firmly embedded in an imaginative reconstruction of the cut and thrust of live interpersonal questioning and debate. Augustine's work is also dialectical in a second sense — each of the stages of the dialectical interchange is cumulative. Insights uncovered as a result of the dialectal sparring provide new platforms for further puzzles and questions. It is also dialectical in yet a third sense as it specifically addresses the situated learner. That is, Augustine the dialectician is engaged not with students in general but with Adeodatus in particular.

Indeed the whole work is generated by a series of questions that on the face of it appear paradoxical. The first question that arises is the purpose of using words. From a contemporary perspective we would not hesitate to answer the question by saying that the primary purpose of using words is to communicate. However, this is not the answer proposed in the *De Magistro*. Instead, Augustine and Adeodatus agree that the purpose of using words is to let somebody know something and hence the basic function of language is to teach.

The structure of the argument in the *De Magistro* follows three paradoxes involved in identifying three conceptually distinct, yet interrelated ways of teaching or communicating knowledge. The three ways of teaching considered are (i) *teaching as reminding*; (ii) *teaching as presenting*; and (iii) *teaching as discovering truth within*.

Teaching as reminding is characterised by the teacher providing signs by means of which the pupil is directed to become acquainted with what is being taught. *Teaching as presenting* moves beyond the use of conventional signs, by directing the student's attention to the realities that are explicitly pointed to, by the signs. *Teaching as discovering truth within* dispenses with the role of the human teacher in favour of God's role as interior illuminator of the student (and the human teacher).

Each way of teaching generates paradoxical questions which centre on the relations involved in teaching—the teacher, what is taught, and the end product or knowledge discovered. (We referred to these in Chapter 1 by means of the proposition: X teaches Y to Z.) The paradox that arises in the practice of teaching as reminding trades on whether what is taught is merely a sign, or a word, or a reality. The paradox that arises in teaching as presenting centres on whether, in such teaching, only a name of something is taught or whether the knowledge of reality is taught. The paradox associated with teaching as discovering truth within lies in how a person achieves certainty. Is certainty derived from the way in which realities are related and understood; or from the way signs are related and understood; or is certainty derived from some relation between signs and realities?

The dialectic of the *De Magistro* traces the paradoxes involved in the three ways of teaching by focusing on an orderly, cumulative address of the following issues: (1) the nature of signs; (2) the nature of *significables* (that is, the realities that signs point to); and (3) the nature of certainty and truth. These issues are dialectically taken up by the questions: (1*) Can anything be taught without signs?; (2*) Can reality be understood when directly indicated by ostension (that is, by pointing or performance)? (The concern here is whether when we point, we become acquainted with the thing or only the sign of the thing at which we point.); (3*) Can words or signs elicit certainty?

The unravelling of these issues and questions hierarchically reveals three principles. Teaching as reminding reveals a *principle of universality* attached to meaning in language. Teaching as presentation uncovers a *principle of value* in the relation between signs and realities. Finally, teaching as discovering truth within yields *certainty of truth* and thus stands as the *fons et origo* of all communication in teaching, learning, and understanding.

The universality of meaning embedded in language for Augustine implies a hierarchy of value which in turn presupposes truth as the ground of communication. Meaning in language is universal because language can be translated from one idiom, say Greek, into another, say Latin. Value is embedded in languages and concepts since we can see that a reality understood is more valuable that the sign used to point to it or the mere appearance of a reality, and that certainty and truth are more valuable than uncertainty. Judgements of truth and the value of such truth, for Augustine, depend upon a principle of Truth which coincides with God.

Augustine's *De Magistro* then is concerned with a meta-level inquiry into teaching insofar as it provides illumination of the Truth. As a result there is little direct discussion of what needs to be taught, the ordering of what is to be taught, the characteristic activities of teaching, or indeed the nature of the learner.[29] Rather, Augustine illuminates all of these dimensions by demonstrating how they can come together in one masterful performance by a gifted student and teacher in dialogue.

Teaching as Reminding

The central argument of the early part of the *De Magistro* concerns teaching as reminding. Augustine's argument is based on the idea that all words *name* and, by implication, that all words are quasi-nouns. Words signify realities either by aiding us to recall a reality or by signifying a reality itself, just as smoke is a sign of fire. But how exactly can teaching as reminding happen? The paradox here is that if someone does not know the reality to which a sign points, then that person also does not understand the sign. Since teaching as reminding of necessity occurs by using signs (most often words), when someone neither understands a reality, nor the sign which points to the reality, then teaching would seem to be impossible.

This paradox provides the context for the entire section on teaching as reminding. Augustine, in dialogue with Adeodatus, seeks to overcome the paradox by finding a principle of universality of meaning in language conceived of as a system of signs. First Augustine considers several objections to the idea that the purpose of language is to teach. At first glance, the activities of 'questioning', 'singing', and 'praying' seem to have no connection with teaching. But it is agreed that questioning is a form of teaching in the sense that questions teach someone what one hopes to know. Singing is distinguished from speaking, and thus from teaching, because its object is the pleasure derived from sound and rhythm. When priests say prayers aloud to a congregation they remind, and thus teach us, about our relation to divine things. However, in silent prayer, words

---

[29] Some of these more practical pedagogical concerns are taken up in Augustine's *De Doctrina Christiana* and *De Catechizandis Rudibus*.

are not vocalised, but are spoken interiorly in the memory which recalls the realities to which the silent words and thoughts refer.

Augustine wants to show that all speech is connected to memory. He does this by arguing that all words are signs, that is, all words signify realities to be remembered. He arrives at this view by analysing three representative but challenging grammatical features of language: the conjunction 'if', the preposition 'from', and the noun 'nothing'. The conjunction 'if' brings to mind a kind of doubt. The preposition 'from' brings to mind the notion of some form of separation. 'Nothing' provides a difficulty because signs, it has already been agreed, stand for realities. 'Nothing' thus cannot refer to what does not exist. Augustine here anticipates Sartre, in suggesting that 'nothing' brings to mind 'some affection of the soul'.[30] By induction from these hard cases, Augustine concludes that all words have a naming function. 'If' names a kind of doubt, 'from' names a form of separation, and 'nothing' names the absence of a presence. Moreover, in each of these cases we achieved clarity by introducing new words to explain the meaning of the original terms. Thus, in each of these cases a sign or word has been taught by means of another sign or word. We have thus not yet moved beyond signs.

This does not exhaust the ways in which signs can be taught. Signs draw our attention towards realities signified, but this can be done also by performance or demonstration. If I am asked what 'walking' is, I can perform the action of walking. But even here confusion is possible, for it is indeterminate whether the performance refers to the person walking, or to the activity performed, or even to the meaning of the word 'walking', such that a speaker is apt to say 'walking' when in the presence of someone performing such-and-such an action. More simply, Augustine's point could be made by saying that a performance of walking could with equal justice be interpreted as a series of interrupted falls.[31]

Augustine is concerned at this point with the distinction between a sign and the reality signified by the sign. Matters are made more complex by the existence of *signs of signs*, as is the case when a word is written. The written word is a sign of a sign. The words, 'Romulus', 'Rome', 'virtue', and 'river' are all nouns but the words

---

[30] *De Magistro* II.3. J. P. Sartre articulates a similar idea in *Being and Nothingness* 9-10 when he talks of planning to meet his friend Pierre in the café. When Sartre arrives Pierre is not there, and Sartre describes this as the absence of Pierre's presence. 'Nothing' always points to the objective lack of a properly present 'something'.

[31] We take this observation from Merleau-Ponty.

used, either in speech or when written, are not the realities pointed to by means of these signs. Augustine refers to these realities targeted by signs as *significables*. The words mentioned are all examples of nouns. The audible word 'noun' is a *sensible sign* whereas the written word 'noun' is a sign of a sign, just as 'word' is, according to Augustine, a sign for 'noun'.

This point is difficult to grasp. Augustine is attempting to show that signs can signify themselves and can also signify other signs. For the first case, note that 'word' is also a word. For the second, note that Augustine thinks that everything signified by 'word' is also signified by 'noun'. This move is designed to support the claim that all signs signify realities (whether those realities be themselves or other things) and are not just empty, conventional parts of language. It is for this reason that Augustine thinks it important to consider linguistic signs that do not immediately seem to refer to realities.[32]

'If', 'or', and 'from' are examples of grammatical conjunction. That is, these three words can all be used to combine simple sentences into compound sentences. But while 'conjunction' signifies these three words, they, in turn, do not seem to signify 'conjunction' because they are examples of conjunctions but individually do not exhaust what it means for something to be a conjunction. So Augustine needs an argument to show how all words may be thought of as quasi-nouns in order for words to be signs that point to realities. He does so by invoking the authority of St. Paul and by appealing, via Cicero, to rules of our use of language. The language of Augustine's argument here is almost impossible to capture in translation (as was mentioned earlier), but the basic point is that all parts of speech, including conjunctions, are called, i.e., named, something—as when we say that some part of speech is a noun, or a verb, or a preposition. As a result these conjunctions function in some respects as nouns—in other words, they refer to realities.[33] 'Noun' and 'word' have the same extension and, at the same time, signify each other. Since signs are both self-referential and signified by other signs, the meanings

---

[32]   Augustine here anticipates—and would disagree with—later analytic philosophers like Bertrand Russell, who developed the view that certain words, such as 'and' and 'or', do not have a semantic meaning but are purely syntactic.

[33]   If this is a fair report of Augustine's argument—and the text is so convoluted that it is difficult to be sure—then it is a not a particularly strong argument. He seems to be arguing that *whatever is named, names*. By parallel reasoning we could claim that *whatever is cut, cuts* or *whatever receives, gives*. These are obviously false claims, the last being especially objectionable to Augustine in light of his theistic commitments concerning creation.

attached to the signs are in principle translatable from one language to another. It is only the vocal sounds *nomen* in Latin (literally, 'name') and *onoma* ('name') in Greek that differ, not their meaning.

Once it has been accepted that all signs are quasi-nouns, that is, they name and thus point to some reality, Augustine may conclude that the meanings of any proposition in language (since meaning is in principle translatable because there are realities referred to by signs) are universal and likewise not tied to a particular linguistic community. Meaning in language then is parasitic on reality and everyone has access to meaning no matter what language is spoken or written. These claims are but provisional steps in the dialectical investigation, and even though they are accepted by the interlocutors, they remain highly contestable. Despite this close alignment of language and reality, Augustine maintains that there is a radical indeterminacy associated with signs and signs of signs, just as later he will show that there is an inherent indeterminacy in teaching as presentation.[34]

It is the principle of universality of meaning which drives the intricacies of Augustine's argument. When engaged in teaching as reminding, the teacher employs signs and, typically, spoken words. The teacher so engaged directs the student's attention to realities with which the student is already acquainted. With this point clarified, Augustine's next step is to inquire into whether a teacher by employing signs can direct the student's attention to realities that are not already known.

Teaching as Presentation

This next stage of the dialectic again begins with a paradox. Teaching is carried out by communicating knowledge of signs that are names pointing to realities. But is knowledge achieved by teaching the sign, since the sign must already be known in some sense in order for it to be meaningful? Can the teacher teach anything about realities directly? Or is what is known—after realities have been indicated by pointing or performance—merely (a) knowledge of a word, or (b) knowledge of reality itself, or (c) knowledge of some relationship between reality and words? To make these difficult questions

---

[34] Augustine in fact anticipates what later analytic philosophers call the indeterminacy of translation. See for example W.V.O. Quine's remarks on the word *gavagai* in his *Word and Object*, Cambridge, Harvard University Press, 1960, ch. 2.

clearer, let us consider examples of (a), (b), and (c). The first two options would lead to unacceptable results for Augustine.

In (a), we can come to the understanding of any given sign by means of other signs that are already known. For example, we can come to learn what 'kleptomania' means by indicating its association with habitual and compulsive stealing, phenomena of which we are already aware. Consider also the case of the translatability of meanings. The German word for 'glove' is *Handschuh*, which is a compound of the German words for 'hand' and 'shoe'. Once we have an understanding of the English word 'glove', we can come to learn that a similar significable is designated by the German *Handschuh*. But this could still leave us unsure as to whether *Handschuh* refers only to what English speakers call a glove. Does *Handschuh* extend to mittens and the hand coverings used by boxers? Or, more perversely, to jewellery worn on the hands? The point here is that familiarity with the transferability of meaning by means of signs of signs, whether in one language or between languages, is indeterminate, and hence we cannot be said to firmly grasp the precise signification of the sign, in other words, to know with certitude the reality to which the sign points.

In (b), imagine that I am trying to teach a student the meaning of the English word 'epicaricacy'. I could show the student any number of classic slapstick comedies, and the student may take delight in these, without ever appreciating the precise focus and underlying phenomenon (i.e., the reality) I wish to indicate, namely the feeling of *Schadenfreude*, or joy taken in the misfortune of others. The experience of the reality overflows the meaning of the term and thus the term remains indeterminate among significables.

In (c) we have the apparent desired object of teaching: a precise fit between sign and signified, or between language and reality, is attained. Here lies the major challenge for Augustine. Can a human teacher ever get beyond signs and teach the realities themselves? At this point Augustine enters into a deeper discussion of this sort of teaching which seems adapted to direct attention to realities, namely teaching as presentation, and of the value to be found within that manner of teaching.

Since teaching as reminding involves the teacher drawing attention by means of signs, and signs of signs, towards realities and signs already known, a new way of teaching is required. This is because neither signs, nor signs of signs, teach knowledge of realities. Augustine examines the Latin phrase *utrum homo, nomen sit* ('whether "man" is a noun'). The dialectical unpacking reveals that the syllables vocally enunciated are not *in* the reality signified. In other words, the syllables *ho* and *mo* are not found in this particular human being before us, nor indeed would these syllables make something to be a man. Reflection also reveals that the naming capacity in language cannot by itself move attention from a word to reality. If I do not already know that 'mushfakery' names the profession of mending umbrellas, the naming function tells me nothing.

However, the rules of grammar, language, and meaning enable a teacher to direct the attention of the student to the reality signified, provided that the reality is in some sense already known. If one already knows the signification or reality of which 'man' is the sign, then the student quickly generalises to the intelligible definition 'rational mortal animal' — at least according to Augustine. Knowledge of the Latin word *homo* ('man') involves knowing the noun, knowing the differentia of the signified — 'rational', 'mortal', and 'animal' — and acquaintance with at least one particular man. The knowledge involved in the signification pointed to by the sign *homo* requires knowledge of all three elements and their relations and, ideally, how that word coheres with the reality signified in its relations and central dimensions.

Augustine argues that knowing a reality and understanding the significance of its associated sign does not depend on our use of words but rather on a prior memory of realities present to us. When engaged in teaching as presentation, instead of making use of signs already understood by the student, the teacher directs the attention of the student to realities already understood. But before exploring the operationalisation of teaching as presentation, Augustine examines the order of dependence and relations among signs and the realities they signify and the values that we attach to each.

If teaching as reminding were the only way we could teach, then nothing could be taught without the use of signs. But indications — teaching as presenting — which are not signs, are genuine ways of teaching. When we do not know what mushfakery is, the teacher can point to (i.e., indicate) what the mushfaker does, and since the elements that go to make up mushfakery are already known, the attention of the student has been brought to bear upon something, the elements of which are known, but the sign of which was unknown.

Augustine's whole discussion of teaching as presenting is permeated by the notion of 'indicating'. Moreover, since the role of memory is crucial to all teaching, learning, and understanding,

Augustine introduces the notion of 'memory of the present' to explain how knowledge of the indicated realities is possible. Sometimes, the teacher when presenting or indicating moves the student's attention to a direct apprehension of realities, neither immediately under consideration nor understood, but capable of being appropriated via images within the memory of the present (or, as we would now say, the imagination). This way of putting the matter helps capture situations like the following. Suppose a teacher wishes a student to attend to some realities that the student has not attended to before. The teacher might say: 'Look at those!' and thus indicate those realities by pointing. The student then attends to the realities before her, and sees a previously unnoticed group of animals. The teacher says: 'Those are wolverines.' The student whose attention has been so directed by the teacher has, first of all, become acquainted with realities she had not experienced before, and subsequently come to learn the appropriate linguistic sign for those realities with which she is newly acquainted. Augustine's discussion of teaching as presentation thus involves an inquiry into teaching without signs or words.

Augustine is also concerned with establishing knowledge of value as it attaches to realities. For Augustine, significables, which are the realities understood, are to be viewed in terms of their importance. He highlights a *principle of valuation* that orders the relations among signs, signs of signs, and the significables or realities that come to be known. He accomplishes this task by appealing to the widely-accepted metaphysical principle that 'whatever exists for the sake of something else must be inferior to that for whose sake it exists.'

If this principle is granted, it is inescapable that realities signified are more valuable than the signs used to point to them. Every sign exists to point to the reality it signifies, so signs are less valuable than what they signify. This principle of value is illuminated by considering what we ordinarily value more. Do we value more a reality itself, or the sign of a reality, or the knowledge of a reality, or the knowledge of the sign of a reality? Augustine uses the examples of 'filth', 'vice', and 'virtue' to establish that the reality *known* is better — more highly valued — than the reality itself. Augustine is thus committed to the position that knowledge plus reality is more valuable than reality alone. Reality trumps signification, just as knowledge of reality trumps knowledge of the signs of reality. It is the orientation towards that which is of greater value that brings out the nobility of teaching as presenting over teaching as reminding.

Gathering these points together, Augustine has shown that teaching as presentation re-collects the elements already known into a new synthesis — memory of the present — which yields a kind of new knowledge. But the question now becomes: Is it possible for a student to be taught anything about realities with which her mind is not at all familiar? This leads us to the final step in the dialectic — teaching as discovering truth within.

Teaching as Discovering Truth Within

A fundamental problem is associated with teaching as presentation. Drawing the attention of a student by indicating or performing is inherently open to error. As mentioned before, if I try to teach the meaning of 'walking' by performing the act of walking, it may be interpreted as a series of interrupted falls. Similarly, to use Augustine's example, drawing on *Daniel* 3:94, a student may be led to understand what *saraballae* are by already knowing (memory of the present) what a head is and what coverings are — hence, a type of head-covering. However, knowing that *saraballae* are head-coverings provides insufficient knowledge because it does not provide us with enough specificity to enable us to distinguish *saraballae* from other similar types of head-covering.

It is this worry that generates Augustine's next step — questioning the degree of our *certainty* in respect to realities known. For Augustine only teaching as discovering truth within confers certainty. Taking a step back, teaching as reminding generally occurs when memory is engaged by attending to signs striking the ear or, in the case of written words, signs of signs striking the eye. Teaching as presentation occurs when the student's attention is drawn to how a given sign relates to a reality by indication. Teaching as discovering truth within likewise requires knowledge of reality by acquaintance with and insight into the indications which undergird sign relations. However, if certainty is to be achieved, that which is to be understood requires not sensibles but *intelligibles*, that is, realities dwelling not merely in the senses but realities as intellectually grasped. In this latter arena of knowledge Augustine is concerned with propositional knowledge and *intuitive knowledge* (i.e., direct apprehension of intelligible objects).

Augustine has already argued that innate rules are necessary in order to understand significations of words which point to realities. These innate rules are both logical and ontological, as with the principle of non-contradiction. They include rules of recognition, which are innate capacities to recognise and judge individuals and kinds and to extract salient features. They are innate because they provide the very conditions of our reasonability. As Aristotle effectively pointed out, we cannot provide a formal argument for the principle of non-contradiction by appealing to a more basic principle since the principle of non-contradiction must be assumed for any rational argument to proceed. Ontological rules operate at the most general level of predication. They involve both the limitations and possibilities open to things due to the particular natures they possess. Thus a human being cannot flap her arms and fly though it is open to birds to flap their wings and do so.

Augustine recognises that certainty comes in degrees. When I understand something I also believe it, but I can believe many things without understanding them. The significations pointed to by the names 'Ananias', 'Azarias', and 'Misael' are well known to those who read the Bible, but Daniel's account of their stories is something believed, not known with certainty. Thus knowledge and belief are different.

This distinction guides the ensuing discussion of the role of the will in knowing. Knowledge of some intelligible realities depends upon the perfection of the will. When truth is known for certain in any act of knowing, God illuminates the mind (recalling the symbolism of creation discussed earlier), but faith, Augustine asserts, is also required to prepare the mind for God's illumination. The will, perfected by faith, opens itself to objects of love, and there are many realities that can only be known if they are loved. These realities include, for Augustine, love of persons, the loving relations characteristic of the communion of the saints, the cherishing of religious sacraments, and more generally truths concerning divine things.

Propositional knowledge is directed both at sense objects or images and at intelligible objects. If I am teaching about sensible things that are present (in some sense), someone may or may not believe what I say — 'It is raining today in Ireland'. The student does not learn from my words unless he or she 'sees' what I am speaking about. When I try to teach something relating to the past my words do not signify realities but rather impressions or images, and are hence open to doubt.

However, when I attempt to teach realities apprehended by the mind I am concerned with intelligible objects which the student can access directly by the light of truth. Here the student apprehends meanings directly by means of the inner teacher, Christ, who illuminates the 'inner man' (*De Magistro* xii.40). The notion of an interior teacher, or interior illumination, may be approached by the rather inadequate but simple experience of sudden intuitive grasping. We have all had the experience of trying to work our way through a difficult problem, as in mathematics, and despite all our efforts and those of our teachers, we simply fail to *see* the solution. Often at some point the light goes on and we break through our frustration in a 'eureka' moment.

Augustine bases his argument on the following observation: 'But after teachers have presented their words about all the disciplines they claim to teach, even including virtue and wisdom, their pupils then examine for themselves whether what has been said is true, contemplating thus by their own abilities interior truth.' (*De Magistro* xiv.45). The student learns interiorly, and no external human teacher can teach in this way. Here the interior teacher is, Augustine asserts, none other than Christ, the eternal Word, Wisdom, and Light of God. The notion of the interior teacher, which is an important theme running through Augustine's writings from his earliest days to his middle and late masterpieces *On Christian Doctrine, Confessions,* and *City of God,* is mentioned only briefly at the end of the *De Magistro*. Here he is concerned to establish the necessity of positing an internal teacher and less worried about the positive development of that notion.

The basic reasoning runs like this: Suppose that a teacher is successful in presenting the contents of his or her thoughts to a student. (Augustine gives good reasons for doubting that this is ever the case, but let us set these worries aside for the sake of argument.) Even granting the ideal case of teaching as presentation, nonetheless such presentation is insufficient for genuine knowledge. This is because the certainty characteristic of Augustine's account of knowledge requires an act of judgement initiated by the learner. This judgement is itself based on a recognition of what is so and what is not so. This recognition comes not from an external teacher but arises internally within the student.[35] But how could the student recognise something without already being in possession of some standard or model against which he or she measures and judges it? A good fit between this standard or measure and that which has been presented results in a judgment on the part of the student that assents to the truth of that which the teacher has proposed. Thus, there must be

---

[35] Compare this with Aquinas' *De Magistro* art. 1, in which he discusses what the student contributes to learning.

some interior teacher, serving as an interior standard and necessary condition for the acquisition of truth grasped with certainty by the student.

The identification of the interior teacher with Christ, the eternal Word of God, present as interior teacher within each and every act of understanding, may be elaborated briefly. There are no limits to the truths human beings may know.[36] While that which is potentially knowable and that which a human may actually know are both infinite, it is unfitting to assert that any human being is omniscient—a possessor of actually infinite stores of knowledge. The necessarily perfect and infinite standard that serves as measure of all truth recognised and recognisable, and that is interior to the student, therefore cannot ultimately be identified with the student. While transcendent infinity and intimate interiority are not compatible with any merely human teacher or learner, these properties are fittingly attributed to the divine. Hence the interior teacher, Augustine asserts, is God, the infinite Word, Wisdom, and Light Who illuminates minds and in Whom all things live, move, and have their very being.

---

[36]   Augustine mentions some nice examples in his *Contra Academicos*, including his famous anticipation of the Cartesian *cogito* argument concerning the certainty of the existence of the self. I know that I exist; and I know that I know that I exist; and I know that ... as far as one may care to repeat.

Augustine: Text

Augustine: De Magistro (On the Teacher)

A new translation by
T. Brian Mooney and Mark Nowacki

Part I

I.1 *Augustine* – What do you think is our purpose when we talk? *Adeodatus* – It seems to me at the moment that we want either to teach or to learn. *Aug.* – The first of these I see clearly and I agree: it is clear that when we talk we teach. But how do we learn? *Adeo.* – How else than by asking questions? *Aug.* – Even then, we want nothing other than to teach. Because if I ask you a question, I interrogate you for no other cause than to instruct you about what it is you want to know. *Adeo.* – You speak the truth. *Aug.* – You see then that when we speak we want nothing other than to teach. *Adeo.* – That is not clear to me. Because if speaking consists of speaking words, we do that too when we are singing. And as we often sing alone, I do not think we are trying to teach anyone, since there is no one there to be taught. *Aug.* – Well, for my part, I think that there is a certain kind of teaching by reminding, and an important one at that, as will become apparent in our discussion. But if you do not think that we learn by being reminded, or that one does not teach by reminding, I will not contradict you. And I assert two reasons for speaking: either in order to teach, or in order to remind others or ourselves. The latter is what we do when we sing. Does this seem correct to you? *Adeo.* – Not exactly. I seldom sing to remind myself of anything, but I do so for pleasure. *Aug.* – I see your idea. But do you not see that what pleases you in song is a certain melody. And since one can add or subtract

melody from words, singing is not the same thing as speaking. For
there is also the melody of the flute and of the harp, and the singing
of birds, and sometimes we ourselves make musical sounds without
words; which undoubtedly can be called music but cannot be called
speaking since it lacks words. Have you any objection? *Adeo.* – None
at all.

I.2 *Aug.* – So then you agree that it is only for teaching or for reminding that we speak? *Adeo.* – I would agree, except that it strikes me
that when we pray, we speak, and it is not permissible to believe that
God either receives teaching from us or is reminded of anything by
us. *Aug.* – Do you not know that the only reason for the precept that
we should pray in our closet behind closed doors, thus indicating the
sanctuary of the soul, is because God does not need to be taught or
reminded by our words in order that He may fulfil our desires?
Whoever speaks, then, wants to give an exterior sign by means of an
articulated sound. But God must be sought and prayed to in the very
depths of the reasonable soul which is called the interior man. This is
what He wants to be His temple. Have you not read in Saint Paul
'Know ye not that ye are the temple of God, and that the Spirit of God
dwelleth in you?' (1 *Cor.* 3.16) and again, 'In the Interior Man there
Christ dwells' (*Eph.* 3.16-17)? And have you not noted the words of
the Prophet: 'Speak in your own hearts and be full of remorse in your
private chambers; sacrifice a sacrifice of justice and have hope in the
Lord' (*Ps.* 16.5-6)? Where, then, can one offer the sacrifice of justice
but in the temple of the soul and in the intimate depths of the heart?
Wherever sacrifice must be offered so too must there be prayer. That
is why when we pray there is no need for words, that is, for articulated words, except perhaps in the case of priests who use words, not
for the sake of God, but for men, so that, thanks to this remembrance,
men may consent to cleave to God. Or what is your view? *Adeo.* – I
fully agree. *Aug.* – You are not perturbed then that the great Teacher,
when teaching his disciples to pray, taught them certain words, so it
seems that he taught them how we should speak when we pray.
Adeo. – No. That does not bother me at all. Because it *is not* the words
that he taught them, but by means of words, he taught the realities
themselves meant by the words, so that they might keep themselves
in remembrance of what they should pray for, and to Whom, as we
have noted, in the sanctuary of their soul. *Aug.* – You understand
well. You have also noticed a further point. I think if we were to hold
that, even without uttering a sound, but thinking only the words, we

nonetheless speak in our minds, even though language does nothing more than remind. Because memory, recalling the words which it retains and turns over, brings out in thought the realities themselves of which the words are signs. *Adeo.* – I understand and agree.

II.3 *Aug.* – We agree that the words are signs? *Adeo.* – Agreed. *Aug.* – But a sign must be something which signifies. *Adeo.* – It cannot be otherwise. *Aug.* – How many words are there in this verse? *Si nihil ex tantu superis placet uerbe relinqui* [If it pleases the gods that nothing be left of so great a city]. *Adeo.* – Eight. *Aug.* – So there are eight signs. *Adeo.* – That is so. *Aug.* – I believe you understand the verse? *Adeo.* – Fairly well. *Aug.* – Tell me what each word signifies. *Adeo.* – I see what *si* [if] means, but I cannot think of any other word that catches the sense of it. *Aug.* – Whatever it might be that is exactly signified by the word, do you have a sense of it? *Adeo.* – It seems to me that *si* [if] signifies a doubt or at least the sense of doubt, and where else can doubt be found but in the soul? *Aug.* – I can accept that for the moment. Move on to the next words. *Adeo.* – What else can *nihil* [nothing] mean than that something does not exist? *Aug.* – Maybe you are correct. But what stops me from agreeing is that something is not a sign, as you just agreed earlier, if it does not signify something; but what is not cannot really be anything. This is because the second word of this verse is not a sign since it does not signify anything. So we were wrong to agree that each word is a sign or that each sign signifies something. *Adeo.* – You are really testing me. But when we have nothing to signify surely it is foolish to use words? When you speak to me I do not believe you utter empty sounds, but whatsoever comes out of your mouth gives me a sign so that I may understand something. This is why you should not, when speaking, utter these two syllables [*ni-hil*] if you do not mean to signify something. If then you see that they are necessary in order to pronounce a word which resonates in our ears, and which teaches and reminds us of something, then all the more you must see what I want to say but cannot explain. *Aug.* – What then is to be done? Should we not instead of saying that this word *nihil* [nothing] signifies a reality which does not exist, rather say that it signifies an affection of the soul when it sees no reality yet finds or thinks that it finds that the reality does not exist? *Adeo.* – Maybe that is what I am trying to explain. *Aug.* – Whatever may be the case, let us move on, before something really absurd happens to us. *Adeo.* – How so? *Aug.* – If 'nothing' holds us back yet we are still detained. *Adeo.* – That would be ridiculous, and yet I see it can come about and has indeed occurred.

II.4 *Aug.* – In due course, God willing, we shall understand more fully this contradiction. Now returning to the verse, tell me and show me if you can, what the other words signify. *Adeo.* – The third word is the preposition *ex* [from], for which we can substitute *de* [from], I think. *Aug.* – I am not asking you to substitute a well-known word for an equally well-known one which means the same thing, if indeed as you think it does mean the same thing. But for the moment let us accept it as so. Surely if the poet had said not *ex tanta... urbe* [from this...city] but instead *de tanta...* [of this...] and I then asked you what *de* signifies, you would say *ex*, because the two words being signs, signify, you think, a single reality. I am, however, seeking the single reality that is signified by these two signs. *Adeo.* – It seems to me that the word signifies a kind of separation of a reality, from some other reality, which is spoken of; it is 'away from' that reality, although that reality is not the same, as one can see in the verse, the city no longer remains but the Trojans could come from there. Be that as it may, they remain as we may say business–people from the city of Rome who are in Africa. *Aug.* – Let me concede that this is indeed so, without seeking to enumerate the many possible exceptions to your rule we might uncover. But at least there is one fact that you can easily point out – since you have explained words by means of words, in other words, signs by means of signs, well-known words and signs by others just as well known – but for myself, I want you to show me, if you are able, what the realities themselves are that these words are signs of.

III.5 *Adeo.* – I am surprised that you do not know, or seem to know, that it really is not possible to respond to what you want. When we are conversing we cannot respond except by using words; you are asking for something, whatever it may be, that certainly does not involve using words, and yet you too ask questions by means of words. First ask yourself something without using words, and I will in turn respond under the same conditions. *Aug.* – I am sure you are right. But if I asked you what is signified by the three syllables *paries* [wall] when one says *par-i-es*, could you not point with your finger? In this way, you would surely see the reality itself of which the three syllables are the sign; and you would be pointing it out, nonetheless without referring to it by using a word. *Adeo.* – That may be so, I can concede, but only for names which signify corporeal realities, if such be available. *Aug.* – But we do not say that colour is a corporeal reality. Is it not instead a quality of a corporeal reality? *Adeo.* – It is. *Aug.* – Why, then, can it still be pointed to with a finger? Do you add the qualities of corporeal realities, in such a way that they too, if they are at hand, may be taught without words? *Adeo.* – When I used 'corporeal reality' I meant everything that is corporeal, in other words, all the qualities that can be perceived by the senses. *Aug.* – Well, hold on. Surely you must make certain exceptions. *Adeo.* – You are right to warn me. I ought not to have said all corporeal realities but rather all visible realities. This is because I accept that sound, smell, taste, weight, heat and other realities that pertain to the other senses cannot possibly be perceived separate from corporeal realities, and so are corporeal as well, but nonetheless they cannot be pointed to by the finger. *Aug.* – Have you never seen that when people are talking they use gestures as if they were talking with deaf people, and how deaf people themselves also use gestures, to ask questions and to reply, and to teach and suggest their desires, or at least a large number of them? Certainly in this case it is not just visible realities that are pointed out, but also sounds, flavours, and other realities of this sort. Similarly, actors in the theatres often draw out, and make comprehensible, whole performances by dancing, without using any words. *Adeo.* – I have no objection, except, not just I, but even the dancing actor cannot show me the signification of *ex* [from] without using words.

III.6 *Aug.* – What you say is probably true. But let us suppose it can be done. You do not doubt, I think, that whatever corporeal movement is used, it would nonetheless still be a sign and not the reality itself. So, while indeed a word would not be explained by a word, a sign could be explained by a sign. And in this way, the monosyllable *ex* [from] and the gesture would signify a single reality; this is what I wanted to be pointed out to me without you using a sign, but rather directly. *Adeo.* – Goodness. How can this possibly be done? *Aug.* – In the same way as is possible for 'wall'. *Adeo.* – But as our reasoning has progressed, even the wall cannot be pointed out except by pointing a finger. The act of extending the finger is not the wall; rather, it is the sign by means of which we see the wall. As far as I am concerned nothing can be pointed out without signs. *Aug.* – Then If I asked you: 'What is walking?' and you get up and perform the act, would you not be using the reality itself to teach me, without words or any other signs? *Adeo.* – Surely. I am embarrassed that I have not seen something so obvious. Thousands of other things occur to me that can be shown straight away without signs, like eating, drinking, sitting, standing, shouting, and innumerable other things. *Aug.* – Good. Tell me then. If I attach no meaning to the word 'walking', and I asked you what you are doing when you are walking, how would you teach me? *Adeo.* – I would perform the same action a bit more quickly so as to attract your attention to what I was still continuing to do, and thereby indicate what I was asked to show. *Aug.* – But do you not know that 'walking' is a different thing from 'hastening'? Whoever walks does not necessarily hasten, and whoever hastens does not necessarily walk. After all, we talk about haste in writing, and in reading, and in numerous other things. This is why if you perform your act more quickly, after my question, I could believe that walking is nothing other than hastening, because of the new element you have added; and, I would be mistaken. *Adeo.* – I accept that a reality cannot be indicated without a sign, if that is what we are trying to do when we are being asked questions. Because, if we do not add anything, our interlocutor will believe that we do not want to point anything out, but are just continuing what we are doing and not paying any attention to him. But if he asks about an act that we can perform, yet at the time we are asked about it we are not performing it, then we can show him after he asks his question by means of the reality itself and not the sign. Perhaps we might make an exception in the case of someone who asked me, when I am speaking, what 'speaking' is. For whatever I say, in order for him to learn something, I must speak. And I will continue my explication until I have made clear what he wants to be shown to him, and without seeking signs beyond the reality itself in order to show it.

IV.7 *Aug.* – Very acutely put. Then we should agree that one can indicate something without a sign, such as acts we are not performing when we are asked questions but can begin to perform immediately after, as well as those in which the performance involves straightforwardly giving signs. That is why, when we speak, we formulate signs, for that is what we mean by 'to signify'. *Adeo.* – Good. *Aug.* – So, when the question is about certain signs themselves, these signs can be indicated by other signs. On the other hand, if the question is about realities which are not signs, these can be indicated by performing (if possible) an action after a question is asked, or by providing signs which can bring to attention the realities themselves. *Adeo.* – Agreed. *Aug.* – So we have a tripartite division. Let us consider, if you do not mind, the fact that certain signs can be indicated by other signs. For words are not the only signs, are they? *Adeo.* – No. *Aug.* – It seems to me that when we are speaking we employ words to signify words or other signs, as we do when we say 'gesture' or 'letter', because the realities signified by these two words are themselves signs; moreover, we can signify another reality which is not a sign, as when we say 'stone'. This word is actually a sign because it designates a reality but this reality signified is not itself a sign. But in this last category, namely, when a word designates a reality that is not itself a sign, this is not pertinent to what we are discussing. We have undertaken the task of considering that category in which signs are indicated by other signs, and we have discovered two divisions, since through signs we teach or bring to mind either the same signs or different signs. Do you not agree? *Adeo.* – It is clear.

IV.8 *Aug.* – Tell me then, for those signs that are words, to what do they pertain? *Adeo.* – To the ear. *Aug.* – And gestures? *Adeo.* – To sight. *Aug.* – And what of when we come upon written words? Must we not understand these words precisely as signs of words? Taken this way, 'word' is an articulated sound which has meaning, but the voice cannot be perceived by any sense other than hearing. So when we encounter a written word, some sign is presented to the eyes yet something that pertains to the ears comes to mind. *Adeo.* – I fully agree. *Aug.* – You will also agree, I think, when saying *nomen* [name] we are signifying something. *Adeo.* – True. *Aug.* – What then? *Adeo.* – That by which each reality is called, as in 'Romulus', 'Rome', 'Virtue', 'river', and many others. *Aug.* – And these four names, do they not signify something? *Adeo.* – They do. *Aug.* – Is there any difference between the words and what they signify? *Adeo.* – A huge difference. *Aug.* – I would like to hear what this difference may be. *Adeo.* – First of all, the names are signs and the realities are not. *Aug.* – Would you be willing to accept that we shall call those realities that can be signified by signs but are not themselves signs, 'significables', just as we call the realities that we can see 'visibles'? This will make our discussion easier. *Adeo.* – I accept. *Aug.* – Well, can these four signs you pronounced not be signified by other signs? *Adeo.* – Do you think I have forgotten? I am surprised you believe so, for we have already established that written words are signs of other signs that we express by means of the voice. *Aug.* – Tell me, what is the difference between these signs? *Adeo.* – Some of them are 'visibles', others 'audibles'. Should we not allow this latter name since we have allowed 'significables'? *Aug.* – I indeed accept it and I am grateful for it. But again, can these four signs not be signified by other audible signs, just as you recall we did for visible signs? *Adeo.* – I remember having said something of this sort recently. I had responded that names signify something, and I suggested four examples. Whatever a name may be, or whatever these four realities may be, they are nonetheless expressed by means of the voice, and I further recognise that they can be understood. *Aug.* – What then is the difference between a sign and the realities signified which are also signs when both pertain to hearing? *Adeo.* – The difference between what we call a 'noun' and the four realities whose signification we are discussing is that the first is a sign of other 'audible' signs, but the other four signs are not signs but realities, some 'visibles', like Romulus, Rome, and river, and others 'intelligibles', like virtue.

IV.9 *Aug.* – I agree and approve. But do you not know that what we call a 'word' is put forward as an articulate sound with a signification? *Adeo.* – I know. *Aug.* – Then, 'noun' is also a word, when it is put forward as an articulate sound with a signification. When we say that an eloquent person uses the right words, surely this person also uses nouns. And when in Terence's work the slave reports to his old Master 'Good words, I pray you', then he has also used many nouns. *Adeo.* – I agree. *Aug.* – So you agree that when we articulate the two syllables *ver-bum* [word] we also signify a noun, so the first word is a sign for the second. *Adeo.* – I agree. *Aug.* – I want you now to respond to a further point. Word is a sign for a noun and noun is a sign for 'river', and 'river' designates something that is visible. You have also explained the difference between the reality and 'river', which is a sign of the reality, and the difference between 'noun' which is a sign for this sign, but then, what do you think is the difference between the sign of a noun, in other words, 'word', and the noun itself of which this is a sign? *Adeo.* – I understand the difference in the following way: the realities signified by nouns are also signified by words, since 'noun' is a word and 'river' is also a word. However, not everything that is signified by noun is also signified by word. This is because, if we take the *si* [if] at the beginning of the verse you offered as well as the *ex* [from] which we were discussing not long ago, our reasoning leads us to these considerations – that some things are words without being nouns, and one can find many other similar words. That is why, if all nouns are words, but not all words are nouns, then to my mind, there is a clear difference between word and noun, that is, between the sign of a sign that signifies no other signs, and the sign of a sign that points to other signs. *Aug.* – But surely you will agree that every horse is an animal yet not every animal is a horse? *Adeo.* – Why should you doubt it? *Aug.* – Well, there is the same difference between noun and word as between animal and horse. But maybe you are reluctant to assent because we use this word *verbum* [word] in a different way to signify a word conjugated in different tenses, as in: I write, I wrote; I read, I have read; and these words are clearly not names. *Adeo.* – You've understood well what caused my hesitation. *Aug.* – Do not let that bother you. Generally, we call all those things signs which designate something else, and among these we also find words. At the same time we speak of 'military signs', which are properly called signs, and in that case we do not use words. Similarly, each horse is an animal but not every animal is a horse, so every word is a sign but not every sign is a word. I think, you would accept that without any doubt. *Adeo.* – I understand now and I definitely agree – there is the same difference between word, generally, and noun, such as we find between animal and horse.

IV.10 *Aug.* – You also know that when we say *an-i-mal* [animal], the three syllables of the noun projected by the voice is different from what it signifies. *Adeo.* – I have accepted this fully both for all signs and significables. *Aug.* – Do you think that all signs signify something other than themselves, just as the three syllables of the word *animal* [animal] do not signify the reality itself at all? *Adeo.* – Not really. Because if we say 'sign', this word signifies not just other signs but also itself. This is so because it is a word and surely all words are signs. *Aug.* – Then when using the two syllable word *verbum* [word], is it not the same thing? For if word signifies any articulate sound that has a signification, then it must also be included in this category. *Adeo.* – Yes. *Aug.* – Is it not the same for *nomen* [noun]? Because it signifies nouns of all sorts and *nomen* [noun] is itself a neuter noun. If I asked you which part of speech 'noun' is, how could you respond except by saying it is a noun? *Adeo.* – Correct. *Aug.* – There are then signs which signify both themselves and other signs. *Adeo.* – Agreed. *Aug.* – Do you think this is also the case for the four-syllable sign when we say *con-junc-ti-o* [conjunction]? *Adeo.* – Not really, because while it is itself a noun, the realities it signifies are not nouns.

V.11 *Aug.* – You have been very conscientious. Now do you see that there are signs which signify each other mutually, in such a way that the one is signified by the other? But this is not really the case with the four syllable word *conjunctio* [conjunction] and the realities signified by it, such as *si* [if], *vel* [or], *nam* [for], *namque* [for indeed], *nisi* [except], *ergo* [therefore], *quoniam* [whereas], and so on. All these conjunctions are signified by the word *conjunctio* [conjunction], but none of them are signified by that four-syllable word. *Adeo.* – I see; and I want to know what signs signify each other mutually. *Aug.* – Do not overlook that when we say 'noun' and 'word' we are using words. *Adeo.* – Yes. I know that. *Aug.* – So, do you not know that when we say 'noun' and 'word' we are using two nouns? *Adeo.* – Yes. I know that too. *Aug.* – You know then that 'noun' signifies 'word' and that 'word' signifies 'noun'. *Adeo.* – I agree. *Aug.* – Can you tell me what differentiates them other than that they sound different and are written differently? *Adeo.* – Maybe I can if I review what I just said. For when we express words, we signify whatever is put forward by articulate voice with some signification. And so it follows that every noun, including the word 'noun', is a word; nonetheless, not every word is a noun, although the word 'word' we are discussing is itself a noun.

V.12 *Aug.* – So, if someone were to assert and demonstrate that every word is a noun, just as every noun is a word, apart from their difference in sound and spelling, how do you think we could distinguish them? *Adeo.* – I could not see how and I should not believe there is any difference. *Aug.* – So, if it is true that whatever articulate sound that has a signification is both a word and a noun, but for some reason, one is a word and the other is a noun, will there not be a difference between word and noun? *Adeo.* – I do not understand how that could be the case. *Aug.* – Well, you do understand that every visible reality is coloured, and that every coloured reality is visible, yet these two have distinct and different significations. *Adeo.* – Yes. I understand. *Aug.* – So similarly, each word is a noun and each noun is a word, though these two words have different meanings. *Adeo.* – I can see that it might come to this. But how it does I am waiting for you to show me. *Aug.* – You notice, I think, that everything enunciated as an articulate vocal sound with a signification strikes the ear so that it can be perceived, and then committed to memory so that it may be known. *Adeo.* – I have noticed as much. *Aug.* – So, two things occur whenever we utter a sound by means of our articulate voice. *Adeo.* – That is so. *Aug.* – Well, what if in these two things, 'word' takes its name from one, and 'noun' takes its name from the other? Since 'word' can be derived from *verberare* [to strike], and 'noun' can be derived from *noscere* [to come to know], in this way the former term is named what it is with regard to the ears and the second with regard to the soul.

V.13 *Adeo.* – I will accept this when you show me that it is correct to call all words nouns. *Aug.* – That is easy, for I think you have learnt and grasp that what is called a 'pronoun' takes on the role of a noun by signifying a reality, but by means of a less complete signification than the noun. This is the definition that you must have repeated to your grammar teacher: the pronoun is a part of speech which stands for the noun itself, albeit less completely, but with the same signification. *Adeo.* – I remember and I agree. *Aug.* – You see then that according to this definition, pronouns stand for nouns and only nouns, as when we say 'this man', 'the king himself', 'the same woman', 'this gold', 'that silver'. 'This', 'that', 'himself', and 'the same' are pronouns. 'Man', 'king', 'woman', 'gold', and 'silver' are nouns which signify realities more completely than pronouns. *Adeo.* – Yes, I see and I agree. *Aug.* – Then give me a few conjunctions as you please. *Adeo.* – Well, *et* [and], *que* [but], *at* [even], *atque* [and even]. *Aug.* – Do you not think that all the ones you have used are nouns? *Adeo.* – Not at all. *Aug.* – Do you not at least think that I was speaking correctly when I said: 'all the ones you have used?' *Adeo.* – Quite right. And now I understand the marvellous way that you have been directing me, that what I uttered were nouns; for otherwise 'all the ones' could not be used correctly. But I still suspect that the reason I thought you had spoken correctly was because these four conjunctions which we are discussing are undeniably also words. As a result we can correctly say 'all the ones' because we have correctly said 'all the words'. But if you ask me what part of speech 'word' is, I will not be able to respond with anything other than 'noun', so your way of speaking was correct because the pronoun stands for the noun.

V.14 *Aug.* – You are probing well, but you are wrong. To correct your error, listen even more carefully to what I am saying, if indeed I can express myself as well as I want to. To use words to deal with words is as complex as rubbing fingers against fingers and for someone other than the one performing the action to recognise which finger is itchy and being scratched. *Adeo.* – I am with you wholeheartedly; but this comparison has made me very attentive. *Aug.* – Of course, words are made up of sounds and letters. *Adeo.* – Yes. *Aug.* – Then we can take up the authority we hold most dear; when the Apostle Paul says: *Non erat in Christo est et non sed est in illo erat* ['In Christ there is neither Yes nor No, but in Him only Yes'] (2 *Cor.* 1.19), I do not think we are to suppose that the three letters sounded when we say *est* [yes] are in Christ but rather the reality signified by these three letters. *Adeo.* – True. *Aug.* – You understand then that when he says 'in Him was Yes' it is as if he said 'in him was what we call Yes', just as if he had said 'in him was virtue' we would take this to mean that what we call virtue was in him. We should not think that he has the two syllables that we pronounce when we say *vir-tus* [virtue] in him but rather what they signify. *Adeo.* – I understand and I am with you. *Aug.* – Well, do you also understand that there is not any difference between saying 'is called virtue' and 'is named virtue'? *Adeo.* – That is clear, and I am with you. *Aug.* – Is it not just as clear that there is no difference between saying that which is in him is called *est* [yes] or is named *est* [yes]? *Adeo.* – Once again I see no difference. *Aug.* – Do you not now see what I am trying to have you see? *Adeo.* – Not really. *Aug.* – Well, can you not see that a *nomen* [name] is that by which a reality is named? *Adeo.* – Nothing is more certain. *Aug.* – So you can see that *est* [yes] is a *nomen* [name] if that which was in Him is named *est* [yes]? *Adeo.* – I cannot deny it. *Aug.* – But if I asked you what part of speech *est* [yes] is, I think you would say, not a *nomen* [noun] but a verb, though our reasoning has taught us that it is also a *nomen* [noun]. *Adeo.* – It is just as you say. *Aug.* – Do you still doubt that all the other parts of speech are also nouns, in the sense we have just shown? *Adeo.* – I do not doubt it now that I acknowledge that they signify something. But in respect to what they signify, if you asked me how each reality is named, I can only respond by saying that they are parts of speech that we do not call nouns, even though reason teaches us to do so now.

V.15 *Aug.* – Are you not disturbed that it might be possible to destroy our reasoning by saying that it attributes authority to the Apostle in realities but not in words? As a result, the foundation of our reasoning might not be as solid as we think. It might be that Paul, while having lived and expounded with so much rectitude, spoke less correctly, misusing 'In Him is Yes' given that he himself proclaimed his lack of skill with words? (2 *Cor.* 11.6) How do you think this opposing view should be refuted? *Adeo.* – I have nothing to object. But I urge you to find someone among the acknowledged authorities on words who, based on this authority, can establish what you wish. *Aug.* – So it seems to you that reason itself, excluding authorities, is less capable of showing that something is signified by every part of speech, in other words, is called something, but whatever might be called something, also names something, and whatever names something is surely itself a noun. One can be certain of this by comparing other languages. Obviously, if you ask how the Greeks name what we name *quis* [who], the answer is *tis* [who]; when asked about what we call *volo* [I fly], the Greeks answer *thelo* [I fly]; when asked about what we name *bene* [well], they answer *kalos* [well]; when asked about what we call *scriptum* [writing], they answer *to gegrammenon* [writing]; when asked about what we name *et* [and], they answer *kai* [and]; when asked about what we name *ab* [from] they answer *apo* [from]; when asked about what we call *heu* [alas!], they answer *oi* [alas!]; and so on for all the parts of speech which we have enumerated, and the question may be asked correctly. But this could not be done if these were not all forms of naming. So following this line of reasoning, the Apostle Paul spoke correctly, and so we can establish, leaving aside authority in every matter of eloquence, that there is no need to look for such persons to back up our view.

V.16 *Aug.* – But perhaps someone who is either too backward or too shameless may not agree; and, on the contrary, asserts that he wants this backed up by authorities who are accepted by everyone and who are the law when it comes to words. Who in the Latin language can be found that is better than Cicero? And yet he, in his magnificent oration called the *Verrine Oration*, calls the preposition *coram* [before] a noun, even though it might be an adverb in that particular passage. It may be that I do not understand that passage very well, and that others might explain it in a different way, but be that as it may, I think there is something that cannot be answered whether by myself or others. According to the traditional teaching of the most respected masters of dialectic, a complete sentence is one which can be either affirmed or denied, and consists of both a noun and a verb. Tullius [Cicero] himself calls this a 'proposition'; and when a verb is used in the third person, it must, the masters say, be in the nominative [naming] case, and they are right to think so. If, then, you consider this with me, when we say 'the man sits', 'the horse runs', you may notice that there are two propositions. *Adeo.* – I do. *Aug.* – You see that in each there is one noun; in the first, 'man', in the other, 'horse'; and in each there is also a verb, in the first, 'sits', in the other, 'runs'. *Adeo.* – Yes. *Aug.* – Now, if I simply said 'sits' or 'runs', you would have good reason to ask me 'Who?' or 'What?', so that I might respond, 'the man' or 'the horse' or 'the animal' or something else, so that when restored to the verb it is a proposition capable of being either affirmed or denied. *Adeo.* – I understand. *Aug.* – Now pay attention. Suppose we see something far away, and are uncertain whether it is an animal or a rock or something else. If I say to you, '*because* it is a man, it is an animal', would I not be speaking rashly? *Adeo.* – Very rashly. But you could say correctly, and without any rashness, '*if* it is a man, then it is an animal'. *Aug.* – Well done. So, in your sentence, 'if' pleases me and pleases you, but in my sentence the 'because' displeases both of us. *Adeo.* – I agree. *Aug.* – Are these two sentences complete propositions: '*If* pleases', '*Because* displeases'? *Adeo.* – They are. *Aug.* – Now tell me, which are the verbs and which are the nouns? *Adeo.* – As far as the verbs go, I see 'pleases' and 'displeases', and the nouns are nothing other than 'if' and 'because'. *Aug.* – So these two conjunctions are nouns that name realities, and this is sufficiently proven. *Adeo.* – Yes, sufficiently. *Aug.* – Can you yourself treat in the same way all the other parts of speech by this same rule? *Adeo.* – I can.

VI.17 *Aug.* – Let us move on now. Given that we have just discovered that all words are nouns and all nouns are words, let me know whether you think that all nouns are 'vocables' [articulate sounds] and all 'vocables' [articulate sounds] words? *Adeo.* – Certainly I do not see any difference between them other than the sound of the syllables. *Aug.* – For the moment I am not going to object, but there are some who distinguish them in respect to meaning, but we do not need to consider their opinions presently. Nonetheless, you surely observe that we have just discovered signs that signify each other mutually, differing merely in sound, as well as those that signify themselves along with all the other parts of speech. *Adeo.* – I do not understand. *Aug.* – Do you not understand that a noun is signified by a vocable and a vocable by a noun, and that as a result, other than the sound of the syllables, there is no difference between them at least insofar as *noun* is taken in a general sense? Though, to be sure, we also use *noun* in a special sense when it is one of the eight parts of speech and it does not contain the other seven. *Adeo.* – I see. *Aug.* – Well, this is what I meant when I said that vocable and noun mutually signify one another. *Adeo.* – I understand that, but I wonder why you said 'signify themselves along with all the other parts of speech'? *Aug.* – Our reasoning earlier taught us that all parts of speech may be called nouns and vocables, in other words, could be signified by both noun and vocable, did it not? *Adeo.* – It did. *Aug.* – When I ask you about the word 'noun', that is, the sound expressed by the two syllables [*no-men*], will you not correctly answer that it is a noun [*nomen*]? *Adeo.* – Yes. *Aug.* – However, does the sign which we express when we enunciate the four syllables *con-junc-t-io* [conjunction] signify itself in the same manner? It is surely not the same, since this noun cannot be counted among the conjunctions which it signifies. *Adeo.* – I accept that as correct. *Aug.* – That is so since it is what I meant when I said that 'noun' signifies itself along with all the other realities which it signifies. You can see this for yourself, for it also works for 'vocable'. *Adeo.* – Easily now. However, it has just occurred to me that noun is used in both a general and a special sense, but vocable is not one of the eight parts of speech. So I think there must also be that difference as well as the difference in sound. *Aug.* – Do you think that *nomen* [name] and *onoma* [name] differ in any other respect than the different sounds of the Latin and Greek languages? *Adeo.* – Here I do not think there are any other differences. *Aug.* – So then we have discovered signs which signify both themselves and each other mutually such that whatever is signified by the one is also signified by the other and that they differ only in sound. We have also uncovered this fourth element, for the first three are understood in respect to noun and word.

VII.19 *Aug.* – I would like you now to review for me what we have discovered in our discussion this far. *Adeo.* – I will do my best. First of all, I remember that we were inquiring into the reason why we speak. We found that we speak in order to teach or to remind, because in questioning we want the person to learn what it is we wish to hear about. Singing, which we seem to do for the pleasure derived, is not really speaking, and thus when praying to God (who we cannot believe needs to be taught or reminded of anything), we use words either to remind ourselves, or so that others may be taught or bring something to mind through us. Then, when we agreed that words are only signs, you quoted the verse: *Si nihil ex tanta superis placet urbe relinqui* [If it pleases the gods that nothing be left of so great a city], asking me to try to explain what each word signified. Although the second word is well-known and obvious, we still could not discover what it means. But since it seemed to me that it is not a word that is empty, and that it is used to teach something to our interlocutor, you suggested that perhaps it refers to some affection of the soul when searching for something and discovering (or believing that it discovers) that something does not exist. Then you humorously side-stepped some deeper questions, of which I am not aware, putting them off for another time. When I tried to explain the third word of the Latin verse *de* [from], you urged me not to proffer a synonym but rather to illustrate the reality which the word points to. I suggested that it was not possible to do so in discussion, but that this might be achieved by pointing with a finger. I suspected that this included all corporeal realities, but we discovered that it works only for visible realities. From that point we moved on, I am not sure how, to the deaf and actors who, by means of gestures and without use of words, can signify not just realities that may be seen, but much more, indeed, almost everything we can speak about. We thus agreed that these gestures are also signs. So we began to look for how we might be able to show, without the use of signs, the realities themselves that the signs signify — thus, 'wall', and 'colour', and every visible object that can be pointed to by a finger were shown to be signs themselves. I wrongly thought that nothing could be discovered without a sign, but we finally agreed that realities can be indicated without signs, as is the case with actions that we are not presently performing, but when we are asked about such actions, after having been asked, can perform them. However, speaking does not fit in this category. If we are presently engaged in speaking, and we are asked what speaking is, it seemed to us very clear that it is easy to show what speaking is by speaking.

VII.20 *Adeo.* – This reminded us that a sign may be indicated by other signs, that something which is not a sign can be indicated by means of a sign, and that without a sign something can be indicated by an action that can be performed when we are questioned. So we undertook to investigate more thoroughly and to discuss the first of these three propositions. That discussion showed that, on the one hand, some signs cannot be signified by means of those signs that they themselves signify, as is the case with the four syllable word *con-junc-ti-o* [conjunction]. On the other hand, some signs can, for in saying 'sign' we are also enunciating a word, and in enunciating 'word' we are also expressing a sign because 'sign' and 'word' are, at the same time, both words and signs. For that category in which signs mutually signify each other, it was revealed that some signs mean not as much, others just as much, and others are identical in meaning. The two syllable word *sig-num* [sign] signifies absolutely everything that signifies something. However, if we say *verbum* [word], this sign does not signify all signs but only that which is vocally articulated. It is thus clear that while 'word' is signified by sign, and 'sign' is signified by word, in other words, the two syllables of the first by the two syllables of the second and vice versa, nonetheless *signum* [sign] has a greater value than *verbum* [word] since more things are signified by the first two syllables than by the second two. Nevertheless, 'word' taken generally, and 'noun' also taken generally, have the same value. This is because, as our reasoning has taught us, all the parts of discourse are also nouns because pronouns can be added. Indeed they all can be said to name something, and there is nothing that cannot, by the addition of a verb, make up a complete proposition. But if 'word' and 'noun' have the same value — everything that is a noun is also a word — they still are not identical in meaning. As our argument showed fairly well there is a difference between them because things are called words for one reason and nouns for another. In the first case, the term was invented to capture the vibration impressed upon the ear, in the second to capture memory in the soul. This can be understood in the very act of talking, for we correctly say: 'What is the *nomen* [name] of this reality?' when we want to commit it to memory, but we do not typically say 'What is the *verbum* [word] for this reality?' There are also signs, the significations of which are not just equivalent but identical, and there are no distinctions between them other than sounding out the letters. In this category we found *nomen* [name] and *onoma* [name]. In the category of signs which mutually signify each other, there was a point I missed: we did not find any sign which does not also signify itself as well as the other realities it signifies. So then, I have recalled everything as best I can. I believe you have spoken throughout with knowledge and certainty, so let me know whether I have presented these matters well and in the correct order.

VIII.21 *Aug.* – Your memory has served you well in presenting everything that I wanted, and I confess that these distinctions now seem to me much clearer than they were when, through our questioning and discussion, we released them from their unknown hiding places. But it is difficult to say at this point where I am trying to lead you with all these detours. It might be thought that we are playing a game, our spirits taking refuge in childish questions; or that we are seeking some petty or mediocre goal; or maybe you do suspect that this investigation will have a worthy reward, and you want to see what it is, or at least you want to hear something about it now. But believe me, this discussion is not some simple amusement, even though we can be playful, so long as we are not puerile in doing so, and we are not seeking some petty or mediocre goal. Yet if I say that that there is a blessed eternal life, that I desire that we be guided there by God, in other words, by Truth itself, by steps and gradually, proportionate to the frailty of our progress, I fear that I would seem ridiculous because I have set out on such a journey by considering signs and not the realities that the signs signify. But please forgive me for playing with you in our preparatory work, since it was not so much frivolous as a way of exercising the development of the strength and acuity of the soul so that we can bear the heat and light of the realm of the blessed life, and to love Truth. *Adeo.* – Please continue just as you started for I never think anything unimportant which you judge is worthy of saying or doing.

VIII.22 *Aug.* – Then let us consider the idea of those signs which do not signify other signs but instead those realities we call significables. First of all, tell me whether 'man' is a man? *Adeo.* – Now it is unclear to me whether you are joking. *Aug.* – But why? *Adeo.* – Because you think the question should be whether 'man' is anything other than a man [*homo*]. *Aug.* – I believe you would think I was playing with you if I was also asking whether the first syllable of this word is other than *ho* and the second other than *mo*. *Adeo.* – Exactly. *Aug.* – But these two syllables together make *homo* [man], or do you deny this? *Adeo.* – I do not. *Aug.* – I am asking you then are these two syllables when joined 'you'? *Adeo.* – Absolutely not. But I see where you are taking me. *Aug.* – Then tell me so that I may not be thought of as insulting you. *Adeo.* – I infer that I am not *homo* [a man]. *Aug.* – What! Why did you not think the same thing when you agreed that the previous inferences were all true and from which this conclusion has been reached? *Adeo.* – I am not going to tell you what I think until I hear your explanation; in asking me if 'man' is man, are you asking me about the two syllables [*ho-mo*] or about the reality signified by them? *Aug.* – Tell me yourself in what sense you take my question; for if it is ambiguous you ought to have been careful not to answer until you were sure of the sense of my question. *Adeo.* – But how could the ambiguity embarrass me since I responded to both senses? Man is definitely man [*homo*], and the two syllables are only two syllables, and that which they signify is nothing other than the reality which it is. *Aug.* – You already know this. But why have you taken only the word *homo* [man] in two senses and not the other words which we have been speaking of? *Adeo.* – I am not at all convinced that I should not have taken the other words in this way. *Aug.* – Leaving everything else aside, consider just my first question. If you had taken it entirely in the sense in which the syllables sound, you would not have answered me because it might seem that I had not really asked any question. But when I just enunciated three words, repeating the middle one, saying *utrum homo homo sit* [whether man is man], you did not take me to mean the first and last words as signs, but rather as the realities signified by them, and this is clear since you responded at once with sureness and confidence that my question could be answered. *Adeo.* – That is true. *Aug.* – Why then did it seem appropriate for you to take the word I repeated both in respect to sound and in respect to signification? *Adeo.* – Fine. Now I take it exclusively in the sense in which something is signified, since I agree with you that we cannot engage in discussion at all, unless once we hear words, we direct the soul towards the realities of which they are the signs. That is why you must now show me how my reasoning erred in arriving at the conclusion that I am not a man. *Aug.* – I would rather ask you the questions once again so that you may come to see your error for yourself. *Adeo.* – Good.

VIII.23 *Aug.* – I will not go over my first questions again since you have already answered them. But consider now more carefully whether the syllable *ho* in *homo* is merely the syllable *ho* and again whether *mo* is just *mo*? *Adeo.* – Here I really do not see any difference. *Aug.* – Do you think that the union of the two syllables makes a man [*homo*]? *Adeo.* – I certainly do not concede that, for we agreed, correctly, that when a sign is enunciated we will attend to its signification, and in considering that, deny or affirm what is said. We have also conceded that the syllables enunciated separately have no signification, they are just sounds. *Aug.* – You accept then, and hold tenaciously in your soul, that responses should be made to questions which are about realities signified by words? *Adeo.* – I do not understand how I should be displeased if words are merely words. *Aug.* – I wonder how you might refute someone who in conversation, so we hear, amusingly suggested that a lion came out of the mouth of his interlocutor. Asking whether what we say comes out of the mouth — something his interlocutor could not deny — he followed up rather easily so that his interlocutor enunciated the word 'lion'. When his interlocutor had done so, he started to make fun of him, since his interlocutor had agreed that whatever we utter comes from the mouth. Moreover, the interlocutor was unable to deny having said 'lion', so the poor fellow seemed to have spewed a terrible beast from his mouth and was a bad man. *Adeo.* — It would not be too difficult to refute that joker because I would not allow that whatever we say comes out of our mouths. When we speak we signify, and when speaking it is the sign of the reality that comes from the mouth, not the reality which is signified, except in those cases in which signs themselves are being signified, a category we discussed earlier.

VIII.24 *Aug.* — I see you are well prepared against such an adversary. Nonetheless, how would you respond if I asked you whether *homo* [man] is a noun? *Adeo.* — What? Nothing is more of a noun than that is. *Aug.* — But when I look at you do I see a noun? *Adeo.* — No. *Aug.* — Would you like me to tell you what follows? *Adeo.* — No, please do not, because I can see for myself that I am not the 'man' that I called a noun when you asked me whether *homo* [man] is a noun. We have agreed that we are to affirm or deny whatever is said in respect to the reality that is signified. *Aug.* — It seems to me that you have not slipped in making that response, because the laws of reason themselves, which are imprinted in our souls, have raised your vigilance. If I were to ask what man is, you would probably reply that he is an animal. However, if I were to ask you what part of speech *homo* [man] is, you would correctly answer, simply a noun. So when *homo* [man] is seen to be both a noun and an animal, the first refers to the sign but the second is said of the reality that is signified. Therefore, when someone asks whether *homo* [man] is a noun, I must respond that it is, because the question put this way indicates that the person asking wants to be answered in the sense in which *homo* [man] is a sign. However, if someone were to ask whether man is an animal, I would agree more readily. But if he were to ask what *homo* [man] is, not mentioning either noun or animal, my soul would settle, according to the rules of the use of language, on what is signified by the two syllables *ho-mo* [man], and so the reply would be animal, or I might go on to give a full definition — rational and mortal animal. Does this seem right to you? *Adeo.* — It does. But once we have accepted that *homo* [man] is a noun, how are we to avoid the unacceptable conclusion asserting that we are not men? *Aug.* – How do you think, other than by pointing out that the conclusion does not follow from the sense in which we agreed that the questioner posed the question? On the other hand, if he holds that he intends the question not to refer to realities, but instead to signs, then we should not be afraid, for why be afraid to agree that he is not *hom-in-em* [a man], in other words, that he is not made up of these three syllables? *Adeo.* – Very true. But why then is the soul offended when it is said *non est igitur homo* [you therefore are not man], since as our discussion has shown this is quite true? *Aug.* – Because I cannot think that the conclusion refers to that which is signified by the two syllables *ho-mo* [man] once the words are enunciated, as a result of that forceful law of nature which, once signs are heard, directs us towards the realities they signify. *Adeo.* – I accept what you say.

IX.25 *Aug.* – I would like you now to understand that signs are dependent upon the realities that they signify. This is so because whatever exists because of something else must necessarily be inferior to that for the sake of which it exists. Or do you think otherwise? *Adeo.* – It seems to me that I should not agree to this too rashly. When we say *coenum* [filth], this noun, I believe, is much superior to the reality it signifies. What is offensive when we hear the sound of the word itself is not so much the sound, since *coenum* [filth] can be changed by a single letter to become *coelum* [heaven]. But we do note a great difference between the realities that are signified by them. This is why I do not want to attribute to the sign that which I loathe in the reality signified. It is for this reason that I think the sign is preferable to the reality, for we prefer what we hear to perceiving the reality with any of our senses. *Aug.* – Most vigilant. Is it wrong then to suppose that realities signified are not to be thought of as more valuable than their signs? *Adeo.* – It would appear so. *Aug.* – Tell me then, what end do you think people wanted to achieve when they put this name on something so nasty and despicable? Do you approve of this or not? *Adeo.* – Well, how can I dare to either approve or disapprove since I do not know what their goal was? *Aug.* – At least you can know what you are after when you utter this word. *Adeo.* – I can indeed. I want to signify the reality which I think needs to be taught or reminded, so as to teach or remind the person I am speaking to of the reality itself. *Aug.* – This teaching or reminding, or being taught or reminded, which you express rightly by the name, or which is expressed to you, should that not be thought to be more valuable than the name itself? *Adeo.* – I accept that the knowledge which is derived from the sign ought to be considered more valuable, but not, I believe, the reality itself.

IX.26 *Aug.* – It is false then that all realities should be thought to be more valuable than their signs, yet according to our discussion, it is not false that those realities that exist because of something else are less valuable than that because of which they exist. The knowledge of filth which caused the noun to be created must be thought to be more valuable than the noun itself, which we discovered was more valuable than the reality of filth itself. Knowledge is more valuable than the sign of which we are speaking for the sole reason that it has been shown conclusively that the sign exists for the sake of knowledge and not knowledge for the sake of the sign. If some glutton, a slave of the belly, as the Apostle calls him (*Rom.* 16.18), were to say that he lives in order to eat, the temperate person who heard him would, being unable to agree, say 'Is it not better to eat in order to live?' These words are inspired by the rule just elaborated, namely that inferior realities exist for the sake of superior ones. The reason for the dissatisfaction is that the glutton valued his life so little that he thought less of it than gluttony, as was made clear by saying that he lived for the sake of eating. Moreover, the advice to eat in order to live rather than to live in order to eat is rightly praised because it highlights what counts as means and what counts as ends, in other words what should be subordinated to something else. In the same way, you and others who can judge things wisely would respond to a person prone to prolixity who says 'I teach in order to talk': 'Man, why do you not talk in order to teach?' If these things are true, as you know they are, you surely can see how much less valuable words should be esteemed than that for the sake of which words are employed, since their use is more important than the words themselves. Words exist so that they may be used, and moreover we use them so as to teach. Just as teaching is more valuable than talking, so too speech is more valuable than words. And again, understanding is more valuable than words. But I would like to hear whether you have any objections.

IX.27 *Adeo.* – I definitely agree that understanding is more valuable than words. But are there any exceptions to the rule just elaborated that everything which exists for the sake of something else is inferior to that for the sake of which it exists? On this I am not so sure. *Aug.* – We shall have a better opportunity to go into this more fully at another time. In the meantime, what you have accepted is sufficient to confirm what I am striving at. You admit that knowledge of realities is more valuable than the signs of those realities. So, knowledge of realities signified by signs is preferable to knowledge of signs alone. Is that so? *Adeo.* – Surely I have not committed myself to allowing that the knowledge of realities is more valuable than the knowledge of signs but not more valuable than the signs themselves. That is why I am afraid I do not agree with you on this point. If the word filth, the noun, is more valuable than the reality it signifies, then the knowledge of the noun should be preferred to the knowledge of the reality, even though the noun itself is less valuable than the knowledge. There are in fact four terms here: the noun, the reality, the knowledge of the noun, and the knowledge of the reality. Just as the first is more excellent than the second, why should the third not be more excellent than the fourth? Yet even if it is not more excellent surely it is not subordinate.

IX.28 *Aug.* – I see you have retained wonderfully everything you have accepted and have presented your views well. However, I think you understand that the three syllable word we say when we utter *vit-i-um* [vice] is better than that which it signifies, yet the knowledge of the noun itself is much inferior to the knowledge of vices. This is why even if you accept and consider the four distinctions — noun, reality, knowledge of the noun, knowledge of the reality — we rightly put the first before the second. When Persius used that noun in his verse, saying, 'But he is stupefied with vice' (*Satyra* 3.33), he committed no vice in versification, but rather added an ornamentation. But when the reality itself that is signified by this noun is present in someone, then that person is indeed vicious. In this way we can see that the third distinction is not more excellent than the fourth, but rather the other way round. The knowledge of the noun *vitium* [vice] exists for the sake of knowledge of vices. *Adeo.* – Do you think that the knowledge of vice is preferable even though vice makes man more miserable? For of all the punishments that men suffer and are conjured up in the imagination of cruel tyrants or by their greed, Persius places this one punishment above all others: the torment of acknowledging vices that cannot be avoided. *Aug.* – In this way you could deny that knowledge of the virtues is preferable to knowledge of the noun virtue, because to behold and not to possess it is torture, and this is how the satirist wanted tyrants to be punished. (*Satyra* 3.35-38) *Adeo.* – May God save us from such madness. Now I do understand that good education, through which understanding comes into the soul, is not to be blamed, but rather that those persons who we should pity most are to be judged, just as Persius judged them, as infected with a disease for which there is no cure. *Aug.* – Well understood. But it should not matter to us what Persius thought. In this matter we should not be subject to authorities. So then, if some form of knowledge is preferable to another in some way, it is not really easy to explain why at this point. I am satisfied nonetheless that it has been established that the knowledge of a reality signified by a sign is more powerful than the sign itself, even if not more than the sign itself. Therefore, let us examine more carefully the category that concerns those realities which we said can be indicated through themselves without signs, such as speaking, walking, sitting, throwing and the like.

X.29 *Aug.* – Do you think that all actions that we can immediately perform after being questioned about them can be indicated without a sign? Or are there any exceptions? *Adeo.* – Considering the entire category of such things again and again, I cannot find anything in this category which can be taught without some sign, except maybe speaking and also perhaps, when questioned, teaching. For whatever I perform when someone asks a question, I see that he cannot learn immediately as a result of my performance, which he wants done for him. If I am asked what walking is while I am resting, or doing something else, and then I immediately perform the act of walking, thus trying to teach without using a sign, how shall I avoid my questioner thinking that 'walking' consists merely in the distance that I have walked? If he believed that, then he would be mistaken, for if someone walked not as far or further than I had, then the questioner would think that this person has not walked at all. And what I have said about this particular word applies equally to all of the others which we thought could be indicated without a sign, except those two we already excluded.

X.30 *Aug.* – I think that is right. But does it not seem to you that speaking is one thing and teaching another? *Adeo.* – Very much so. If they were the same no one could teach without speaking, but we teach many things by means of signs which are not words, so who can doubt that there is a difference? *Aug.* – Are teaching and signifying the same or are they different? *Adeo.* – I think that they are the same. *Aug.* – But is it not correct to say that we signify so as to teach? *Adeo.* – Yes. *Aug.* – If someone said that we teach in order to signify, then would this position be easily rejected by the previous statement? *Adeo.* – That is so. *Aug.* – If then we signify so that we may teach, and do not teach so that we may signify, then teaching and giving signs are indeed different. *Adeo.* – That is true, so I did not answer well when I suggested that they are both the same. *Aug.* – Now tell me whether the person who teaches what 'teaching' is does so by signifying, or by some other means? *Adeo.* – I do not see how it could be otherwise. *Aug.* – So you were wrong when questioned just now since you said that teaching about realities can be achieved without signs; however, we can see that not even in this case can teaching occur without signs. You have agreed that teaching is one thing and signifying is another. And if, as appears to be the case, they are different, and teaching can be accomplished only by means of signifying, then 'teaching' cannot be indicated by performance, as you thought. So we have discovered nothing as yet, save 'speaking', which signifies both itself and other things, and which can be taught by performing. But since speaking is itself a sign, it is not very clear whether anything can be taught without the use of signs. *Adeo.* – I have no reason to object.

X.31 *Aug.* – We have established then that nothing can be taught without using signs and that knowledge ought to be more valuable to us than the signs by means of which we come to know, and this despite the fact that not every reality signified is greater than its sign. *Adeo.* – So it seems. *Aug.* – Recall then what a tiny goal has been reached by such lengthy, circuitous discussion. Since we started this discussion, which has continued for quite a long time, we have worked to resolve three problems: Whether anything can be taught without signs? Whether some signs ought to be preferred to the realities they signify? And, whether knowledge of realities is better than knowledge of their signs? However, there is a fourth point I would like to briefly hear about from you. Do you think that our conclusions are established beyond all doubt? *Adeo.* – I would certainly like to have achieved some certainty after all these doubts and running about, but your question bothers me somewhat — I am not sure why — and stops me from agreeing. I suspect you would not have asked me this question unless you had some objection, and the difficulty is so deep that I cannot explore it fully or answer with certainty, for I am worried that something lies hidden in these complexities which escapes the sharpness of my insight. *Aug.* – I think you do well in being doubtful, as it is indicative of a cautious spirit and this is a great custodian of serenity. It is really difficult not to be worried when views that we hold easily and with passionate belief can be undermined by counter-considerations, and thus, it would seem, can slip from our grasp. It is a good thing to agree to matters that have been examined well by reason, but so too, it is dangerous to suppose that some matter is known when it is not. We should be vigilant when matters we took to be well established and firmly held are undermined, in case we succumb to distrust and hatred of reason and that it might seem our confidence in truth itself is not warranted.

X.32 *Aug.* – But come, let us move on and consider more thoroughly whether you are right in doubting any of our conclusions. Suppose that someone who is ignorant of fowling [bird-catching], which is carried out using twigs and bird-lime, comes upon a fowler armed with his instruments as he walks along, though he is not engaged at that time in fowling, and catching up with him, and in wonder and reflection, were to ask himself, as he might well do, what was the purpose of the man's equipment. If the fowler, noticing that he is being watched, were to perform his art, skilfully using the twig and, noticing a bird close-by, if he were to lure, approach, and catch it with his stick and falcon, would then the fowler not have taught this spectator by means of performance and without use of signs, the very thing that the observer wanted to know? *Adeo.* – I am afraid that he would be in the same position as the person I mentioned earlier who inquires about walking, since it does not seem to be the case that the specificity of fowling can be shown fully by this performance. *Aug.* – It is easy to remove this worry because I can add a stipulation that the observer is intelligent enough to understand the whole of the craft from what he saw. It suffices for our purpose that some people can be taught about some matters without the use of signs, though not all matters. *Adeo.* – I could add that if that person were sufficiently intelligent he would also come to understand fully what walking is when a few steps are performed. *Aug.* – I have no objection and indeed I agree with the truth of your point. You can see that both of us have now agreed that some people can be taught some things without using signs and that a while ago we were wrong to hold that nothing whatsoever could be indicated without using signs. Now after these remarks, consider that not just one reality or another, but thousands of realities can be entertained by the soul, and these can be indicated by realities when no sign has been presented. Why then should we still have doubts, I ask you? This is not to mention the innumerable performances of men in every theatre in which realities themselves are presented without signs. And consider the sun and its light pervading and clothing all things, the moon and other stars, lands and seas, and all the countless things that come to be through these. Are they not all exhibited and shown in themselves, by God and nature, to those who can discern them?

X.33 *Aug.* – When we consider this more carefully, then maybe we will find that nothing can really be learnt by means of signs. When someone presents a sign to me, if I do not know what reality it is a sign of, it can teach me nothing. And if I already know the reality, what then does the sign teach me? When I read (Daniel 3.94): *Et saraballae eorum non sunt immutatae* ['And their *saraballae* are not changed'], the word *saraballae* cannot show me anything about the reality it signifies. If it names some kind of head-covering, then when I hear the word, have I learnt either what a 'head' is or what 'coverings' are? I already knew these, and it is not when someone names them, but when I actually see them, that I come to understand for myself. Moreover, when the two syllable word *ca-put* [head] struck my ear for the first time, I knew as little about its signification as I did when I first heard or read *saraballae*. But when *caput* [head] was repeated often, and I observed and noted when it was said, I realised that it referred to a reality already well-known to me by sight. Before I found this out the word was merely a sound to me, and I realised it was a sign when I understood the reality of which it is the sign; a reality which I learnt about, as I said just now, not from its sign but by seeing. So then, the sign is understood after the reality is known, rather than it being the case that the reality is known when its sign is given.

X.34 *Aug.* – To understand this better, suppose that we now hear the sound *caput* [head] for the first time, and we do not know whether it is just a sound or if it signifies something, and we ask what *caput* [head] is. (Remember, we want to understand, not the reality signified, but rather knowledge of the sign itself, and we clearly lack knowledge insofar as we do not know what the sign is a sign of.) If then, in answer to the question, the reality is pointed to by a finger, we see the reality and thus come to learn the sign that we had previously only heard but not understood. So there are two things in signs: sound and signification. We surely perceive the sound by means of the vibration which strikes the ear and not by the sign itself, whereas we learn the signification when we see the reality signified.

Pointing a finger indicates nothing other than the reality pointed to, and it points not to a sign but rather to that part of the body that is called *caput* [head]. Therefore, I did not learn anything about reality, because I already knew this, nor did I learn the sign in this way, since the act of pointing was not directed at the sign. But I am not really so concerned with the act of pointing a finger because it seems to me that this is a sign of a gesture rather than of realities indicated. It is similar with the adverb *ecce* [look], because we tend to point the finger when we use this adverb as if just one sign of indication were insufficient. What I am really trying, if I can, to convince you of is this: above all we learn nothing, as I just said, by means of those signs we call words. In other words, we learn the meaning of the sign, which is hidden in the vocal sound, when the reality itself that is signified is understood—this is the manner in which the signification comes to be known.

X.35 *Aug.* — Moreover, what I have just said about *caput* [head], I must also say about 'coverings' and countless other realities. But even when I have come to know them all, I may still not know what *saraballae* are. If someone were to indicate what they are by a gesture, or a drawing, or by showing me something similar to them, I am not saying that he would not be teaching me (though I could easily show this if I wanted to elaborate further). However, I am saying something relevant to the point we are discussing — that he has taught me nothing by means of words. If someone, while in my presence, seeing these *saraballae*, brings them to my attention by saying, *ecce saraballas* [look at these *saraballae*], I would learn something of which I was previously ignorant, not as a result of the words spoken, but by seeing the reality, and in this way come to understand and to remember the meaning of the noun. When I learn about the reality itself I am not relying on the word of someone else but on my own eyes, though it may be that I trust the words of others so that I might pay attention, in other words, so that I might discover what is to be seen.

XI.36 *Aug.* — So far as words are to be valued, they invite us to search for realities by reminding us, but they do not present us with realities to be known. On the other hand, whoever teaches me something places before my eyes, or any other corporeal sense, or even to the soul itself, those realities I desire to know. So from words we can only learn words, or rather the sound or noise of words. Even for realities that are not signs, and thus cannot be words, I cannot know that the sound I hear is really a word unless I know what it signifies. So, knowledge of words is perfected by knowledge of realities, but by merely hearing words we do not learn anything about realities. We do not learn words that we already know, and we cannot say that we learn those words that we do not know unless their signification is already understood. This occurs not by hearing words when they are enunciated, but rather by understanding the realities that are signified. It is sound reasoning, and truly said, that when words are pronounced we either already know what they signify or we do not; if we already know, then we remember rather than learn, but if we do not know, we are not even reminded, though perhaps we are prompted to ask questions.

XI.37 *Aug.* – However, what if you were to say: 'We cannot know what head-coverings are unless we see them, yet we remember the sound of the noun, and we cannot fully know the noun itself until we understand the realities themselves'? Nonetheless, we accept the story about the boys who vanquished both the king and the fires by virtue of their faith and religion, and that they sang praises to God, thus meriting honour from their enemies. Yet have we learnt about them in any other way than through words? I think so, since we already know what all these words signify. I already know what three boys are, what a furnace is as well as fire, what a king is, and what 'unhurt by fire' is, along with everything that is signified by these words. However, I am as ignorant of Ananias and Azarias and Misael as I am about *saraballae*, and the names do not, and could not, help me know these men. Everything we read in these stories about what occurred at that time is written down, and I confess that I believe rather than know these to be the case; and those writers whom we believe knew the difference between believing and knowing. As the Prophet says: 'If you do not believe, you will not understand.' (*Isaiah* 7.9). He would not have said this if he had not thought that believing and knowing were different. Therefore, what I understand I also believe, since everything I understand I believe, but I do not understand everything I believe. I am not blind to the fact that there is utility in believing many things which I do not know, and among them is the utility in the story about the three boys. While the majority of things remain unknown to me I nonetheless acknowledge the utility of believing.

Part II

XI.38 *Aug.* – Now, of all the things that we understand, we consult, not the words that are expressed in an exterior fashion, but rather the interior custodian, truth, within the soul, perhaps because we have been alerted to do so by means of words. Moreover, the one who is consulted, is He who is the Teacher, Christ, who is said to dwell in the interior man, in other words, the immutable Power and eternal Wisdom of God, to whom every rational soul pays heed. But to each is revealed only so much as can be received depending upon the perfection of the will. If someone is deceived, this is not a result of some defect in consulting Truth, just as it is not a defect in external light when the eyes of our bodies are often deceived. We make use of external light in respect to visible realities so that it may reveal them to us in so far as we have the capacity to discern them.

XII.39 *Aug.* – We need light so that we may, through our bodily senses, perceive colour and other realities; we need the elements of this world and also those bodies of which we are sensually aware; we need the senses themselves which the soul uses to recognise and interpret realities of this kind. We also need interior truth, so that our reason can know intelligible realities, for what proof can be given to show that we learn anything by words other than the sound which strikes the ear? All realities that we perceive are perceived either by means of a bodily sense or by the soul. We refer to the first of these as sensibles and the latter as intelligibles, or as our authorities would say, carnal realities and spiritual realities. If we are asked about sensibles, we can answer, provided that the realities sensed are close by, such as when we are questioned while gazing at the new moon, about where it is, or what sort of reality it is. If the questioner does not see, he believes our words, or maybe often does not believe them, but he learns nothing unless he actually sees what is being talked about. If he does learn, he does so by means of his own senses perceiving the realities themselves, and not by means of the words articulated. The same words are heard both by the person who sees and the person who does not see. However, if we are asked not about realities that are immediately at hand but about realities we have previously sensed in the past, here we are speaking, not of realities in themselves, but of images derived from these realities and imprinted in memory. I am not at all sure how we can speak of these images as being true when we can see that they are merely images, unless this is so because we do not speak of what we see or what we sense, but instead of what we have seen or have sensed. We carry these images of realities in the recesses of memory like documents of realities previously sensed, contemplating them in the soul, and so we can speak of them in good conscience and not falsely. But these documents are private, and if someone hears about them, and if he too has experienced and sensed them, he learns nothing from my words; rather, he remembers what is said by means of the images in his own memory. But if he has not perceived the realities that we speak of, it is clear that he believes, rather than knows, by means of the words.

XII.40 *Aug.* – But if we are dealing with realities perceived by the soul by means of reason and insight, that is, intelligibles, these are said to be realities that we apprehend immediately in that interior light of truth by which the inner man himself is illumined and filled with joy. But then whoever is listening, if he also sees for himself those realities with the pure and hidden eye, then he knows what I speak of by his own meditations and not because of my words. As a result, even though I speak truly about reality, I still cannot teach someone, for he must contemplate truth for himself. He is taught not by my words but by realities that he sees and that God reveals to him inwardly. So, if he is questioned about these realities, he can answer. There can be nothing more absurd than supposing he is taught when I speak, because even before I speak he can explain those realities if he were asked about them. It is often the case that he who is questioned denies something, and then when questioned further, goes on to affirm what he has already denied. This happens due to a weakness in discernment, since he cannot consult the [interior] light about the whole issue. While he cannot see the whole all at once, when questioned about the parts that make up the whole he can, one step at a time, become enlightened about the whole by means of his questioner's words. If he is guided in this way by the words of the questioner (even though he does not fully grasp the whole by such verbal teaching) he nonetheless, by means of questions ordered in this way, can teach himself inwardly according to his own ability. Just as in our recent discussion, when I asked you if anything could be taught by words, the question at first seemed absurd to you, because you did not have a complete view of the issue, and so it was appropriate for me to order my questions in a manner such that your own powers could come to listen to their inner teacher. So once you admit that those things I have spoken about to you are true, and you are certain about them, so too must you admit that you had knowledge about them. But where did you learn these things? You might respond that I taught them to you. To this I would reply, what if I were to assert that 'I saw a man flying'? Would my words carry the same certitude for you as if I had said 'Wise men are better than fools'? You would surely deny this. You would assert that you do not believe the first statement, or if you do believe it, you do not know that it is true, but that you do know the latter statement with a high degree of certainty. In this way you would understand that you have not learnt anything from my words; neither in the first case, in which you did not know what I affirmed, nor in the second, which you knew very well, since you were able to respond confidently and with clarity to my questions, stating what you did not know or what you did know. Finally, taking the matter as a whole, you recognised and agreed that each of the parts were clear and certain, so you now know the falsity of what you had denied. When we say something, the hearer either does not know whether what was said is true or false, or he knows that it is false, or he knows that it is true. In the first case, either he will believe, or he will suppose it to be so, or he will doubt it; in the second case, he will either oppose or reject it; and in the third he will affirm it. In none of these cases does the hearer learn anything as a result of what is heard; when I have spoken, he who does not know if my words are true, as well as he who knows they are false, and he who would give the same answers when asked, none of them has learnt anything by means of words.

XIII.41 *Aug.* – On this account it follows that, in the case of those realities discerned by the soul, anyone who cannot discern them listens in vain to whoever does discern them, with the exception that it is useful to believe them while ignorance persists. In so far as someone can discern those realities grasped by the soul, he is in an interior way a disciple of truth, and in an exterior manner a judge of the speaker or at least of what is said. For quite often a hearer knows what has been said while the speaker himself does not know. Take, for example, a disciple of Epicurus, who thinks that the soul is mortal, but who repeats the arguments of wiser men who hold that the soul is immortal, in the presence of an audience conversant with spiritual realities. If someone hears the speaker, he will judge the truth of what is said, even though the speaker does not know the truth. Indeed, on the contrary, what he thinks is false. Should he be thought to teach what he does not know? Nonetheless, he uses the same words that also serve the one who does know.

XIII.42 *Aug.* – And so, there is little left for words, for they do not even indicate the soul of the speaker, since it is uncertain whether the speaker knows what he is saying. Concerning also liars and deceivers, you will easily understand that their words do not reveal what is in their souls but rather conceal it. I do not, of course, in any way doubt that truthful men by means of words try, and to some extent do, open up their souls; they would succeed, we all agree, if liars were not permitted to speak. However we have often experienced, both in respect to ourselves and others, that words do not correctly express our thinking. I think this happens in two ways. Sometimes, when something has been committed to memory and repeated often, it may be spoken while we are thinking about something very different. This often happens when we are singing a hymn. Sometimes, against our own will, we commit a slip of the tongue, and in this case as well signs are expressed about realities that are not really in our souls. Even liars also think about the realities they speak of, so even if we do not know whether they are expressing the truth, we do know what they intend to say, provided they do not make one of the two mistakes just mentioned. If anyone contends that this only happens now and again, and that it is easy to spot when it happens, I make no objection, though quite often it is hidden and it has often escaped my notice when I have been listening.

XIII.43 *Aug.* – In the same category there are other cases which are very prevalent and occasion countless disagreements and strife. This occurs when someone who is speaking signifies the reality which he is thinking of but does so only to himself and to some others, but his words do not signify the same thing to his interlocutor nor to others. If someone were to say in our hearing that brutes are superior in virtue [*virtus,* 'virtue' or 'power'] to men we could not accept this, and we would vehemently refute it as false and repugnant, though perhaps the speaker meant by *virtus* ['virtue', or 'power'] just bodily strength, and thus is expressing what he thinks, without lying or being mistaken about the reality and without having something else turning around in his soul. He is expressing in language words that he has memorised and he has not committed a slip of the tongue. He simply calls the reality he was thinking about by a name other than the one by which we call it. We should at once agree with him if we could see his thoughts which he had not expressed well with the words spoken when stating his opinion. It is said that defining terms can fix this error. If in our question we define *virtus* ['virtue' or 'power'], it would become clear that the conversation is about the word and not about the reality; but even if I allowed this, I must ask how often do we find people who are good definers? Moreover, there are many who dispute the art of defining, but this is not the right place to deal with them, and in any case I do not approve of them.

XIII.44 *Aug.* – I am leaving out the fact that we hear many things poorly and enter into lengthy and multiple debates about these. So, for example, recall when you were recently talking about the Punic word which I said signified 'mercy', but you had heard from those who know the language well that this word signified 'piety'. I resisted this suggestion, asserting that you had forgotten what you had heard because it seemed to me that you had said not 'piety' but 'faith', even though you were seated close to me and the two words are not similar enough in sound to deceive the ear. For a long time I thought that you did not know what had been said to you, but it was I that did not know what was said. If I had heard you properly, it would not have seemed to me at all absurd that 'piety' and 'mercy' in Punic are expressed by one word. These sorts of things happen often, but as I said we should overlook them for fear of blaming words instead of the negligence of listeners or indeed for fear of becoming agitated by human deafness. These issues I have just enumerated are more troubling when, even though we speak the same language as the speaker and the words are clearly heard in Latin, we still do not understand the thoughts that are being expressed.

XIII.45 *Aug.* – Be that as it may, I now relent and admit that when words are heard by anyone who knows them, then the hearer should be assured that the speaker has been thinking about the realities which they signify. But is it the case that for that reason he also learns whether the speaker is speaking the truth, which is the question we are addressing at the moment?

XIV.45 *Aug.* – Teachers surely do not profess that it is their own thoughts which are perceived and grasped rather than the disciplines which they convey by speaking? Who is so foolishly curious as to send his son to school in order to learn what the teacher thinks? Teachers express by means of their words all the knowledge that they profess to teach, but virtue and wisdom —these cannot be grasped by words. For those who are called pupils need to consider whether what is said is true, contemplating according to their own abilities interior truth. It is in this way that they learn, and on discovering that what has been said to them is true, they offer praise, not realising that they are praising not so much teachers but rather learners, if indeed the teachers themselves know what they are speaking of. However, men are mistaken in calling people teachers who are not such, mostly because there is no delay between the time of speaking and the time of thinking; and because after the speaker has reminded them, they learn immediately in an internal way what they believe they have been taught in an exterior way by he who prompts them.

XIV.46 *Aug.* – At some other time, God-willing, we will consider further the whole issue of the utility of words which when you think about it is no small matter. For the moment, I have warned you not to attribute more to words than is proper. Hence, we should not just believe but also come to understand that it has been truthfully written on divine authority that we should not call anyone on earth a teacher, because 'there is one in Heaven who is teacher of us all' (*Mat.* 23.8-10). What 'in Heaven' means He will reveal to us by means of signs, and in an exterior way, in order that we can turn inwards to Him and so become enlightened. To know and love Him is the blessed life, and this is what everyone claims they are seeking even though there are few indeed who may rejoice in having discovered it. But now, please tell me what your view is of my whole long discourse? If you have come to accept that what has been said is true, then if you had been asked about each of the statements, you would reply that you did know them. You must see, therefore, from whom you have learnt about these issues. Certainly it is not from me, to whom you would have answered correctly if questioned. However, if you do not know that these things we have spoken about are true, then neither I nor He has taught you: not I, since I cannot teach anyway; and not He, because you have not yet the power to learn. *Adeo.* – As for me, I have learnt by being reminded by your words that a man is merely prompted by words so that he can learn, and it appears that only a very small part of what a speaker is thinking is expressed in his words. Moreover, whether what is said is true, He alone teaches us Who, when He spoke in an exterior way, reminded us that He dwells within us. So now, by His favour, I shall love Him more ardently as I progress in understanding. Nevertheless, I am especially grateful for the discourse you have delivered without interruption, for you anticipated all of the objections that worried me. You omitted nothing that caused me doubt, nor is there anything concerning which the hidden oracle of which you have spoken has not confirmed for me in your words.

CHAPTER 3.1

Aquinas: Commentary

Thomas Aquinas

Thomas Aquinas, the Angelic Doctor of the Catholic tradition, has had a massive influence on the philosophical and theological teachings of Christianity. It is difficult to overstate the degree to which he has influenced the ways in which the Christian faith is intellectually understood, lived in concrete practice, and transmitted from one generation to the next.

Born in 1224/1225, he was of noble extraction from the counts of Aquino, distantly related to Emperor Frederick II ('Frederick Barbarossa') as well as the kings of Aragon, Castile, and France. His family intended him to become the abbot of the most famous abbey in Europe at that time, namely Monte Cassino — a destiny frustrated by his fateful choice of joining a new religious order that made its living by begging and preaching, the Dominicans.[1] After studying the liberal arts at the University of Naples, in 1245 he continued his studies under Albertus Magnus (Albert the Great) in Paris. He received

[1]   Many stories surround his family's reaction to Thomas' taking of the Dominican habit — he was placed under house arrest by his family for almost two years, and attempts to induce him to give up his calling by having a prostitute seduce him were spectacularly unsuccessful. For details of Aquinas' life and educational background we have drawn upon the authoritative study by J. P. Torrell, *Saint Thomas Aquinas: Vol. 1: The Person and His Work*, trans. R. Royal, Washington D.C., Catholic University of America Press, 1996; and also the somewhat dated but still excellent J. Weisheipl, *Friar Thomas D'Aquino: His Life, Thought, and Works*, Oxford, Basil Blackwell, 1974. For additional biographical details and general surveys of Thomas' thought see F. C. Copleston, *Aquinas*, Harmondsworth, Penguin Books, 1955; E. Gilson, *The Christian Philosophy of St. Thomas Aquinas*, trans. L. K. Shook, South Bend, University of Notre Dame Press, 1994; E. Stump, *Aquinas*, London, Routledge, 2005; *The Cambridge Companion to Aquinas*, ed. N. Kretzmann and E. Stump, Cambridge, Cambridge University Press, 1993; and *Thomas Aquinas: Contemporary Philosophical Perspectives*, ed. B. Davies, Oxford, Oxford University Press, 2002. The chronology of Thomas' life presented here follows Torrell with some modifications from Weisheipl.

his first teaching appointment at the University of Paris in 1252 and became a master of theology in 1256. After almost a decade in Italy, in Orvieto and Rome (1259–1268), he took up a second teaching appointment at the University of Paris (1268–1272). Thomas Aquinas died at Fossanova on his way to the Council of Lyon in 1274. He was formally elevated to sainthood in 1323 by Pope John XXII and proclaimed a Doctor of the Church in 1567 by Pope Pius V.

He was physically large, both with respect to his height and his girth. Despite his size, he was known to have spent very little time sleeping or eating, and probably ate only once per day.[2] He also travelled extensively, and is estimated to have covered a good 15,000 kilometres — most of it on foot.[3] He was known to be of happy countenance and affable disposition. He was reported to have been exceedingly humble and patient, and in the often acrimonious public debates of the day, was notable in that even his staunchest opponents conceded that he never hurt anyone through words.[4]

It was not uncommon for him to dictate to three or four secretaries on diverse subjects at the same time.[5] His mind was so well organised, it is reported that, overcome with exhaustion from his work, he would occasionally fall asleep but still continue dictating until the subject had been finished.[6]

Aquinas wrote voluminously over the course of his lifetime.[7] Posterity remembers him primarily for his magisterial *Summa Theologica*, which became the definitive expression of the marriage of Aristotelian philosophy and Christian theology. But in the end he was essentially a man of prayer and a mystic. Indeed, he seems to have thought that prayer was a necessary precondition of under-

---

[2] Torrell, *op. cit.*, p. 282.

[3] As a sign of their humility Dominican friars were expected not to ride horses. Moreover, since the Dominicans were a mendicant order, Thomas would be expected to have to rely on charity for food and other necessities.

[4] See Torrell, *op. cit.*, pp. 280-281.

[5] Weisheipl, *op. cit.*, pp. 137 & 243-244; Torrell, *op. cit.*, pp. 241-242. Other examples of Thomas' extraordinary powers of concentration are mentioned in Weisheipl, *op. cit.*, pp. 235-236, 300-301.

[6] Weisheipl, *ibid.*; Torrell, *op. cit.*, p. 242.

[7] Counting only indisputably authentic works in an electronic database of his writings, Aquinas wrote 8,686,577 words. Including contested works, the total goes over 11 million. See A. Kenny, *Aquinas on Mind*, London, Routledge, 1994, pp. 10-11. See also the entry for 'Aquinas, St. Thomas' in *The Oxford Companion to Philosophy*, ed. T. Honderich, Oxford, Oxford University Press, 1995.

standing and the intellectual life.[8] After a mystical experience at Mass, he put down his pen forever, explaining that: 'I cannot do any more. Everything I have written seems to me as straw in comparison to what I have seen.'[9]

Educational Context of Aquinas

Elementary education in Aquinas' day consisted in reading, writing, singing, a bit of grammar, and knowledge of the calendar.[10] After completing a course in elementary education, the student would advance to the study of the seven liberal arts.[11] The liberal arts were divided into the *trivium* and *quadrivium*, dating back to Martianus Capella's *On the Marriage of Mercury and Philology* (5th Century). The three 'trivial' arts were grammar, dialectic (or logic), and rhetoric. These arts all concerned language and elegance of expression within language. The four 'quadrivial' arts were arithmetic, geometry, astronomy, and music. These were traditionally understood to be occupied with the study of 'things' as opposed to language, for instance, geometry could be used to measure the earth. They also may be understood as being related to one another as theory to application, in which their interrelationships were emphasised. Astronomy drew upon the theoretical resources of geometry to describe the motions of the heavenly bodies. Music entailed study not only of musical theory, but typically involved also learning to play the monochord (a one-stringed instrument played by plucking). As was well known since the time of Pythagoras, different notes on a monochord are related by strict arithmetic proportions: to play a note precisely one octave higher, one simply shortened the string by half. It is from these arithmetic relations that musical intervals are still described today in terms of quarter-tones and fifths.

After falling into disarray during the so-called Dark Ages, the classical liberal arts were revived during the Carolingian period

---

[8] See Torrell, *op. cit.*, p. 284.

[9] Quoted in Torrell, *op. cit.*, p. 289. See also Weisheipl, *op. cit.*, pp. 320-327.

[10] That Aquinas benefitted from his early instruction in music is evident from a number of hymns he composed, including *Pange lingua* ('Sing My Tongue', from which the famous *Tantum ergo sacramentum* is extracted), *Verbum supernum* ('Word on High'), *Adoro te devote* ('With All My Soul I Worship Thee') and *Lauda Sion* ('Praise Zion'). Many of these are still commonly sung. For discussion see Weisheipl, *op. cit.*, 176-185.

[11] We know the names of some of Thomas' teachers at this time, including Pietro Martini (who taught Thomas grammar) and Peter of Ireland. The latter was an eminent intellectual of the time. See Weisheipl, *op. cit.*, p. 17.

under the impetus of Alcuin of York and with the direct patronage of Charlemagne.[12] From the early ninth century there was a slow and steady diffusion of increased professionalism in education through a system initially focusing upon cathedral schools. These schools were attended not just by students drawn from their immediate communities, as parish priests were instructed to teach any promising youths to read and, where appropriate, to recommend that they be sent on for further study at the cathedral schools.

From the cathedral schools and the guild system[13] eventually arose universities, where masters and students came together for the purposes of instruction and the diffusion of learning.[14] This was a novel institution and perhaps one of, if not the most, important contributions of the mediaeval period to western culture. Certainly it is difficult to imagine contemporary intellectual culture without the university.

While the broad structure of the trivial and quadrivial arts stayed in place, in practice they were defunct as a balanced educational pedagogy by the early 13th century. In Aquinas' day grammar and rhetoric were dealt with in a perfunctory manner and little time was spared for the formal study of arithmetic and geometry. By way of contrast there was a general explosion in the proportion of the curriculum devoted to dialectic. The reason for this may be summarised in a single name: Aristotle.

The recovery of Aristotle's writings had a stunning impact on European intellectual culture, which suddenly found itself confronted with a vast, coherent, and technically sophisticated intellectual system that included works in formal logic, rhetoric, the natural sciences — including biology, zoology, psychology, meteorology, and astronomy — as well as ethics, politics, and metaphysics.[15] The

---

[12] The Dark Ages for Europe extended roughly from 500 to 1000. The latter half of this period coincided with the flourishing and high point of Islamic civilisation.

[13] The mediaeval guilds drew inspiration from as far back as ancient Egypt. Schooling in the mechanical arts required membership in a guild in which apprentices were initiated by masters into the secrets of their crafts. See S. A. Epstein, *Wage Labor and Guilds in Medieval Europe*, Chapel Hill, University of North Carolina Press, 1991.

[14] The classic historical treatment of the rise of the universities is H. Rashdall, *The Universities of Europe in the Middle Ages*, 3 vols., Oxford, Clarendon Press, 1895.

[15] Following Aristotle, Aquinas suggests that different philosophical subjects are suitable for different ages of student and that there should be a logical progression in the order of studies, e.g., that physics should be studied before

process whereby the thought of ancient Greece entered Europe is a fascinating adventure that cuts across multiple cultures, religions, and ethnicities. Greek works were first translated into Arabic by Syrian Christians living under the rule of Islam. Muslim and Jewish intellectuals, including some of the finest minds of both traditions — Ibn Sina, Ibn Rushd, al-Ghazali, Moses Maimonides, to name but a few — commented on the translated works and composed their own responses. The Arabic works made their way to Muslim-occupied Spain and Sicily, where they were translated again from Arabic into Latin. The result was a heady mix of classical learning blended with the more contemporary reflections of generally monotheistic but non-Christian scholars.

The greatest challenge facing the universities of Aquinas' day was what to do with this overwhelming wealth of material that was too important to ignore yet potentially hazardous to the propagation of the faith. In addition to clear scholarly challenges, such as separating out what was original to the Greek thinkers and what was an accretion from later scholars, there was the pressing matter of determining how to respond in cases where what Aristotle taught was clearly incompatible with the faith. For instance, Aristotle maintained that the world we inhabit is eternal and has always existed in much the same state that we find it. This would imply that there have always been human beings, which seems to threaten the Christian notion of God as creator.[16] Other theses conflicted with Christian orthodoxy, such as the opinion suggested in Aristotle and elaborated by Ibn Rushd that all humans share the same intellect, which is at odds with the Christian understanding of personal, as opposed to collective, immortality and life after death.[17]

Church officials were quick to notice that the authority of Aristotle, in consequence of his wisdom and accuracy in so many mat-

---

metaphysics. For discussion see J. F. Wippel, *Metaphysical Themes in Thomas Aquinas*, Washington D.C., Catholic University of America Press, 1984, pp. 95-97.

[16] Aquinas wrote on this subject several times and devoted a brief treatise to it — his *De aeternitiate mundi* ('On the Eternity of the World'). For relevant texts see St. Thomas Aquinas, Siger of Brabant, and St. Bonaventure, *On the Eternity of the World*, 2nd ed., trans. C. Vollert, L. H. Kendzierski, and P. M. Byrne, Milwaukee, Marquette University Press, 1984.

[17] A succinct response is given by Thomas in his *De unitate intellectus contra Averroistas*. For translation and commentary see R. McInerny, *Aquinas Against the Averroists: On There Being Only One Intellect*, West Lafayette, Purdue University Press, 1993. See also E. P. Mahoney, 'Aquinas's Critique of Averroes' Doctrine of the Unity of the Intellect,' in *Thomas Aquinas and His Legacy*, ed. D. M. Gallagher, Washington D.C., Catholic University of America Press, 1994, pp. 83-106.

ters, was so great that on these key subjects students might accept his views uncritically and in so doing abandon the teaching of the Church. What was needed was a constructive engagement with Aristotle, one both respectful and sensitive to the critical challenges posed by his thought. Aquinas' own teacher, Albertus Magnus, was at the forefront of this endeavour. It was while he worked as Albert's assistant that Aquinas first came into extensive contact with the works of Aristotle.

Scholastic Method

One of the difficulties many contemporary readers come up against in understanding mediaeval authors is related to the form or manner of presentation of philosophical inquiry. There are several distinct formal modes of pedagogy and questioning. These emerge from the classroom experience as well as the broader university context and practices, and take characteristic literary forms. They may be seen as subcategories of the *lectio* (or academic lecture) and *disputation*.

The *lectio*, which is the antecedent of the standard academic lecture, was originally a direct reading of an authoritative text, such as Aristotle's *Metaphysics*, accompanied by clarifications and commentary by the teacher.[18]

Disputations took various forms, and it is hypothesised that some of Aquinas' disputations that have come down to us arose directly out of his classroom experience. For instance, Torrell hypothesises that during a schoolday Thomas and his bachelor (what we would now call a graduate student) would spend an hour over a *lectio* with the younger students, followed by a second hour wherein the bachelor took the lead. After a morning thus spent and a brief break, students, bachelor, and teacher would return to discuss a series of questions arising either naturally from the text or from the interests of the students. These questions would then be looked at from all sides by the bachelor together with the students, and then would receive a formal summation by the teacher. Over the course of several weeks, a thematic unity in the questions would arise. A report would be made, cast in final form by the master, and then pub-

---

[18] For an account of the mediaeval *lectio* and Thomas' works arising from his duties as a lecturer, see Weisheipl, *op. cit.*, pp. 116-122.

lished.[19] The whole process is characterised by a communal inquiry, the object of which is the attainment of truth under the guidance of both authoritative sources and abstract reason.

More formally, the disputed issue is framed as a question, or *quaestio*. Bazan defines the *quaestio* as 'a regular form of teaching, apprenticeship, and research, presided over by the master, characterised by a dialectical method, which consists in bringing forward and examining arguments based on reason and authority which are furnished by the participants and conflict over a theoretical or practical problem. The master must arrive at a doctrinal solution by an act of determination that confirms him in his magisterial function.'[20]

Other forms of academic disputation occurred at regular intervals in the universities. Some of these involved series of questions promulgated beforehand by the master, who would develop his own position and then answer any objections originating from the audience, or from formal respondents. The most extreme form of the disputation is the famous *quodlibet*. Quodlibetal disputations, 'disputations on anything', opened the master to any random question posed by the audience. In form, the mediaeval disputations may be likened to that other well known institution, the joust. Participants would enter the lists of the academic tourney, and there was a great deal of public reputation at stake.

The traditional style of the disputation follows the general rubric of fixing on controversial questions (*dubitationes* or *quaestiones*), followed by an elaboration of possible objections, and finally a summation aimed at achieving a resolution of the central difficulty. The form is nothing other than the most rigorous application of what is now called analytic philosophy. Nevertheless the methodological approach differs to the extent to which appeals to authority are canvassed. Aquinas' own elaboration of the methodological problem indicates very strongly the psychological depth of the method as well as its ultimate appeal to reason. Aquinas describes the disputation as follows:

> Any activity is to be pursued in a way appropriate to its purpose. Disputations have one or other of two purposes.
>
> One sort is designed to remove doubts about whether such and such is so. In disputations of this sort you should above all

---

[19] See Torrell, *op. cit.*, pp. 61-62. For an alternative account of the mediaeval disputation with particular reference to the *De Veritate* from which Aquinas' text for this volume is taken, see Weisheipl, *op. cit.*, pp. 123-128.

[20] Quoted in Torrell, *op. cit.*, p. 60.

use authorities acceptable to those with whom you are disputing; with Jews, for example, you should appeal to the authority of the Old Testament; with Manicheans, who reject the Old Testament, you should use only the New; with Christians who have split from us, e.g. the Greek, who accept both Testaments but reject the teaching of our saints, you should rely on the authority of the Old and New Testaments and of those church teachers they do accept. And if you are disputing with people who accept no authority, you must resort to natural reasons.

Then there is the professional academic disputation, designed not for removing error but for teaching, so that those listening may be led to an understanding of the truth with which the magister is concerned. And here you must rely upon reasons, reasons which track down the root of the truth and create a real knowledge of how it is your assertions are true. Otherwise, if professors settle questions by bare authority, listeners are told indeed that such and such is so, but gain nothing in the way of knowledge or understanding (*scientiae vel intellectus*), and go away empty.[21]

In addition, Aquinas was very sensitive to the legitimate claims and boundaries of disciplines. Aquinas would therefore have been a staunch opponent of those moderns who, in the name of faith, reject claims within the sciences arrived at by proper methods of reasoning. We would expect him, for instance, to reject the position of those who, on the basis of a literal reading of *Genesis*, reject evolution via natural selection.[22] For example, in response to a series of questions posed by Baxianus de Lodi and his pupils comprising a heterogenous mix of metaphysical, theological, and scientific matters, Aquinas begins his reply by observing that a 'number of these articles [i.e., questions] pertain more to philosophy than to faith. We do a great disservice to the *doctrina pietatis*, when we affirm or we

[21] *Quodlibet* IV. Text adapted from that quoted in J. Finnis, *Aquinas: Moral, Political, and Legal Theory*, Oxford, Oxford University Press, 2004, pp. 11-12.

[22] Moreover, what was understood by the mediaevals as a literal interpretation is different from what we commonly take that term to mean now. For the mediaevals, a literal interpretation is one expressing the primary intention of the author, and thus Augustine could write that the six days of creation in *Genesis* could stretch over untold thousands of years, and this in a work entitled *A Literal Commentary on Genesis*. This does not mean that Aquinas would necessarily accept the particular variations of evolutionary theory currently on offer, as he would reject any theory that positively excluded divine providence.

reprove in its name things that do not belong to it as if they were related to *sacra doctrina*.'[23]

When published, a disputation was recast in a standardized form. The questions posed within the debate would be gathered into *articles*, which usually take the form of yes/no questions. Each article would then be subdivided into at least four sections. The first section consists of a list of numbered *objections* to the position adopted by the magister. The objections are then followed by the *sed contra* ('on the other hand...'), wherein the magister would briefly state his position and list authorities he took as agreeing with him. Then comes the *respondeo* ('I reply that...'), wherein the magister develops his view more fully, typically relying on natural reason instead of arguments from authority. Finally, there are numbered responses (*ad primum...* 'to the first...') to each of the objections. Given the lively nature of the disputed questions, this structure can become more complex.

Text of Aquinas' *De Magistro*

The text that has come down to us as the *De Magistro* ('On the Teacher') is Question 11 of the larger work, *Disputed Questions on Truth* (*De Veritate*).[24] We possess the dictated original manuscript for questions 2 through 22 of the work. This is good news not only with respect to ascertaining the scholarly accuracy of the text but also because Aquinas' handwriting is of legendary difficulty to decipher.[25]

Aquinas' *De Magistro* follows the standard format of the mediaeval disputation which we have just discussed. However, in order to make the central ideas more accessible to contemporary readers, we have departed from the traditional arrangement and have presented his work in flowing paragraphs. We fully accept that much of scholarly interest is lost as a result of this editorial decision (not least of which is the dynamic reproduction of the animated cut and thrust of live public debate and inquiry), but we defend this decision on the grounds that we are anxious to communicate with an audience who may not be familiar with the conventions of mediaeval philosophy. Our aim is to have readers engage Aquinas

---

[23] *Responsio de 30 articulis*, quoted in Torrell, *op. cit.*, p. 169.

[24] His views are tersely reiterated in his *Summa Theologica*: see *S.T.* I, 89.I & 117.I, and *S.T.* II-II, 181.3.

[25] Frustrated paleographers have, for generations, referred to Thomas' handwriting as *littera inintelligibilis* ('unintelligible hand') and he is commonly acknowledged as having the worst handwriting of any known mediaeval author.

as a contributor to contemporary debates within the philosophy of education.

There are those who point out (with some Pickwickian justice) that Aquinas never formulated an explicit philosophy of educa-tion.[26] It is however fair to say that he does consider quite carefully one fundamental aspect of education, teaching. To appreciate the significance of Thomas' views on teaching it will be worthwhile to situate them within his general epistemology and metaphysics.

In the *Summa Theologica* Aquinas, drawing on Augustinian and Neoplatonic sources, provides us with an image of the circle of enlightenment.[27] God is the principal source of knowledge. God radiates out an intellectual light which permeates the entire created order. Understanding is assimilated or attenuated depending on where a being is situated in the ontological hierarchy. Those beings ontologically 'closer' to God participate more fully in the intellectual light and those further away to a lesser extent. It is in this sense that Aquinas thinks of God as our first teacher.

Angels understand more clearly than man and can better fulfil the function of teacher due to their greater ontological proximity to the Divinity. A human being, standing as bridge (*pontifex*) between the material and spiritual orders can know certain things in a manner not available to angels (especially in respect to sensible particulars). A human being uses sense perception of particulars as a foundation for building up a knowledge of universals. This general picture is the one within which the *De Magistro* is set. The first question addressed is whether only God can properly be called a teacher or whether human beings also deserve that appellation. There is one further key background issue that is helpful for the understanding of the *De Magistro*, namely Aquinas' psychological theory. However, we defer discussion of this to our next section.

---

[26] See, for instance, A. MacIntyre, 'Aquinas's Critique of Education: Against His Own Age, Against Ours', in *Philosophers on Education: Historical Perspectives*, ed. A. O. Rorty, London & New York, Routledge, 1998. MacIntyre's claim that 'Aquinas had no philosophy of education' (*op. cit.*, p. 96) is somewhat disingenuous and could be applied to all four of our selected authors. One might also, with equal justice, assert that Aquinas had no explicit philosophy of religion, though it would be difficult to find any philosopher within the past thousand years who has exerted a greater influence on the philosophy and practice of the Christian faith.

[27] See *S.T.* I.89.1.

Understanding Aquinas' *De Magistro*

Over the course of the four articles of the *De Magistro* Aquinas inquires into the reciprocal activities of teaching and learning: what it is to be a teacher, what it is to be a student, and the way of life characteristic of the teacher. At first glance, the questions that Aquinas poses look puzzling. For instance, even a generous-minded contemporary reader is likely to find it more than a little odd to find that approximately one-third of the work is devoted to understanding how angels can teach. But while Aquinas is perfectly serious about the angels, what he has to say even in this section of the *De Magistro* cannot be dismissed as a quirky mediaeval effusion. This is because Aquinas is not just doing theology but rather is introducing an extended thought experiment, the range and power of which can be felt even by those who do not share his religious convictions. Talking about angels frees him to clarify what is going on in human learners as they move towards greater understanding. Instead of being an odd detour, discussing angels turns out to be an efficient platform for elaborating what is going on within students as they learn. It also provides an interesting springboard for speculation on what might be possible for human teachers to achieve as teachers.

In what follows we will present a brief overview of each of the four articles of the *De Magistro*. The purpose here is to express some of Aquinas' concerns in a more contemporary idiom. Our aim is not to give a full and detailed exposition of all of his arguments but rather to provide sufficient resources for the text to be read with understanding.

Article 1 – Can a human teach and be called a teacher, or just God alone?

In this article Aquinas is concerned to distinguish the different senses in which it is appropriate to say that someone is a teacher. We might consider Aquinas' succinct question as shorthand for a series of interrelated questions:

1) Can God teach?
2) In what distinctive sense does God teach?
3) Can human beings teach?
4) In what distinctive sense do human beings teach?
5) What does the learner contribute?

Aquinas argues that it is correct to say that human beings teach. But he qualifies his answer in important ways. This is because it is not proper to say that a human being is a teacher in every respect. No human teacher could ever be a sufficient cause of everything that the student learns. Aquinas thinks that human teachers do not create knowledge in their students. For any learning to occur, it is necessary for the student to contribute something. This common-sense observation is captured in a variety of maxims, including the observation that you can lead a horse to water but you can't make it drink. One might ask: From what source does the horse get whatever it contributes to drinking? One possible answer: from its Creator, who gives the horse its equine nature. In parallel fashion, Thomas thinks that we should look for distinctively divine contributions to the activity of learning in human nature. God gives the student those powers and capacities that suit him or her for learning, and as success in teaching requires actual learning on the part of the student, successful teaching entails a willing and active receptivity on the part of the student. (Aquinas develops this theme in greater detail in later articles, especially article 3.)

For all the Scholastic terminology, this is a very quotidian insight. Teaching requires certain capacities in the learner. For instance, no matter how gifted the human teacher, it is impossible to teach a lizard or a cat advanced particle physics. Why? Because the basic nature of lizards and cats does not suit them for such a task. They lack the necessary natural capacities. Nor is it possible to teach a three-year old human advanced particle physics. In this case, though, the limitation is not due to a natural incapacity. After all, at least some human beings do become particle physicists, and these physicists typically learn their discipline from human teachers. Rather, what seems to be lacking in children are those specific factual foundations and trained intellectual skills (what we have earlier referred to as know-that and know-how) required for a working knowledge of particle physics. There must, it seems, be a positive foundation upon which the potential learner's understanding is to be built.

As Aquinas notes, following Aristotle, all learning comes from pre-existing knowledge.[28] But if all learning presupposes prior learning, does this not present us with a terrible puzzle? While we can explain knowledge of, say, calculus on the basis of a prior knowledge of arithmetic, and knowledge of arithmetic on a prior knowledge of how to count, how do we learn to count? Surely knowledge

---

[28]　See Aristotle, *Posterior Analytics*, I.1.

of this sort is not directly impressed within us at birth:[29] there are human cultures that never develop sophisticated counting systems. That is, there are cultures that do not have specific words for higher quantities.[30] Yet there is something natural about counting: even those who lack the words are generally able to distinguish different quantities and sort them into more and less.

The tack Aquinas takes, in a manner sensitive to the concerns Augustine raises on this issue, is to characterise the sorts of actualities or positive features that must be present for humans to learn. The brief answer Aquinas gives (which is certainly open to further refinement and empirical research) nevertheless remains relevant. First, human learners require a natural capacity to *abstract* features of things. Thus, we need some capacity that allows us to, at first implicitly, and later explicitly, give voice to the idea of a being or a thing. Second, human learners require an ability to focus their attention on just some features of a thing and leave out others. That is, we must be capable of recognising *salience*.[31] Aquinas unites these two capacities into what in his technical vocabulary is called the *agent intellect*.[32]

Third, human learners must maintain at least an operational or implicit commitment to those *general principles of reasoning* that fit one for understanding the way the world actually is. Thus, while it is possible to deny in words the principle of non-contradiction, it is not possible to do away with this principle in practice, especially if one has any commitment to expressing thoughts in language.[33] This

---

[29] This is controversial, for some philosophers have held that certain forms of knowledge are innate. Possible examples might include Plato, Augustine, Descartes, and Leibniz. The notion of innate knowledge runs counter to a central tenet of Aquinas' empiricist epistemology which holds that all human knowledge begins in the senses, though there are innate capacities for knowing that must be present for the senses to do their job within the process. J. S. Mill takes Aquinas' empiricist account to even more extreme lengths, adopting an associationist psychological account and denying all forms of innate knowledge.

[30] For instance, it is argued by some anthropologists that the Pirahã (an Amazonian tribal group) do not have words for numbers greater than two. See D. Everett 'Pirahã' *Handbook of Amazonian Languages*, vol. 1, eds. D. C. Derbyshire and G. K. Pullum, Berlin, Mouton de Gruyter, 1986; and M. C. Frank *et al.*, 'Number as a cognitive technology: Evidence from Pirahã language and cognition,' *Cognition* 108, 2008, pp. 819–824.

[31] See article 3.

[32] We discuss the agent intellect in more detail below.

[33] The principle of non-contradiction (PNC) runs as follows: that *it is impossible for something to both be and not be in the same respect at the same time and in the same manner.* Aristotle presents three versions of the PNC in *Metaphysics* IV, 3-6. The

adherence to the first principles of reasonability concerns what Aquinas terms the *possible intellect* in operation.[34] According to Aquinas, these cognitive features—abstraction, salience, general principles of reasoning—are natural gifts implanted by God in all human beings, though they may be present in different degrees in different humans.

Other cognitive features need to be present and possessed by the potential learner before any actual learning can take place. For instance, a fourth feature, emphasising the subjective contribution of the learner, might be noted. Aquinas would say that successful teaching requires that the human learner be *properly disposed* to acquire knowledge. A learner must be open to teaching and willing to take an interest in what is taught. 'Pay attention!' says the teacher, but it is more of a request than a command. Neither God nor man may force a learner with respect to this fourth necessary feature of understanding. This is so because human learners are free agents and so their choices concerning their own learning are decisive.[35]

To summarise Aquinas' final position, God is the original teacher who furnishes human learners with the first three cognitive features mentioned above. Only God, as the author of human nature, may be said to teach in these ways. Or, as Aquinas puts it, only God may properly be said to teach human beings *interiorly*. The notion of God as an interior teacher is premised on the idea that humans have the nature that they have with the characteristic capacities that suit them for understanding—a nature created by God. An interior teacher is able to teach in an exterior manner as well, by proposing external sensible signs that direct the attention and awaken the powers of the learner.

However, there is still room for the human teacher, who presents objects of learning for the student in an exterior way. At the simplest level, human teachers might present or point to an object and say its name. Thus, the sign in speech for 'a spherical object one plays with'

PNC has been challenged by modern dialetheists. See, for example, Graham Priest, 'To be and not to be—that is the answer. On Aristotle on the Law of Non-Contradiction.' *Philosophiegeschichte und Logische Analyse* 1 (1998), 91–130. Although we cannot argue for this here, we reject Priest's position.

[34] The possible intellect is discussed in greater detail below.

[35] Aquinas is very clear that human freedom is sacrosanct. Thus, for instance, in matters of conscience he holds that it is a mortal sin to do what may be the objectively correct thing when doing so goes against one's conscience. Thus, conversions cannot be forced and parents must be allowed to raise their children within their own faith. See *S.T.*III.68.10.

is 'ball'. Over time, we are able to teach more indirectly, presenting signs in speech that students interpret, as we find in a lecture. In all cases the human teacher presents exteriorly that which the student grasps by a willing interior act of understanding via the cognitive powers mentioned above.

Article 2 – *Whether anyone should be called a teacher of himself?*

In this article, Aquinas is again on the side of common opinion: 'Without doubt a man can, through his implanted light of reason and without a teacher or aid of outside instruction, come to a knowledge of many unknown things, as is evident in everyone who acquires knowledge by discovery. A man is thus in a way a cause of his own knowledge.' Yet, immediately following this comment, Aquinas writes: 'Still, he cannot be called his own teacher or be said to teach himself.'

Why does Aquinas make this claim? Because in this article he wishes to call our attention to what makes teachers special and distinct from their students. Recall that in the previous article we found a defence and elaboration of the student as an active contributor in the act of understanding. In article 2, we see what the teacher (ideally) contributes to the development of understanding. Thomas does this by showing us what the learner, qua learner, lacks; namely, knowledge and understanding.

It may seem a bit obvious, but it is important to point out that a student cannot both know something and not know that same something at the same time and in the same way. For instance, nobody could both actually know that Aquinas was Italian and not actually know that Aquinas was Italian. But with this bland observation, we are in a position to clarify what kinds of agents teachers and learners are. While a student is capable of learning from his or her environment—and in this sense, too, Nature is our teacher—this is not, in the full and proper sense, what it means to teach. For teaching, properly speaking, must involve giving—nothing can give what it does not have (*nemo dat quod non habet*).

The teacher already has what the learner receives, and in this we see the nobility of the teacher. From the richness of what is already possessed, namely knowledge, the teacher may well-order and well-present that which is to be given so that the gift of knowledge may be better received and more firmly possessed. This does not threaten the dignity of the learner, who must actively receive that which is given.

Article 3 — Whether man can be taught by an angel?

Aquinas uses this question to situate his discussion of human psychology within the context of teacher and learner. By carefully noting how the learner learns, we can gain a better appreciation of how a teacher may successfully teach, and gain richer insight into the sort of expectations we should have concerning our students.[36]

Aquinas was an acute cognitive psychologist (here we take up the discussion deferred earlier) and many of his insights are still relevant in contemporary discussion. A quick reading of article 3 reveals that Aquinas uses familiar words in ways that are slightly unfamiliar to us. The majority of his technical vocabulary was in fact inherited from the classical Greek philosophical tradition, and from Aristotle in particular. Many of the words he uses are with us today: we still talk about natures, species, forms, and essences. We even speak about cognition in terms that Aquinas would find familiar: to this day we talk about ideas and concepts, and we distinguish intuition and intuiting from reason and reasoning. We find it important to take account of sensation, imagination, and intellect, and we see these three as distinct yet interrelated cognitive faculties. There are, however, some differences in how we use these words and how Aquinas employs them. He also uses words with which non-specialists are likely to be unfamiliar. For instance, what are *phantasms, sensible species*, and *intelligible species*? How is the *agent intellect* distinguished from the *possible intellect*?

The general psychology Aquinas defends is empiricist. He believes that for human beings knowledge begins in the senses: we learn by seeing, hearing, touching, smelling, and tasting. The task of the philosophical psychologist is to note all of the important steps in the process whereby we come to move from sensing things to knowing them. Once we have noted all of the important steps, then we will be in a position to ask for more detail (perhaps using modern science) concerning how those different steps come about.

Suppose that we see a cat. According to Aquinas, the *sensible species* is the likeness of that exterior object (the cat) as it is present in our senses. It may seem perfectly obvious, but of course we cannot

[36] For this section we have found the following reference works helpful: R. E. Brennan, *Thomistic Psychology: A Philosophic Analysis of the Nature of Man*, New York, The Macmillan Company, 1941; W. B. Monahan, *The Psychology of St. Thomas Aquinas*, Worcester, Trinity Press, 1935; S. L. Brock, *Action and Conduct: Thomas Aquinas and the Theory of Action*, Edinburgh, T&T Clark, 1998; R. Pasnau, *Thomas Aquinas on Human Nature*, Cambridge, Cambridge University Press, 2002; and A. Kenny, *Aquinas on Mind*, London, Routledge, 1994.

literally have the cat in our eye: it would be too big! So what we have must be some likeness or image of that cat. But the image of the cat does not stay only in our eye. We most likely need to integrate the sensible species received in the eye with the sensible species received in our other senses. For instance, we might hear the cat meow, so we need to combine the sensible species impressed upon our ears with the sensible species impressed upon our eyes. There are other things we can sense that we know from different senses, as when we perceive the size and shape of a cat with our eyes and also with our touch when we pat it.[37]

The complete, integrated sensory image—in our example, the image we build up of the cat we see, touch, smell, and hear—is called a *phantasm*. The faculty dedicated to receiving and manipulating phantasms is called the *imagination*. We find echoes of this way of speaking in contemporary English, for we say that we have images in our imagination, and that we fantasise or fancy things, which is another way of saying that we imagine them. The main difference is that what we today call the imagination is something Aquinas calls the *creative imagination*, which is only part of the whole faculty dedicated to sensory images.

The phantasms present in the imagination are still particular. That is, we have an image before us, but do not as yet understand the common or universal features embedded within the image. We cannot recognise this image as being an image of a cat until we know what a cat is and recognise that there could be more than one cat in the world. In other words, we need to *abstract* those common, repeatable features found in our phantasm of the cat before we can be said to truly understand it.[38]

The cognitive faculty that abstracts the repeatable, common features from phantasms is called the *agent intellect*. The agent intellect works like an X-ray, illuminating and pulling out what is universal in the phantasms. The products of this abstractive activity by the agent intellect are called *intelligible species*. Other, more familiar names that Aquinas uses for intelligible species are still with us: they are concepts or ideas.

The faculty that receives and manipulates concepts is the *possible intellect*, so-called because there is no limit to the sorts of ideas or con-

[37] As an historical aside, the sensory faculty whose task it is to notice these multiple-sensible features like size and shape is called the *common sense*.

[38] As we have seen, this is similar to the position adopted by Augustine in his *De Magistro*.

cepts it can take on or potentially understand. In most cases, when Aquinas writes about the intellect, what he is referring to is the possible intellect, and this is the more usual way of speaking nowadays. So, if the sensible species is the object in the world considered as present to the senses, then the intelligible species will be that same object considered as present to the intellect.

Within the possible intellect we could make further distinctions and identify various sub-faculties, but Aquinas does not go into such detail in this article. He does, however, think it important to distinguish two operations of the intellect. The ordinary operation of the human intellect, in which we proceed stepwise from one concept to another, is called *reasoning* or *ratiocination*. When we think through and deduce the steps within a logical argument (an example of know-that), or when we think through what we need to do to bake a cake (an example of know-how), we are *reasoning*. This operation is characteristic of human beings, and it is in virtue of our seemingly unique power to reason that Aristotle defined human beings as rational animals.[39]

In addition to reasoning, there is another way of knowing that involves an immediate grasping of truth. For instance, there is no way of giving formal, reasoned, proof of the Euclidian proposition that when equals are added to equals, the results are equal; nor of the principle of non-contradiction, namely that it is impossible for something to both be and not be in the same respect at the same time and in the same manner. When we recognise the truth of these principles we are not using our reasoning powers but rather our *intuition*. The act of *intuiting* something as true is familiar to all of us: it is the 'ah-ha!' or 'eureka!' moment when something dawns upon us, and we suddenly understand.

Given this technical apparatus, we are in a position to draw out what Aquinas teaches in article 3. His main concern is to situate the angelic mode of teaching between the divine and human ways of teaching, and in so doing bring out its characteristic features. Thomas' final position will be that angels are able to teach in a more interior way than human teachers, but in a less interior way than God.

Aquinas begins by setting aside consideration of those ways in which angels might teach that are essentially the same as the ways human beings teach. Angels might, for instance, take on a physical

---

[39] In addition to being rational and animal, Aristotle often includes the fact that we are social.

body and speak to us, and then we would learn by hearing the angel the same way we would from hearing a human being.[40] Next, Aquinas recapitulates his discussion of the mode of teaching proper to God alone. Only God can teach in a fully interior way, bestowing fundamental cognitive capacities to human beings as author of their nature.

While an angel cannot create human beings, and hence cannot be an interior teacher in the fullest sense, an angel can teach in a more interior way than human beings by directly strengthening the operation of our cognitive faculties. To use an analogy, an angel can help focus our agent intellect and clarify our intellectual vision, much as employing a magnifying glass clarifies our power of sight. We see more clearly, and hence more truly, when we see by means of a magnifying glass, yet a magnifying glass is not a replacement for our vision but rather an aid of it, and achieves its effect by building on our natural capacity of sight.

One implication of Aquinas' view is that a direct strengthening of the pupil's basic cognitive structures is not open to a teacher qua teacher. We might, however, wish to further qualify his point by noting that there may be dimensions of basic cognition that could be addressed medically. This would be entirely consistent with Thomas' position, as he fully accepted that there were physical components to cognition (as evidenced by the fact that a blow to the head can interfere with thinking), and so he would be happy to make room for medical advances.

Another implication of Aquinas' discussion is that even angels cannot force the student to learn. No one — not an angel, and certainly not a human teacher — can force the free judgment of a student. It is possible, Aquinas reasonably goes on to say, for an angel to help call a student's attention to what needs to be learnt by impressing phantasms on the imagination. This is an elevated version of the technique humans use: pinch someone, and they are most likely to pay attention to the spot pinched. Again, there is a practical lesson here for human teachers: pedagogy must be suited to what is taught, for the order and the mode of presenting images to students impacts their ability to abstract what they need to learn.

---

[40] A biblical example would be the angel Raphael conversing with Tobias.

Article 4 — Whether to teach belongs more to the active life or to the contemplative life?

This article concerns teaching as a calling, with its own distinctive virtues and satisfactions. Teaching is, for Aquinas, more than something one does; it is a way of being, and should be recognised as such. To be a teacher is to embrace a way of life that defines who one is and what one does. To be a farmer involves embracing a way of life; to be a weekend gardener does not. To be a doctor involves embracing a way of life; to volunteer for the ambulance brigade does not. Of course there is nothing wrong with gardening or volunteering — these are, in fact, very good things to do. But with respect to the demands of gardening or volunteering, one can legitimately claim to garden or volunteer without taking on either of these as fundamental constituents of one's identity. Such is not the case for farmers, doctors, priests, lawyers, — or teachers.[41]

This brings us back to the idea of teaching as a vocation, that is, a 'calling out' for those who respond to the summoning to participate in a complete way of life. Note that the very form in which Aquinas poses his question contains an implicit critique of those who would become teachers for reasons extrinsic to the nature of teaching itself. Ways of life contain internal goods, and such goods are routinely correlated with roles and responsibilities that are characteristic of that way of life. So, if one becomes a teacher primarily for extrinsic reasons — perhaps the prospect of steady life-time employment beckons, or the possibility of long vacations or favourable working hours — then, while there is nothing objectionable in these things in themselves, to put any of these extrinsic goods first would be to subvert the nature of teaching. While teaching is occasionally a chore, a challenge, and a burden, it should never be just a job.

Given that teaching, properly understood, is a distinct way of life, (and given that, in the previous articles Aquinas has gone some way towards explaining what a teacher does, what a learner does, and the respective dignities of each as loci of their own characteristic contributions to understanding,) it remains for Aquinas to look into the nature of teaching as a vocation. What is the essential nature of teaching considered as a way of life?

A characteristic concern of much of mediaeval philosophy, which has sources both in Aristotle and the New Testament, is the distinction between two differently oriented ways of life. By the *contempla-*

---

[41] There are other plausible candidates for the list. Newer professions such as computer programmer might be suitable for inclusion.

tive life, Aquinas does not necessarily mean a way of life open only to 'deep' individuals and sages. Rather, the contemplative life is a way of life that finds its completion in an interior act. A priest's life is essentially contemplative, finding its completion in prayer, however much that individual might minister to his flock's needs through corporeal works of mercy. As Aquinas puts it, the end of the contemplative life is the *consideration of truth*. The *active life* is not necessarily a life abuzz with frenetic activity, but rather is a way of life that finds its end and fulfilment in exterior acts. A life dedicated to politics is active, even though a statesman's actions should be anything but mindless. As Aquinas puts it, the end of the active life is the *good of one's neighbours*.

Both ways of life are found in the teacher, for a good teacher is concerned with truth. But ultimately the end of the act of teaching is the good of the pupil, and as such teaching as a vocation belongs more to the active life than to the contemplative, though it requires commitment to contemplation for its support and fullest realisation.

Aquinas: Text

Aquinas: De Magistro (On the Teacher)

Abridged and adapted as flowing text from the translation of Mary Helen Mayer[1]

The four articles of the *De Magistro* take up four points of inquiry, namely: (1) Whether man can teach and be called a teacher, or just God alone? (2) Whether anyone can be called a teacher of himself? (3) Whether man can be taught by an angel? (4) Whether teaching pertains to the active or to the contemplative life?

ARTICLE 1

Whether man can teach and be called a teacher, or just God alone?

Can a man teach and be called a teacher, or just God alone? It might seem that God alone teaches and ought to be called a teacher.[2] In *Matt.* 23.8 it is written: 'One is your master,' and preceding this, 'Be not called Rabbi,' on which the *Gloss* says, 'Lest you attribute divine honour to men, or usurp to yourselves what belongs to God.' Further, knowledge is a certain form of the soul, and nothing can form

---

[1] M. H. Mayer, *The Philosophy of Teaching of Saint Thomas Aquinas*, New York, Bruce Publishing Co., 1929.

[2] In the Latin text, Aquinas begins each section with a numbered list of possible objections to the position that he will later adopt. He follows this with a brief catalogue of authorities and, sometimes, terse arguments for his own view. He then presents his full considered view, followed by a numbered list of replies to the original objections. To facilitate comprehension for modern readers, we have reformatted Aquinas' work into flowing text. We have therefore collapsed and reordered some of the originally distinct objections and replies, when we have deemed doing so appropriate, so as to more clearly bring out Aquinas' main arguments.

the soul of man except God alone, as Augustine says. Also, God alone purges the soul of guilt: 'I am He that blot out thy iniquities for my own sake.' (*Isa.* 43.25.) As guilt is in the soul, so is ignorance. Therefore, God alone purges the soul of ignorance, and so it seems that He alone teaches, not man.

However, while the Lord prescribed that His disciples should not be called masters, this was not absolutely prohibited. We are only forbidden to call a man a teacher in a way that attributes to him the principal part of teaching which belongs to God, as that would be to put our hope in the wisdom of men and in those things we hear from men, instead of in God. Therefore, a man can teach another and be called a teacher, not just God alone.

When it is said that nothing can form the soul except God, the soul's essential form is referred to, without which it is formless, whatever other forms it may have. But the essential form is that form by which the soul is turned to the Word [Christ] and clings to It, through which alone the rational nature is said to be formed.

Guilt is in the affections, on which God alone can make an impression, as will be evident in the next article, but ignorance is in the intellect, on which even a created power can make an impression. The agent intellect impresses the intelligible species on the possible intellect, which is a medium through which sense impressions and man's teaching can cause knowledge in our souls. Therefore a man, not just God alone, can teach another.

One might think that a man cannot teach another because, if a man teaches, he does so only by means of some signs. For even though some realities seem to be taught by themselves, by performance (for example, if when somebody asks what it is to walk, someone walks), this is still not sufficient unless some sign is added. Augustine, in his book *De Magistro*, explains why signs are needed for a man to teach another: each reality has many aspects, and so in a performance, it is not known (without the addition of signs) how far that performance holds in regard to any aspect of that reality, whether in regard to the substance of the reality or in regard to some other aspect of it. So a man can only teach another by means of signs. But it is not possible to arrive at a knowledge of realities through signs because the knowledge of realities is more potent than the knowledge of signs, and furthermore, the knowledge of realities stands in relation to knowledge of signs as ends to means. Since an effect cannot be greater than its cause, it seems that no man can give to another a knowledge of realities, and hence, cannot teach him.

Also, if a man proposes signs of some realities to another, either the one to whom the signs are proposed already knows those realities of which they are the signs, or he does not. If he already knows them, he cannot be taught them; but if he does not know them, then because the realities are unknown, the meanings of the signs cannot be known. Someone who does not know what rocks are cannot know what the noun 'rock' signifies. When the signification of a sign is unknown, we cannot learn anything by means of it. If, then, a man does nothing more in teaching than propose signs, it seems that a man cannot be taught by another man.

However, the understanding of realities is not brought about in us through an understanding of signs but rather through an understanding of principles (though these in turn are proposed to us by means of some signs). It is the understanding of principles, not the understanding of signs, that causes in us a knowledge of conclusions.

Those realities about which we are taught by means of signs we do know to some degree, but to some degree we do not know. For example, if we are being taught what 'man' is, we must know beforehand something about man, either the fact of his animality or of his substantiality, or at least of his existence, which cannot be unknown to us. Likewise, if we are being taught any conclusion, we must first know the subject and the predicate and what these signify. We must also have prior understanding of the principles through which the conclusion is taught. Therefore, 'all learning comes from preexisting knowledge', as Aristotle says, and so a man can teach another man, not just God alone.

Another reason one might have for thinking that a man cannot teach another man is that the knowledge purportedly being taught was either already in the one learning or it was not. If it was not in him and is caused by another, then one man would have caused knowledge in another, but this is impossible. It is impossible because the subject of knowledge is the intellect. But sensible signs, through which alone it seems that man can be taught, are not received into the intellect but remain in the sensitive faculty. Therefore, one man cannot cause knowledge in another man who does not have that knowledge. But if the knowledge was already in the man who learns, it was either in perfect actuality and so cannot be caused (because what is already present cannot become present), or it was there only as potential knowledge. But potential capacities cannot be brought to actuality by any created power for they are planted in nature by God alone, as Augustine says. Therefore, it seems that a man can in no way teach another man.

However, the cause of knowledge is not the signs but the process of discursive reasoning from principles to conclusion. While the signs are received in the sense faculty, the intellect can abstract from them the essence, which it then uses in producing knowledge.

Also, in the one who is being taught, knowledge pre-exists not in complete actuality but, as it were, in potency. The understanding of universal concepts is naturally implanted in us and likened to 'seeds' of all subsequent understanding. Although these seeds cannot be developed to actuality by a created power since they are infused by God, a created power may educe into actuality what is originally and virtually in them. Therefore, a man can teach another man.

Another reason one might have for thinking that a man cannot teach another is that knowledge is a kind of accident.[3] But an accident does not change the subject in which it inheres. Hence, since teaching seems to be a transfusion of knowledge from teacher to pupil, one cannot teach another. Further, if one man teaches another, the teacher must cause a change in him from knowing potentially to knowing actually. Therefore, the pupil's knowledge must be raised from potential knowledge to actual knowledge. But what is raised from potency to actuality is changed. Therefore, knowledge or wisdom will be changed, which is contrary to Augustine, who says that 'Wisdom coming to man is not itself changed but changes man.'

However, when a teacher communicates knowledge to a pupil, the knowledge in the teacher is not numerically the same knowledge as the knowledge produced in the pupil. Rather, the knowledge in the pupil is merely similar to the knowledge which is in the teacher, but raised from potentiality to actuality. Therefore, a man, not just God alone, can teach another man.

Further, wisdom is of two sorts: created and uncreated. Both sorts are infused in man, and because of this endowment, a man can change for the better by developing them. Uncreated wisdom cannot, indeed, be changed in any way; created wisdom can be changed in us extrinsically but not intrinsically. That is, wisdom itself may be

[3]   Accidental features are features that a thing can gain or lose yet still remain the same kind of thing. For instance, a man's hair can turn grey yet he remains a human being. Essential features are those features a being must necessarily possess in order to remain the same kind of thing, such as being a mammal for a human.

considered in two ways: on the one hand, with respect to the eternal realities with which it is concerned, wisdom is entirely unchangeable; on the other hand, with respect to the existence which it has in the man, it is changed extrinsically when the man is changed from having wisdom in potentiality to having it in actuality. The intelligible forms, of which wisdom consists, are both likenesses of realities and forms which perfect the intellect. Therefore, since created wisdom can be changed from potentiality to actuality, a man, and not just God alone, can teach another man.

Another reason one might have for thinking that a man cannot teach another man is that knowledge is caused interiorly in the soul, not exteriorly in the senses. But, in *Rom.* 10, the *Gloss* on 'Faith cometh by hearing' says: 'Though God teaches interiorly, yet the preacher proclaims from without.' Therefore, it might seem that a man is taught by God alone and not by another man. Further, as Augustine says, 'God alone has a teaching chair in heaven, Who teaches truth interiorly, but another man stands in the same relation to the teaching chair as a farmer does to a tree.' But the farmer is not the maker of the tree but its cultivator. Therefore, a man cannot give knowledge, but only dispose another to knowledge. Knowledge is a representation of realities in the soul, since knowledge is said to be an assimilation of the knower to the reality known. But one man cannot represent in another's soul the likenesses of realities, for then he would operate interiorly in him, which belongs to God alone. If a man is a true teacher, he must teach the truth. But whoever teaches the truth illumines the soul, since truth is the light of the soul. Therefore, if a man teaches then he illumines the soul. But a man cannot do this, since God is He 'Who enlighteneth every man that cometh into this world.' (*Jn.* 1.9) Therefore, it seems that a man cannot teach another man.

However, just as a physician, although he works exteriorly while nature alone works interiorly, is said to cause healing, so a man is said to teach, although he announces exteriorly while God teaches interiorly. Augustine, when he maintains in the *De Magistro* that God alone teaches, does not mean to deny that man teaches exteriorly, but to insist that God alone teaches interiorly.

The knowledge received from teaching constitutes intelligible forms, which are impressed in the pupil directly by the pupil's agent intellect, and only mediately, or indirectly, by the teacher. The teacher proposes the signs of intelligible realities from which the pupil's agent intellect forms abstractions which are in turn impressed upon his possible intellect. Hence, the words of the teacher, either heard or viewed in writing, have the same relation to causing knowledge in the intellect as anything outside the soul has, because from both, the intellect takes the intelligible content. Yet the words of the teacher have a closer relation to causing knowledge than the perceptible realities outside the soul in so far as words are signs of intelligible forms.

Man can truly be called a teacher, teaching truth and enlightening the soul, not by means of infusing the light of reason, but rather as aiding the light of reason to the perfection of knowledge by means of those realities that he proposes exteriorly, as was spoken of in *Eph.* 3.8-9: 'To me, the least of all the saints, is given this grace,...to enlighten all men that they may see what is the dispensation of the mystery which hath been hidden from eternity in God.' Therefore, a man, not just God, can teach another man.

Another reason one might have for thinking that a man cannot teach another man is, as Boethius says, that through teaching, the soul of man is only stimulated to know. But he who stimulates the intellect to knowing does not make it know, just as one who stimulates another to seeing with his bodily sight does not make him see. Therefore, one man does not make another know, and hence cannot properly be said to teach him.

However, intellectual sight and bodily vision are not the same. Bodily vision is not a discursive power such that from certain of its objects, it arrives at others. All of its objects are visible to it as soon as it is turned towards them. Hence, someone who has the power of sight looks towards all visible realities in the same way, much as one who has habitual knowledge directs attention towards what he habitually knows. The one looking does not need someone else to excite him to see, except insofar as his gaze may be directed by the pointing of a finger, for example. But the intellective power, since it is discursive, does infer some realities from others. As a result, it does not have the same relation to all intelligible realities that it considers. It sees certain self-evident realities directly and immediately, and in these are implicitly contained other realities that it does not immediately see. The intellective power can come to see these implicitly contained realities only through the exercise of discursive reason, by making explicit that which is implicitly contained in principles. Therefore, before the intellect has habitual knowledge, it is not only in accidental potentiality to know such realities but even in essential potentiality, for it needs a mover which will lead it into actuality through teaching.[4] He who knows something habitually, however, does not need this service of a mover. The teacher, then, excites the intellect to know those realities which he is teaching as an essential mover, leading it from potentiality to actuality; but he who presents something to the bodily sight excites it as an accidental mover. Someone who already has habitual knowledge can, in this way, be caused by someone else to think about something.

Another reason one might have for thinking that a man cannot teach another man is that knowledge requires certitude of understanding; otherwise it would not be knowledge but opinion or belief, as Augustine notes in his *De Magistro*. But one man cannot cause certitude in another man by means of any sensible signs that he proposes, for what is in the senses is more obscure than what is in the intellect, and certitude is always produced in relation to something clear and distinct. Further, since knowledge is understanding with certainty, a man receives knowledge from another insofar as he is made certain through the assertions of that other. But a man cannot be made certain by that which he hears another man asserting; otherwise it would be necessary that whatever is said to anyone by a man should be held as certain. But a man is made certain only inasmuch as he hears truth speaking interiorly, and it is to this interior truth he refers even about those realities which he hears from another man, so that he may be certain. Therefore, man does not teach, but only truth which speaks interiorly, which is God. Therefore, one man cannot teach another.

However, all certitude of knowledge arises from certitude of principles. Conclusions are then known to be valid when they are resolved into their principles. Therefore, the fact that anything is known with certitude is possible because of the light of reason divinely implanted in us, by which God speaks within us. As was said, certitude of knowledge is from God alone, Who endowed man with the light of reason through which he knows the principles from which certitude arises. It does not arise from man's exterior teaching, except inasmuch as while teaching he resolves conclusions into principles. From such an exterior teacher, however, we could not reach certitude of knowledge if there were not in us certitude of principles

---

[4] Aquinas is here trading upon traditional Aristotelian notions of levels of potency. Humans are able to learn a language (while worms are not); a child thus suited by nature to acquire a language is said to be in *passive potency*. A human who has learnt a language but is not speaking it is said to be in *active potency*. Knowledge of this latter sort is also called *habitual knowledge*.

into which conclusions are resolved. Therefore, even though a man cannot cause in another man the certitude required for knowledge, a man may teach another man, and not just God alone.

Another reason one might have for thinking that a man cannot teach another is that knowledge requires both the intelligible light and intelligible forms. But neither of these can be caused in one man by another, because this would necessitate that a man create something, since it seems that simple intelligible forms cannot be produced except through creation. But man cannot create, and therefore, it seems that a man cannot cause knowledge in another man, and hence, cannot teach him.

However, a man teaching exteriorly does not infuse the light of the intellect, but is, in some way, the cause of the intelligible forms, inasmuch as he proposes to us certain signs of intelligible content which the intellect receives from the signs and stores in itself.

Another reason one might have for thinking that a man cannot teach another man is that no one learns by means of the assertion of another man that which even before the assertion he could have answered if he were asked. But a pupil, even before the teacher speaks, could answer, if asked about those things which the teacher proposes. For he would not be taught by the assertion of the teacher unless he was confident that things were truly just as the teacher proposed. Therefore, it seems that one man is not taught by the assertion of another man.

However, before being taught a pupil who is questioned might answer concerning the principles by means of which he is being taught, but not concerning the conclusions that someone is teaching him. Therefore, he does not learn the principles from the teacher but only the conclusions. Therefore a man, not just God alone, may teach another man.

Drawing upon our authorities, there are some further reasons to think that man, and not just God alone, can teach and be called a teacher. In 2 *Tim.* 1.11 it is said: 'Wherein I am appointed a preacher … and a teacher.' Further, in 2 *Tim.*3.14 it is said: 'But continue thou in those things which thou hast learned, and which have been committed to thee.' The *Gloss* says: 'From me as though from a true teacher.' In *Matt.* 23.8-9 it is likewise said: 'For one is your Teacher … and one your Father.' But the fact that God is the Father of all does not exclude man from being called father. Therefore, neither is man excluded from being called teacher. Further, on this point *Rom.* 10.15 says: 'How beautiful are the feet of them that preach the gospel of peace', concerning which the *Gloss* says: 'Those are the feet that illumine the church.' Now, this is spoken of the Apostles. Since, therefore, to illumine is the function of a teacher, it seems that it belongs to man to teach. Further, Aristotle says that a being is perfect when it can generate beings like itself. But knowledge is a kind of perfect understanding, hence a man who has knowledge can teach another. Finally, Augustine says: 'As the earth, which before sin was watered by a fountain, and after sin depended on rain descending from the clouds, so the human soul, which is typified by the earth, before sin was enriched from the fountain of truth, but after sin needed the teaching of others like the rain descending from the clouds.' Therefore, after sin, a man can be taught by another man.

More generally, it may be noted that there is the same diversity of opinion about the following issues; namely, eduction of forms into existence, acquisition of virtue, and acquisition of knowledge.

Some have said that all sensible forms are from an external agent, that is, from a substance or separate form, which they call the giver of forms or the agent intellect, and that all inferior natural agents are nothing more than agents which prepare matter for the reception of forms. Similarly, Avicenna claims that the cause of morally good habits is not our action, but that action impedes the contrary of the habit and thus prepares for it, so that the habit comes to us from the substance which perfects the souls of men, which substance is the agent intellect or a substance like it. In the same way, they say that knowledge is not caused in us except by a separate agent; in light of which Avicenna says that the intelligible forms flow into the soul from the agent intellect.

Some are of the opposite opinion; namely, that all forms are innate in realities and that they do not have an outside cause, but are manifested only by external action. For they suppose that all natural forms are in act, lying hidden in matter, and that the natural agent does nothing else than draw these out from their latent state into manifestation. In the same way, some even suppose that all habits of virtue are naturally innate in us and through action impediments are removed, and in this way, as it were, the aforesaid habits lie hidden, just as rust is removed by polishing to show the brightness of the metal. Similarly, some have said that knowledge of all realities is connatural to the soul and that through teaching and external aids to knowledge of this kind, nothing else happens than that the soul is led to a remembrance or a consideration of those realities which it knew before. Hence, they say that to learn is nothing else than to remember.

But both of these opinions are wrong. The first opinion excludes proximate or secondary causes, since it attributes all effects appearing in lower realities to first causes alone. This detracts from the universal order which is woven together by the order and connection of causes, while the First Cause from the abundance of its own goodness confers upon other realities not only that they may be, but also that they may be causes. The second opinion results in the same difficulties, since removing a hindrance is only moving extrinsically and accidentally. If lower agents do nothing other than lead from a hidden state into manifestation by removing impediments, it follows that all lower agents do not act except extrinsically and accidentally.

Therefore, according to the teaching of Aristotle, a middle course between these two positions must be held in each of the foregoing cases. Natural forms indeed preexist in matter, but not in actuality as the second opinion held, but only in potentiality, from which they are educed into actuality. This is accomplished by an extrinsic proximate agent, not only by the first cause, as the first opinion supposes. Likewise, according to Aristotle, the habits of virtues preexist in us in certain natural tendencies which are, as it were, beginnings of virtue, and afterwards, through their exercise, are brought to their due development. Likewise we must say, about the acquisition of knowledge, that there preexist in us some potentialities of knowledge; namely, the first conceptions of the intellect which are recognised immediately by the light of the agent intellect by means of the forms abstracted from sense presentations, whether these conceptions be complex as with axioms or simple as in the ideas of being, or unity, or something of this nature which the intellect grasps immediately. From these universal principles all principles follow as from seminal capacities. When, therefore, from these universal intellections, the soul is led to know particular realities in actuality that before were known potentially and, as it were, under the aspect of the universal, then someone is said to acquire knowledge.

It must be kept in mind that within natural beings something may preexist potentially in a twofold manner: in one way, in active, complete potentiality, that is, when the intrinsic principle is sufficiently able to bring it to full actuality, as is evident in healing, for through the efficacy of nature in the sick person, he is brought back to health. In another way, a reality can preexist in passive potentiality, as when the intrinsic principle is not sufficient to educe it into actuality, as is evident when fire is made from air, for this cannot be done through any power existing in air. When, therefore, something exists in active, complete potentiality, the extrinsic agent acts only by helping the intrinsic agent and by ministering to it those things by means of which it comes forth into actuality, just as a doctor in healing is a minister to nature which does the principal work — ministering by aiding nature and by applying the medicines which nature uses as instruments for healing. But when something preexists only in passive potentiality, then the extrinsic agent is that which does the principal work in bringing it from potency to act, just as fire makes, from air, which is fire in potentiality, fire in actuality. Knowledge, therefore, preexists in the learner, not in purely passive potentiality, but in active potentiality, otherwise a man could not acquire knowledge by himself.

Just as a person may be cured in a twofold manner, through the operation of nature alone or through nature with the aid of medicine, so there is a twofold manner of acquiring knowledge, the first when natural reason by itself comes to a knowledge of the unknown, which is called 'discovery'; the second when someone extrinsically gives aid to natural reason, which is called 'learning by instruction'. Now, in those things which are done by nature and art, art works in the same way and by the same means that nature does, for just as nature, for someone suffering from cold, induces health by warming him, so too does the physician. Hence, art is said to imitate nature. Similarly, in the acquisition of knowledge it happens that the one teaching leads another to knowledge of the unknown in the same way as the learner would lead himself to an understanding of something unknown by discovery.

Now, the process of reason in one who arrives at an understanding of something unknown by discovery involves the application of general, self-evident principles to various matters, and proceeding from them, to particular conclusions, and from these to others. Hence, according to this, a man is said to teach another man because the teacher proposes to the student by means of signs the same discursive natural reasoning process which he himself goes through, and thus the natural reason of the pupil comes to an understanding of the unknown through the aid of what is proposed to him as with the aid of instruments. Just as a physician is said to cause health in a sick person through the operations of nature, so too a man is said to cause knowledge in another man through the operation of the learner's own natural reason—and this is to teach. Hence, one man is said to teach another man.

As Aristotle says, 'a demonstration is a syllogism that makes someone know.' But if someone proposes to another those realities which are not included in self-evident principles, or which though included are not immediately evident, he does not cause knowledge in him but perhaps opinion or belief. However, even belief is caused by innate principles because those realities which necessarily follow from self-evident principles themselves must be held as certain, and those things that are contrary to self-evident principles must be rejected entirely. But, with regard to other matters he may either assent or not. But this light of reason by means of which principles of this kind are known by us is implanted within us by God, being, as it were, likenesses of uncreated truth reflected within us. Hence, since no human teaching can be efficacious save by virtue of this light, it is evident that God alone is He Who teaches interiorly and principally, just as nature alone heals interiorly and principally. Nevertheless, a man is properly said to cure and to teach in the aforesaid manner.

ARTICLE 2

Whether anyone can be called a teacher of himself?

The second point of inquiry is whether anyone can be said to be a teacher of himself. And it seems that a man can properly be said to teach himself. One reason for this is that an action ought to be attributed to a principal, rather than to an instrumental, cause. The principal cause of any knowledge produced in us is the agent intellect, and a man who teaches exteriorly is a kind of instrumental cause, proposing to the agent intellect the instruments by means of which it leads us to knowledge. Therefore, the agent intellect teaches, rather than a man who does so in an exterior way. If, therefore, on account of exterior instruction the one who speaks is said to be the teacher of the one who hears, much more ought he who hears on account of the light of the agent intellect be called a teacher of himself.

Again, to teach is more proper to God than to man. Hence, in *Matt.* 23.8 it is said, 'One is your Teacher.' But God teaches us inasmuch as He gives us the light of reason by which we can judge concerning all realities. No one learns anything except that he arrives at certitude of knowledge. But certitude of knowledge is in us because of principles naturally known by the light of reason. Therefore, it is particularly proper to the light, which is the light of the agent intellect, to teach, and therefore the act of teaching ought to be attributed especially to that light interior to each man. Therefore, a man may be the teacher of himself.

But against this, note that while God knows explicitly everything that man is taught by Him [and hence the function of teaching can be fittingly attributed to God], it is otherwise with regard to the agent intellect. Although the agent intellect is more of a principal cause in some respects than is a man who teaches extrinsically, nevertheless complete knowledge does not preexist in the agent intellect as it does in the teacher. Therefore, the agent intellect is not properly a teacher, and a man cannot be a teacher of himself.

Another reason to think that man may be called his own teacher is that it is more perfect to know something by discovery than to learn from another. If, therefore, the name of teacher is applied to that manner of acquiring knowledge by which one learns from another, so that one may be called a teacher of another, all the more should the name of teacher be applied to the way of learning by discovery, so once again someone may be called his own teacher.

The mode of acquisition of knowledge through discovery is more perfect on the part of the one receiving such knowledge, inasmuch as he is thereby distinguished as being more apt for learning. Nevertheless, from the perspective of what causes knowledge, the more perfect mode is teaching, because the teacher explicitly has the knowledge as a whole and can lead the pupil to that knowledge more quickly and easily than could the student do for himself. This is because the pupil knows the principles of knowledge only generally. Therefore, contrary to what was said above, teaching is a more perfect cause of knowledge than discovery.

Another reason one might have for thinking that a man may be his own teacher is that, just as one is led to virtue by oneself and by others, so is someone led to knowledge both by himself through discovery and by another through instruction. But those who arrive at the works of virtue without an extrinsic instructor or lawgiver are said to be a law unto themselves, as we read in *Rom.* 2.14: 'When the Gentiles, who have not the law, do by nature those things that are of the law...(they) are a law to themselves.' Therefore, he who acquires knowledge through himself also ought to be called a teacher of himself. Further, the teacher is the cause of knowledge as the physician is of health, as was said. But a physician can heal himself; therefore it might seem that man can teach himself.

However, law has the same relation to practical matters as a principle of reasoning has to speculative matters, but not the same as a teacher to a pupil. Hence, it does not follow that if someone is a law unto himself that he can be a teacher to himself. Moreover, a physician heals insofar as he possesses health, not in actuality, but rather in the knowledge of his art. The teacher, on the other hand, teaches inasmuch as he has knowledge in actuality. Hence, he who does not have health in actuality can cause health in himself because he has health in the knowledge of the art of healing; but it is not possible that someone have knowledge in actuality and yet not have it, which would have to be the case for a man to be taught by himself. Therefore, a man cannot be a teacher of himself.

Furthermore, Aristotle says that it is impossible for the one teaching to learn because it is necessary for the teacher to have knowledge and for the learner not to have it. Teaching implies a relation of superiority and subordination, just as lordship does. But relations of this kind cannot exist between a person and himself, for no one can be a father of himself or a lord of himself. Therefore, a man cannot be called a teacher of himself.

Speaking generally, without doubt a man can, by means of his implanted light of reason, and without a teacher or exterior aid, come to a knowledge of many unknown realities, as is evident for anyone who acquires knowledge by discovery. A man is thus in a way a cause of his own knowledge. Still, he cannot be called his own teacher or be said to teach himself. For we find two kinds of principal agents in nature. One kind of agent is that which has in itself everything which it causes in the effect, either in the same way, as in the case of univocal causes, or in a superior way, as in the case of equivocal causes.[5] But there are some agents in which there preexists only a part of the result which is brought about. Take, for example, movement, or the heat found in some warming medicine which either actually or virtually causes healing. The heat is not the healing entirely but only partially.

Now, in the first kind of agent [in which everything it causes in the effect preexists in it], the actuality is fully realised, but not in the second kind [in which only a part of what it causes in the effect preexists in it], because a cause acts insofar as it is in act. Hence, since the sec-

[5]   An example of a univocal cause could be reproduction, in which a parent has offspring of the same kind. An equivocal cause could be the sun drying out mud: the heat found in the sun is similar to, but different from, the heat found in the drying mud.

ond is not fully the cause of the effect but only partially so, it will not be a cause in the fullest sense.

Teaching implies the perfect activity of knowledge in the teacher. Hence, he who is a teacher must have explicitly and perfectly the knowledge which he causes in another, as it is to be received in someone who learns. But when knowledge is acquired by means of an internal principle, that which is the active cause of knowledge [the agent intellect] does not have the knowledge to be acquired except partially. That is, it has the knowledge to be acquired only as seminal sources of knowledge, and these are general principles. From such imperfect causality the name of teacher or master, properly speaking, cannot be attributed, and therefore, no man can be called a teacher of himself.

ARTICLE 3

Whether man can be taught by an angel?

The third point of inquiry is whether man can be taught by an angel, and it seems that he cannot. If an angel teaches, he must teach either interiorly or exteriorly. But he does not teach interiorly, for that belongs to God alone, as Augustine says. Nor does an angel teach exteriorly, it seems, because to teach exteriorly is to teach through some sensible signs, as Augustine says in the *De Magistro*. But the angels would have to appear to the senses if they were to teach us with sensible signs of this kind, but that happens only outside the ordinary course of nature and is, as it were, miraculous.

However, an angel who teaches invisibly does indeed teach interiorly in comparison to the teaching of a man who proposes his teaching to the pupil's exterior senses. But, in comparison to the teaching of God, Who works within the soul by infusing light, the angel's teaching is to be considered exterior.

But the angels teach us interiorly only insofar as they make an impression on the imagination. Phantasms impressed on the imagination are not sufficient for the actual function of the imagination unless we pay attention to them. But an angel cannot force us to pay attention because attention is an act of the will, on which God alone can make an impression. Therefore, not even by making an impression on the imagination can an angel teach us, since we cannot be taught via the imagination except by actually imagining something.

Further, the intellect of an angel is more removed from the intellect of a man than is a man's intellect removed from his imagination.

But the imagination cannot receive that which is in the human intellect, for the imagination can only receive particular forms, which the intellect does not contain. Therefore, the human intellect does not have a capacity for those realities which are in the angelic intellect, and, therefore, a man cannot be taught by an angel.

However, although the attention of the will cannot be forced, the attention of the sensitive part can be prevailed upon, as when someone is pricked, he must pay attention to the wound. Thus it is with all other sensitive powers which employ corporeal organs. Such [non-voluntary] attention suffices for imagination. Therefore it is possible for a man to be taught by an angel.

And, on the contrary, the human imagination can receive that which is in the human intellect, but in another fashion. Similarly, the human intellect can receive that which is in the angelic intellect, but after its own fashion. Although the human intellect is more adapted to the imagination in the same human subject (since they are both powers of one soul), yet in the same way it is more adapted to the angelic intellect because they are both immaterial. Therefore, an angel can teach us.

One might think that we cannot be taught by angels [without their appearing to the senses] except insofar as they enlighten the intellect. But it seems that they cannot enlighten the intellect because angels do not bestow the light of reason, which is from God alone and natural to the soul; nor do they bestow the light of grace, which God alone infuses. Further, to teach belongs to the One Who enlightens every man born as is evident from the *Gloss* on *Matt.* 23: 'One is your Teacher'. Yet this is not proper for an angel but for the Uncreated Light alone, as is evident from *Jn.* 1.9. Therefore, angels, with or without appearing visibly, cannot teach us.

In reply, it can be said that the *Gloss* on *Matt.* 23 is speaking of that mode of teaching that is proper to God alone, and such teaching we do not ascribe to an angel. However, while it is true that an angel infuses neither the light of grace nor the natural light in us, angels can strengthen the divinely infused natural light, and in this way they can teach us.

When someone is taught by another, the learner must examine the concepts of the teacher so that he comes to understand in his own soul by using the same reasoning process that the teacher himself employed. But a man cannot see the concepts of an angel. This is because he cannot see concepts themselves, just as he cannot see concepts in another man. Much less could he see them in an angel, because of the greater difference between man and angel than between man and man. Nor, again, can he see concepts in sensible signs unless the angel appears to the senses, which possibility we are not here considering. Therefore, it seems that an angel cannot teach us.

However, just as in natural beings a univocal agent is one which impresses a form in the same way in which it has that form, and an equivocal agent is one which impresses a form in another way than it has it, so it is with teaching. A man teaches another man as a univocal agent, that is, he gives knowledge to another man in the same way that he has it, namely, by deducing causes from effects. Hence, it is necessary that the concepts of a teacher be made evident to the one learning through some signs. But an angel teaches as an equivocal agent, for an angel understands intellectually [i.e. intuitively] what to man is arrived at by way of reasoning. In being taught by an angel, the angel's concepts are not made manifest to man. But in man's own way, there is caused in him the knowledge of the realities that the angel knows in a very different way, and so man can be taught by an angel.

Another reason to think that we cannot be taught by angels is that whoever teaches another leads him to truth and thus causes truth in his soul. But God alone causes truth, because truth is an intelligible light and simple form, and does not come into existence gradually. This means it cannot be produced except by creation, which is proper to God alone. Since angels are not creators, as Damascene says, it seems that they cannot teach.

However, he who teaches does not cause truth but the understanding of truth in the learner, for propositions which are taught are true before they are known since truth does not depend upon our knowledge but upon the existence of realities. Therefore, even though angels cannot create truth, they can teach by causing understanding of truth in the learner.

It might also be objected that an unfailing illumination can proceed only from an unfailing light, for when the light is removed, the subject ceases to be illuminated. But in teaching, an unfailing illumination is needed because knowledge embraces necessary things, which are eternal. Therefore, teaching only comes from an unfailing illumination. But the angelic light is not of this kind, since their light would fail if it were not divinely preserved. Therefore, it might seem that an angel cannot teach.

In reply, although knowledge acquired through teaching concerns unfailing [eternal and necessary] realities, knowledge itself can fail [i.e. cease to be]. Therefore it is not necessary that the enlightenment of teaching come from an unfailing light. But even if it is from an unfailing light, as from a first principle, the fallible created light can be a middle principle, and so it is not necessarily excluded.

It is said in *Jn.* 1.38 that when Jesus asked: 'What seek you?' the two disciples of John who followed Him answered: 'Rabbi, where dwellest thou?' The *Gloss* here says, 'By this name [Rabbi] they showed their faith', and another gloss reads: 'He asked them not in ignorance but that they might gain merit by their reply. And when He asked them what they sought, they wanted a person not merely a thing.' From this it is seen that in their response they confessed that He was a person and by this confession they showed their faith. In doing this they gained merit. But the merit of Christian faith consists in this, that we confess that Christ is a divine person. Therefore, it seems that to be a teacher belongs only to a divine person.

However, among the disciples of Christ there is noted a certain development of faith so that at first they respected Him as a wise man and a teacher but afterwards listened to Him as God teaching them. Hence, a gloss a little below that passage says, 'Because Nathanael learned that Christ, though absent, had seen what he had been doing in another place, which is a sign of divinity, he professed that Christ was not only a teacher but the Son of God.'[6]

Another reason one might think angels cannot teach us is that whoever teaches must disclose the truth. But, since truth is an intelligible light, it is better known to us than an angel. Therefore, we are not taught by an angel since what is better known is not learned by the less known.

However, an angel does not make manifest an unknown truth to us by making known its own substance, but rather by proposing to us another truth that is better known or by strengthening the light of the intellect.

Another doubt may be gathered from Augustine who says that our soul is formed immediately by God without any creaturely mediation. But an angel is a creature. Therefore, nothing is interposed between God and the soul, in its formation, that stands as superior to the soul yet inferior to God, such as an angel. Further, as

---

[6]   The implication of this passage is that since human beings can come to learn from both God and from man in the single Person of Christ, then angels, who occupy a middle place between God and man, can also teach us.

our will reaches even to God Himself, so our intellect can reach to the contemplation of His essence. But God Himself directly forms our will by means of the infusion of grace with no angel mediating. Therefore, He also forms our intellect by teaching with no mediating angel. Hence, it seems, a man cannot be taught by an angel.

But, Augustine did not intend to say that the angelic intelligence is not of a more excellent nature than a man's, but only that an angel does not come between God and the human soul, such that the human soul, through union with the angel, receives its ultimate form, as certain people have proposed. (They also say that man's ultimate blessedness consists in this, that our intellect should be joined to an intelligence whose blessedness consists in union with God Himself.)

Moreover, in us certain powers are constrained by both their subject and their object, such as the sensitive powers, which are excited by the stimulation of the sense organ and by the strength of the sensible object. But the intellect is not constrained by its subject, since it does not employ a bodily organ. Instead, it is constrained by its object, because the efficacy of a demonstration obliges a man to assent to a validly derived conclusion. The will, however, is not constrained either subjectively or objectively but is moved by its own instigation to this or that. Hence, only God, Who works interiorly, can make an impression on the will; but on the intellect, a man or an angel can make an impression by representing to us objects by which the intellect is constrained. Therefore, an angel can teach us in this way.

Another reason one might have for thinking that angels cannot teach us is that all understanding occurs by means of some species. If, therefore, an angel teaches a man, he must cause some species in him by means of which he may come to know. But this is not possible except by creating the species (which is in no way proper to an angel, as Damascene says), or by illuminating species within the phantasms so that intelligible species result in the possible human intellect. But this would seem to return to the error of those philosophers who propose that the agent intellect, whose office it is to enlighten the phantasms, is a separate substance. Hence, one might think, an angel cannot teach.

Further, the light by which a reality is illumined ought to be a suitable light, just as corporeal light is suitable for colours. But angelic light, since it is purely spiritual, is not a suitable light for the phantasms, which are in a way corporeal as they are retained in a corporeal organ. Therefore, the angels cannot teach us by illuminating our phantasms.

However, the fact that something is spiritual does not prevent it from being suitable to act upon something corporeal because nothing prevents the lower from being acted upon by the higher. Therefore, the angelic light, which is spiritual, can illuminate corporeal phantasms since the spiritual is higher than the corporeal. Moreover, an angel neither creates species in our soul nor illumines the phantasms directly. But when the angel's light is united with the light of our own intellect, our intellect can more effectively enlighten the phantasms. Even if an angel did illuminate the phantasms directly, it would not follow that the position of those philosophers is true. For although it is the function of the agent intellect to illuminate the phantasms, yet it can be said that this is not due to it alone.

There is another reason for doubting that angels can teach us. Everything that is known, is known either through its essence or through its likeness. But understanding, by which a reality is known in its essence by the human soul, cannot be caused by an angel, for thus it would be necessary that virtues and other realities which are contained within the soul must be impressed by the angels themselves, since such realities are known through their essences. Similarly, neither could understanding of realities which are known through their likenesses be caused by angels, since the realities to be known are more closely related to the likenesses in the knower than an angel is. Hence, it seems that in no way can an angel be the cause of a man's understanding, and this is to teach him.

On the contrary, an angel is not the cause of a man's understanding insofar as a man knows realities through essences, but can be the cause insofar as a man knows them through likenesses. This is not to say that an angel is closer to realities than the likenesses are, but that an angel causes the likenesses to be present in the soul either by moving the imagination or by strengthening the light of the intellect.

Another reason one might have for thinking that angels cannot teach us is that although a farmer in an exterior way encourages nature to produce natural effects, he is not called a creator, as is evident from Augustine. Therefore, with equal reason angels ought not to be called teachers and masters although they stimulate the intellect of man to know.

A final objection is that, since an angel is superior to a man, if he teaches, his teaching ought to be superior to man's teaching. But this is not possible, for a man can teach about realities which have causes determined in nature, but other realities, such as future contingencies, cannot be taught even by angels, since by their natural knowledge angels are ignorant of these realities, because God alone has knowledge of the future. Therefore, it seems that angels cannot teach man.

On the other hand, while 'to create' implies a first cause, which is proper to God alone, 'to make' implies causality in general. It is the same with teaching in reference to knowledge: God alone is called a creator, but God, an angel, or a man can be called a maker or a teacher. Even with respect to those realities that have causes determined in nature, an angel can teach more realities than a man can, since an angel knows more realities, and those realities which an angel teaches he teaches in a superior manner. Hence, an angel may teach us.

A number of authorities agree that an angel can teach a man. Dionysius says: 'I see that the angels first taught the divine mystery of the humanity of Christ and afterwards through them the grace of that knowledge descended to us.' And Augustine says that some receive the teaching of salvation immediately from God, some from angels, and some from men; therefore, an angel can teach. Also, what an inferior can do, a superior can. But an angel is superior to a man, and the order of divine wisdom is not less among the angels than in the heavenly bodies which influence realities lower than themselves; therefore, an angel can teach a man.

Moreover, that which is in potentiality can be educed into actuality by that which is in actuality, and that which is less fully actual can be educed into fuller actuality by that which is already in more perfect actuality. Since an angelic intellect is more fully in actuality than a man's intellect, a human intellect can be educed into a fuller actuality of knowledge by means of an angelic intellect; and, therefore, an angel can teach. Further, both the sun that shines its light, and someone who opens a window that obstructs the light, are said to illuminate a house. Although God alone infuses the light of truth in our soul, nonetheless an angel or a man can remove an obstruction to receiving that light. Therefore, not only God but an angel or a man can teach.

More generally, angels in their dealings with men operate in a twofold manner. In one way, according to our natural capacity, that is, when an angel appears to a man sensibly either by taking on a body or in some other way, and teaches him with audible words. We will not inquire about this mode of teaching by an angel, because in this way an angel does not teach differently from how a man does. But in another way, an angel deals with us according to its own nature, that is, invisibly. How far a man can be taught by an angel in this latter way is the object of this question.

It must be kept in mind that since an angel is between God and man, as befits its rank an intermediate way of teaching is proper to the angel, one that is inferior to God's teaching but superior to man's. But the nature of an angel's teaching cannot be understood unless we can understand the nature of God's teaching and man's teaching.

To make this clear we must recognise that there is this difference between the intellect and bodily sight: concerning what it knows, bodily sight has all its objects equally and immediately available to it. Because this sense is not a discursive power, it is not obliged to arrive at knowing one object by means of another. However, for the intellect, not all intelligible realities are equally and immediately available for knowing. Some intelligible realities it sees immediately, and some others it does not see except by first examining other principles. Thus, then, a man gains knowledge of the unknown in two ways, namely, by the intellectual light, and by the primary concepts that are intuitively known and which are compared to the light of the agent intellect as tools to a builder. In respect to both, God is the cause of man's knowledge in the most excellent way possible, because He endows the soul itself with the intellectual light and impresses upon it knowledge of first principles, which are like seeds of knowledge (just as He impresses on other natural beings their seminal principles for all the effects they produce). But a man, being equal according to the order of nature to other men in the kind of intellectual light they possess, can in no way be the cause of knowledge in another man by increasing that light in him.

But knowledge of unknown realities is caused through principles intuitively known. Therefore, a man is, in a way, the cause of another man's knowing, not by giving him a knowledge of principles but by educing into actuality that which is implicitly and potentially contained in the principles by means of sensible signs shown to the external senses. But because an angel naturally has a more perfect intellectual light than man, he can be the cause of knowing in a man in both ways, although in an inferior way to God but in a superior way to man.

Concerning this light, although an angel cannot infuse the intellectual light as God does, he can, however, strengthen the infused light to make a man understand more perfectly, for when anything which is imperfect in some way comes into contact with something more perfect, in that respect its power is strengthened. This is seen even in bodies, for a body which is given [a particular] position is strengthened by another body giving and fixing it in its position, and is compared to it as actuality to potentiality.

Concerning principles, an angel can teach a man, not indeed by giving a knowledge of principles as God does, and not by proposing the deduction of conclusions from principles with the aid of sensible signs as man does, but rather by forming certain species in the imagination. These can be formed by stimulating the corporeal organ, as is evident for those asleep and the insane, who, according to the diversity of the phantasms arising in their imaginations, experience different images. Thus, by the mingling together of species it comes about that an angel shows what he knows through images of this kind to the one in whom the species are mingled, as Augustine says.

ARTICLE 4

Whether teaching pertains to the active or to the contemplative life?

The fourth point of inquiry is whether teaching belongs more to the active or to the contemplative life. One might think that it pertains to the contemplative life, for as Gregory says, 'The active life fails with the body.' But to teach does not fail with the body, because the angels, who have no bodies, teach. Therefore, it seems that teaching pertains to the contemplative life.

Further, as Gregory says, 'He is busy with the active life so that he may come later to the contemplative life.' But contemplation precedes, and teaching follows; therefore, it would seem that to teach does not pertain to the active life but to the contemplative life.

However, against this, the active life fails just as our body fails, because it requires labour and ministers to the infirmities of our neighbours. On this Gregory says, 'The active life is wearisome because it is spent in the sweat of the brow, which two things will not be in the future life.' Nevertheless, there is a hierarchical activity among the celestial spirits, as Dionysius says, and this is another activity different from the active life which we pass on earth. Hence, the teaching which will take place there will be different from the teaching in this life.

Gregory also says that, 'Just as a good order of living tends to lead us from the active to the contemplative, so it is useful for the majority of men that the soul should turn from the contemplative to the active, so that the active life may be more perfectly pursued because the contemplative life has inflamed the soul.' It must be recognised that the active life precedes the contemplative in respect to those acts that are in no way compatible with the contemplative life; but in respect to those acts which take their subject matter from the contemplative life, it is necessary that the active life follow the contemplative.

From the same authority it might be thought that teaching pertains more to the contemplative life. Gregory says that 'while the active life is busy with work, it sees less.' But he who teaches must see more than he who merely contemplates. Hence, it might seem that to teach pertains more to the contemplative than the active life. And, by similar reasoning, it might be argued that the active life deals with temporal realities whereas teaching deals especially with eternal realities, and that teaching about these eternal realities is more excellent and more perfect. Once again, it would seem that teaching does not pertain to the active but rather to the contemplative life.

By way of reply, note that while the vision of the teacher is a principle of his teaching, teaching itself consists more in the communication of knowledge of the realities seen than in the vision of them. Hence, the vision of the teacher pertains more to action than to contemplation. Furthermore, with respect to temporal realities, teaching is compatible with the contemplative life, as will be explicated below.

There is a final reason one might have for thinking that teaching pertains more to the contemplative life than the active life. The same reality that makes each thing perfect in itself enables it to be a giver of a similar perfection to another thing. For example, fire, through the same heat, is both warm and warming. But for someone to be perfect in the consideration of divine things pertains to the contemplative life. Therefore, it might seem that teaching, which involves transferring the same perfection of knowledge to another, pertains to the contemplative life.

However, all that this argument proves is that the contemplative life is a principle of teaching, just as heat is not the act of warming but the principle of warming. And so, conversely to what was argued, the active life arranges for the contemplative life.

So, as Gregory says: 'The active life is to give bread to the hungry, to teach the ignorant with the word of wisdom.' Moreover, the works of mercy pertain to the active life. But to teach is numbered among the spiritual works of mercy; therefore, teaching pertains to the active life.

In general, the contemplative life and the active life are distinguished from each other by their subject matter and by their ends. The subject matter of the active life concerns temporal things with which human life deals. The subject matter of the contemplative life concerns the knowable reasons for those realities upon which the contemplative dwells. This diversity of subject matter arises from the diversity of ends, for in all subjects the matter is determined by the requirements of the ends. The end of the contemplative life is the consideration of truth, for we are now dealing with the contemplative life. I mean the consideration of uncreated truth according to the capacity of the one contemplating it, which in this life is beheld imperfectly but in the future life perfectly. Hence, Gregory says that the contemplative life begins here so that it may be consummated in the future life. But the end of the active life is activity, which is directed to the utility of our neighbour. In teaching, however, we find a twofold subject matter, and as a sign of this two accusatives are employed as objects of the verb which expresses the act of teaching.[7] One of these accusatives pertains to the matter taught; the other accusative to him to whom the knowledge is given. By reason of the first subject matter, teaching pertains to the contemplative life; by reason of the second to the active life. But in view of its end, teaching seems to pertain to the active life alone, because the ultimate subject matter, in which it attains its intended end, is the material of the active life. Hence, teaching pertains more to the active than to the contemplative life, although it also pertains to the contemplative life.

[7] Aquinas is here describing what we discussed in chapter 1 under the rubric of 'X teaches Y to Z'. To understand the nature of the X, he is here unpacking the meanings of Y and Z.

Newman: Commentary

John Henry Newman

Newman was born in London, England on the 21st of February 1801 and died at Edgbaston, Birmingham on the 11th of August 1890.[1] He received his early education at a private boarding school in Ealing which he first attended in 1808 aged seven years. From his youth he was an avid reader of the Bible and would be nurtured in his religious sentiments both within his family and school life — confessionally, he was brought up within the Church of England. In 1817 he took up a place at Trinity College, Oxford. However, partly due to concerns over his father's difficult financial situation, he initially did not excel, receiving a third-class honours degree in 1821.

Despite his lack of formal academic success, he was elected as Fellow of Oriel College (then perhaps the most prestigious of Oxford colleges) in 1822. In 1826 Newman became a Tutor at Oriel, where one of his most significant pedagogical legacies was his resolute defence of the small or individual tutorial. Newman, against much of the practice of his time, was deeply concerned to maintain the pastoral and mentoring role between teacher and pupil, thus emphasizing his adherence to the necessary relation between master and pupil. He writes: 'the personal influence of the teacher is able in some sort to dispense with an academical system ... [however,] an academical system without the personal influence of teachers upon

[1] The details of Newman's life presented here are indebted not just to Newman's voluminous correspondence and autobiographical work but to two major secondary sources: I. Ker's magisterial *John Henry Newman: A Biography*, Oxford, Oxford University Press, 2009; (first edition published 1988); and J. L. May, *Cardinal Newman*, New York, The Dial Press, 1930. A useful, though somewhat hagiographical discussion may be found in the Catholic Encyclopedia, available on-line at http://www.newadvent.org/cathen/10794a.htm. References to Newman's *The Idea of a University* not selected in this book are taken from the edition of M. J. Svaglic, Notre Dame, University of Notre Dame Press, 1982.

pupils, is an arctic winter; it will create an ice-bound, petrified, cast-iron University.'[2]

Newman converted, or in his own eyes, reverted to Catholicism in 1845. As a major intellectual force within the Anglo-Catholic movement, Newman's embracing Roman Catholicism occasioned much public comment and criticism. In response to attacks on his personal integrity, in particular by Charles Kingsley, Newman responded with what came to be recognised as one of the classic compositions of English literature, the *Apologia pro vita sua*.[3] This work, together with his *An Essay in Aid of a Grammar of Assent*[4] and the earlier works composed during his Anglo-Catholic period (especially the *Tracts for the Times*[5]) assured Newman a permanent place in English letters. He subsequently established the Oratory of St. Philip Neri, and was made Cardinal by Pope Leo XIII in 1879. On September 19th 2010 Pope Benedict XVI officially proclaimed his beatification — the penultimate step on the road to sainthood.

The Idea of a University, published in 1873, is the culmination of a long meditation starting in 1852 with Newman's nine lectures entitled *Discourses on University Education*. Again, in 1858 Newman returns to the topic of university education in his *Lectures and Essays on University Subjects*. The 1873 publication is thus the revised version of a long investigation of almost twenty years.

Between 1850 and 1870 the public debate on what education entails — university education in particular, but also earlier schooling — occupied some of the finest minds of the Victorian age. John Henry Newman, John Stuart Mill, Henry Sidgwick, Thomas Henry Huxley, and Matthew Arnold are only a few of the key contributors to this debate.[6] While the debate ultimately focused on the status of liberal education, it had a much wider social and political agenda.

---

[2]   Newman, *Historical Sketches*, London, Longmans, Green and Co., 1899, vol. iii. 14, pp. 74-5.

[3]   See J. H. Newman, *Apologia pro vita sua*, ed. I. Ker, London, Penguin Books, 1994.

[4]   See *An Essay in Aid of a Grammar of Assent*, Notre Dame, University of Notre Dame Press, 1979.

[5]   A recent edition is the four-volume *Tracts for the Times*, by J. H. Newman, J. Keble, J. B. Pusey, et al., Charleston, Nabu Press, 2010.

[6]   For Newman and Mill see the selections in this book. Also see H. Sidgwick, 'The Theory of Classical Education,' originally published in *Essays on a Liberal Education*, ed. F.W. Farrar, London, Macmillan, 1867; T. H. Huxley, *A Liberal Education; And Where To Find It*, Charleston, BiblioBazaar, 2006; M. Arnold, *Culture and Anarchy*, New Haven, Yale University Press, 1994. The debate continues today. See, for example, Michael Oakeshott, *Rationalism in Politics*, ed.

The outcome of the debate, in both theory and practice, was a vindication of liberal education; a vindication that, in modified forms, has lasted until relatively recently in Great Britain. Liberal education, the ideal Newman argues for with such rhetorical appeal, had enormous prestige in Victorian England because in the imagination of the Victorian mind it was allied with the Church of England and central to the training of clergy. It was also entrenched in the training and examination system that produced some of the greatest political leaders in Parliament and the wider political bureaucracy, including the administration of the Empire on which the sun never set.

According to the common Victorian conception, a liberal education is one that is not to be thought of in terms of the breadth of its curriculum, but as one primarily distinguished by contrast with a servile or menial education. Indeed, this is precisely the distinction that the ancient Greeks and Romans had in mind. It was the education of a free person, normally from a wealthy elite family, who was not forced to use that education as a means to achieving a livelihood. Throughout western history it carried a prestige that sharply contrasted with what the Victorians disparagingly called 'Instrument Knowledges' — the sorts of education directed towards technological, mechanical, and more broadly, utilitarian concerns with making a living.[7]

In the 19th century about two thirds of the graduates of Oxford University and almost half of Cambridge University graduates became clergymen, illustrating the link between the prestige of the Church of England and those who had been liberally educated. The form of liberal education may have differed in its accentuations, such as the emphasis on classics at Oxford, mathematics at Cambridge, and philosophy in the Scottish universities, but its aim remained the same — as Newman puts it, liberal education produces

---

T. Fuller, London, Liberty Fund, 1991; *The Voice of Liberal Learning: Michael Oakeshott on Education*, ed. T. Fuller, New Haven, Yale University Press, 1989; Leo Strauss, 'What is Liberal Education?', in *Liberalism Ancient and Modern*, Ithaca, Cornell University Press, 1968; and M. C. Nussbaum, *Not For Profit: Why Democracy Needs the Humanities*, Princeton, Princeton University Press, 2010.

[7]   See M. Sanderson, 'Vocational and Liberal Education: a historian's view', *European Journal of Education*, 28, 2, 1993, pp. 189-196. Interestingly, the prestige associated with liberal education and corresponding denigration of the 'servile' arts appears to be a largely British phenomenon. France accords due respect for both branches of learning through its *grandes écoles* – Ponts et Chausées (1715) and *École Polytechnique*; the same respect is accorded in Germany in its *Technische Hochschulen*, not to mention the case of the Massachusetts Institute of Technology in the United States. See Sanderson, *op. cit.*, pp. 191-192.

'a cultivated intellect, a delicate taste, a candid, equitable, dispassionate mind, a noble and courteous bearing in the conduct of life.'

Those who have received such an education are able to bring the qualities of their minds to bear in an open and flexible way to any problem that arises. In this way, Parliament as well as the administrative bureaucracy derives the fruits of this education. Cambridge mathematicians such as Pitt and Palmerston, and Oxford classicists like Peel and Gladstone, provide proof that the qualities of mind developed by means of a liberal education can operate with social results in the practical sphere.[8] Such a view extended beyond Parliament and the bureaucracy, as the *India Act* of 1853 required that formal examinations in liberal subjects be taken by anyone wanting a position in the Indian Civil Service. Even the company Shell based its recruitment policies on the same criteria as the British Civil Service.[9]

The prestige and elitism of liberal education indeed became entrenched even in the forms of schooling in Great Britain. Robert Morant, in a set of regulations drawn up in 1904, made classics compulsory at all British grammar schools. The very existence of the hierarchically tiered education system (the distinction between grammar and comprehensive schools) is inherently linked to the status of liberal education and its social, political, and intellectually elitist underpinnings. Despite massive increases in student numbers between 1914 and 1938 (from 187,000 up to 470,000) and widespread calls for more vocational schooling, the liberal educational ideal remained intact. The 1944 *Education Act* captures well the mind-set: 'the primary purpose of education … must aim first and foremost at helping to produce persons not ciphers.'[10]

---

[8] William Pitt the Younger was Prime Minister twice and also Chancellor of the Exchequer in which role he oversaw far reaching tax reforms designed to reduce the national debt; Henry John Temple (Lord Palmerston) was British Prime Minister, Secretary For War, and Home Secretary. Among his many achievements, his role in the eventual abolition of the slave trade is significant; Sir Robert Peel was also Prime Minister and Home Secretary but is perhaps best known for his creation of the Metropolitan Police Force; William Ewert Gladstone was Prime Minister and Chancellor of the Exchequer, each four times. Joseph Schumpeter refers to him as 'the greatest English financier of economic liberalism.' J.A. Schumpeter, *History of Economic Analysis*, London, Allen & Unwin Ltd, 1954, p. 402. Also see Sanderson, *op.cit.*, p. 190.

[9] See, Sanderson, *op.cit.*, p. 190, and R.W. Cohen, Evidence to XVIII R.C. *Civil Service, the Employment of University Graduates in Business*, London, 1913.

[10] Quoted in Sanderson, *op. cit.*, p. 191.

With these background considerations in mind, two key factors need to be emphasised for understanding *The Idea of a University*. First, Newman is concerned to validate the centrality of the study of theology in a university. Indeed, it is this conviction that partially motivates the establishment of a Catholic university in Dublin. Newman's argument is as masterful as an exercise in rhetorical tact as it is compelling in its logic (if we grant his premises). The political controversy over the establishment of a Catholic university in Ireland required Newman to carefully balance the competing interests of several stakeholders. The Archbishop of Armagh, Paul Cullen, having been directed by Rome, required the university to be emphatically Catholic. Irish nationalists required the university to be emphatically Irish. Archbishop Murray of Dublin was not committed to the idea of a Catholic university in his city, considering the whole venture impractical.[11] Newman also had to consider the interests and concerns of those at Oxford University (predominantly members of the Anglican communion) since the new university was to be modelled on Oxford, as well as for reasons of ecumenical propriety. Newman draws the various oppositions together by pointing to the shared commonalities accepted by all sides. It was the Vicar of Christ who originally gave both Ireland and England the faith as well as the civilisational fruits borne of that faith.[12] Since all of the branches of knowledge are mutually interdependent, theology, the study of reality in relation to divine things, must be a part of the university curriculum. Since Newman's audience largely accepted that God was the author of all things, it followed that anything studied must in principle fall under that discipline which considers things in their relation to the divine. Furthermore, any member of the Christian communion would acknowledge that there are truths articulated within theology that are not articulated, or at best only partially articulated, within any other discipline. Any institution that aspires to call itself a university, namely a place where universal knowledge is taught, cannot justly call itself such while deliberately leaving out a subject acknowledged to constitute a significant part of the general fabric of truth.

The second factor, though also having a theological dimension (since some utilitarians were criticising the relation between liberal

---

[11] See Ker, *op. cit.*, pp. 377 & 383.

[12] Ker, *op. cit.*, pp. 29-32.

education and its confessional framework[13]), is much more closely aligned with the profound social and political changes Great Britain had been undergoing since the advent of the industrial revolution. Jeremy Bentham's version of utilitarianism initiated a radical critique of elitism, since in Bentham's view every person's pleasure counts equally in the evaluation of what utility demands, namely the greatest happiness for the greatest number. This democratisation of human interests was also allied to the outcome-driven orientation of utilitarianism. What matters for Bentham and Benthamite utilitarians (such as James Mill, the father of John Stuart Mill) are the results of actions and states of affairs.[14] This idea privileges results over the cultivation of habits of mind, the latter being something which advocates of liberal education such as Newman see as something desirable for its own sake and in principle independently of its outcomes.

It is the combination of these intellectual factors together with the *material conditions* of advancing industrial and market capitalist society that led to the perception that more specialised and professional forms of education were urgently required. Indeed, by 1850 new institutional forms of university were beginning to appear such as the Bentham-inspired University of London in which the focus of learning was moving away from (in some respects) the traditional liberal education. Among the voices in this debate Newman is the most strident in articulating a vision of the university as a locus of a liberal education, firmly based in the study of literature and the classics as objects of contemplation, noble and worthy in themselves, and apart from their admitted benefits.

Understanding *The Idea of a University*

As we have seen, the early parts of *The Idea of a University* are concerned with the polemics of the debates on the role of theology within a university and also with respect to theology's role within wider society. Newman concludes by noting that since a university must teach all sciences, theology must be included as theology satisfies the formal requirements of a science. For Newman, all sciences are interconnected and mutually interdependent. Theology, even in respect to factual matters, exerts an influence on the other sciences and its omission prejudices the proper teaching of all the rest.

[13]   Ker, *op. cit.*, pp. 382-83.

[14]   For a good contemporary discussion of utilitarianism see J. J. C. Smart and B. Williams, *Utilitarianism: For and Against*, Cambridge, Cambridge University Press, 1973. Also see our introduction to J. S. Mill in this volume.

Finally, he thinks that if theology is excluded, it will not merely leave a hole in the fabric of studies, but its provenance will be usurped by other disciplines. This is a prophetic move on Newman's part since this is exactly what has occurred: science, for instance, has trespassed its proper domain, and we now find scientists claiming authority in matters in which they lack the intellectual training, requisite formation, and sensitivity with respect to the history and propositional content of that which they presume to judge.[15]

Newman, in Discourse V, argues that the main purpose of a university is to create an *atmosphere* of intellectual activity within which students learn to seek knowledge as an end in itself, that is, not for some extrinsic purpose such as gaining employment. He thinks in keeping with the very name 'university', such an institution should strive to be a place where universal knowledge is taught. He holds that all branches of knowledge are intimately connected. This is because they are ultimately derived from the Creator, God, who brought all things to be via a single comprehensive act. As the unitary act of creation issues from a supremely intelligent creator, it has a reasonable, intelligible structure and all parts are harmonised in respect to the intention of their author. Since God is also Wisdom and Truth, all human *intellectual* endeavour is ordered towards a unified end — the attainment of truth.[16]

All branches of human knowing thus 'complete, correct, [and] balance each other' as they strive towards comprehensive understanding of the rich yet unified end intended by God. The practical implication of these ontological and epistemological insights is that a university must embrace all departments of knowledge that help illuminate our situated appreciation of the Divinity's creative activity. A wide range of studies are thus required to foster the appropriate intellectual atmosphere. Newman labels the pursuit of such studies *liberal education*, bringing out in a particularly emphatic way the *intrinsic* desirability of such an education for the well-rounded and flourishing human being.

Newman focuses upon those disciplines that most enlarge the mind and soul in virtue of their inherent universality. In conse-

---

[15] The works of Richard Dawkins and Stephen Hawking leap to mind. See R. Dawkins, *The God Delusion*, New York, Houghton Mifflin, 2006; and S. Hawking and L. Mlodinow, *The Grand Design*, New York, Bantam Books, 2010.

[16] Here Newman is echoing a Platonic thesis which Augustine would recognise, namely that to be is to be intelligible; he is also echoing the first chapter of Aquinas' *Summa contra Gentiles* I.

quence, he devotes less time and effort in discussing professional disciplines such as medicine. This is not because such disciplines are unworthy or useless, but rather because of the narrowness of their scope. The object of study befitting a seat of universal learning is universal knowledge, that is, general knowledge, such as will fit its possessor for the widest and most comprehensive sorts of human accomplishment. Newman's focus is squarely upon the kind of person that one can *become* as a result of having received a liberal education, rather than what one *does* with one's education.

The atmosphere that pervades an institution devoted to universal knowledge is importantly one that is generated by both focused inquiry within disciplines and cross-fertilisation among disciplines. Newman stresses the positive value of conflict and intellectual rivalry. The university as a whole is a community of inquirers and each discipline raises questions and suggests answers which prompt responses from other disciplines. This atmosphere inculcates a *habit of mind* whose attributes include freedom, equitableness, calmness, moderation, and wisdom — what Newman calls a *philosophical habit*.

But what does Newman mean by *liberal education*, and what value does such an education have? Newman distinguishes between *useful knowledge* and *liberal knowledge*. The former consists of knowledge directed to external ends, examples of which include mercantile knowledge and knowledge of the mechanical arts. The latter consists of knowledge desirable for its own sake, and which does not require justification outside of itself. An example particularly congenial to Newman is theology, within which the nobility of the realities contemplated and their inherent lovability sufficiently justify pursuit of the discipline whether it has practical (that is, useful) consequences or not. Liberal knowledge is its own end.

In elucidating the value and desirability of a liberal university education, Newman argues that knowledge acquisition is a good in itself, and that it is in our nature to desire to know for its own sake. He appeals first to the philosophical tradition, which has ever recognised the intrinsic value of liberal knowledge. But he then adds that this is the common opinion of the educated portion of humanity in his day. The justification for the acknowledged value and desirability of liberal knowledge is ultimately ontological: liberal knowledge answers to a fundamental orientation and direct need of human nature. There is no perfection of human nature without knowledge.[17]

While Newman is concerned to defend the intrinsic value of liberal education, he is by no means antithetical to the instrumental benefits that it also confers. Liberal knowledge is both instrumentally valuable and intrinsically so. One can be instructed in useful knowledge, but liberal knowledge requires an elevated state of mind attained only through systematic cultivation of pure inquiry. On this last point Newman offers two clarifications: first, invoking the authority of Cicero, he notes that requisite cultivation of refined intellectual inquiry should not impinge upon our fundamental duties to others. That is, we have a duty to feed our family before we feed our mind. Second, Newman reiterates that he is not disparaging useful knowledge. Useful knowledge, he is happy to admit, improves everyone's welfare. In his critique Newman simply means to bring out what useful knowledge lacks, and in so doing illuminate not only the place for liberal knowledge but also to show how we should not rest content with merely useful or instrumental knowledge.

One potential objection to Newman's account is of ancient provenance. Cato the Elder valued all things in light of what they produced. Thus, he thinks that it is wrong to say that we seek knowledge purely for its own sake because all knowledge seems to evoke an external end. It is this external end that should be construed as the source of desirability and value. A more recent example of a thinker who might advance an objection like this is Thomas Hobbes, who believes that all goods are instrumental goods. Thinking conducted in the pursuit of such goods is *ipso facto* instrumental thinking, and hence of value only insofar as it helps attain instrumental goals. For Newman this misconstrues the human condition. It is a bit like thinking that the *benefits* one derives from a love relationship (such as pleasurable caresses) are the reasons *why* we love someone, when in reality we love someone for his or her own sake.

Central to Newman's account of the intrinsic value of liberal knowledge are his examples of aesthetic contemplation. It is a commonplace to observe that aesthetic appreciation is independent of utilitarian purpose. When we see a beautiful painting or encounter a

---

[17] This is a perennial theme in Greek philosophy and was articulated forcefully by both Augustine and Aquinas.

fog at sea, there is a disinterested quality to the experiences.[18] To use a contemporary example, there is a major difference between appreciating the Mona Lisa that we visit at the Louvre in comparison to the use of the image of the Mona Lisa as part of an advertising campaign. In the former case our appreciation is disinterested; in the latter it is not.

Newman's motivating assumption is that philosophical knowing, including both the philosophical habit of such knowing as well as its synthetic qualities in respect to specific items of knowledge, is the characteristic good of the intellect, perfecting it and making it excellent of its kind. It is this insight that allows Newman to reject the version of the principle of utility stemming from Francis Bacon. Bacon was preoccupied with scientific investigation and with putting scientific knowledge to use for the benefit of human beings. As with Cato, the Baconian theory founders on its Procrustean account of the goods of human knowing.

Newman has identified liberal knowledge with philosophy. By this he means to highlight not just the sort of knowledge obtained but the manner in which it is obtained. He calls attention to the habits of mind fostered by dialectic and the activity of reasoning. The aim of achieving universal knowledge requires skill in its articulation, so that what is known becomes a kind of enthymeme, pregnant with those conclusions already carried within it.

In drawing attention to the characteristic habits and methods employed in coming to possess liberal knowledge, Newman makes two brief yet highly significant observations in passing. First, habits become one with their possessor: the habits one possesses define one's character as an individual, and one's character, though built up by habit, is the most inward and profound possession of an individual. If the object of acquiring liberal knowledge is to achieve a truly philosophical habit, the educational process must elicit the deepest powers of the learner. Second, Newman sees the former point as providing the distinguishing mark of the university as a place of education as opposed to a place of instruction. In the former, the deepest powers of the student are educed; in the latter, the student receives facts and is trained in various forms of know-how.

---

[18] See for this idea the classic paper by E. Bullough, 'Psychical Distance as a factor in Art and an Aesthetic Principle', *British Journal of Psychology*, 5, 1912. A similar account is developed by G. Katkov, 'The Pleasant and the Beautiful', *Proceedings of the Aristotelian Society*, XL, 1939-40, 176-206.

One of the deepest criticisms of taking philosophy as the focus of university education is that the experience of millennia shows that philosophers fail to deliver what they promise, namely that they would make their students good by educating them into virtue.[19] When Newman turns to the role of the university and liberal education in its relationship to morality, he departs significantly from the philosophical tradition represented by Augustine and Aquinas. Augustine and Aquinas thought that education is centrally concerned with the formation of moral character. To think that education could be detached from formation in the moral virtues was for them anathema. Somewhat surprisingly, this detachment is embraced by Newman. Once the end of university education has been identified as the cultivation of a habit of mind and liberal knowledge, formation in the virtues has been foregone as an object, let alone the primary object, of university education. It is ironic that in his justification for the creation of a Catholic university Newman provides the intellectual basis for modern secular education.

As noted, Newman is sensitive to the charge that philosophical learning does not necessarily result in an ethical character. Formal study of philosophy, including moral philosophy, does not suffice to elicit proper motivations or control of the passions within its students.[20] The gathering of knowledge is one thing, the cultivation of virtue another.

What characterises someone possessed of an excellent intellect? In the most universal sense, a perfected intellect is one which allows its possessor to 'reason well in all matters, to reach out toward truth, and to grasp it.' Newman asserts that the label we apply to an individual who has achieved intellectual excellence of a general sort, which manifests itself in a fine sensibility, discriminating taste, and facility for judging, is: *gentleman*. Thus, Newman argues, the end product of liberal education is not the saint or the scientist or the shoemaker but the gentleman. And being a gentleman is valuable, though the excellences characteristic of a gentleman, and in light of which the gentleman's value is apparent, are not identical to those of the genuinely moral agent. Moreover, if the saint is the highest

---

[19] This is hardly a new observation. It is the subject of extended discussion by Plato in respect to the relationship between Socrates and Alcibiades.

[20] On this point Newman is in good company. Plato, Aristotle, and Aquinas all hold that moral philosophy is of little use with respect to the direct formation of the moral virtues. Justification for the study of ethics must be found elsewhere.

human type, then the gentleman is not the highest goal of human flourishing.

Both Augustine and Aquinas thought that some truths can only be appropriated by those already possessing the requisite virtues, and that faith is a necessary condition for the attainment of some truths. To cite an example from Elizabeth Anscombe, it is often said that the homeless are invisible. In a painfully straightforward way this is true. Unless someone has been formed in the virtues that make one apt to recognise and respond to their plight, the salient features of homelessness are overlooked and they remain invisible.[21]

These insights are not explicit in Newman's *Idea of a University*, and the idea that grace builds on nature is not accounted for within his educational scheme, though he is committed to such ideas from a confessional viewpoint. Newman is particularly concerned with arguing for the value of a liberal education in terms congenial to a wider audience. As a result, his inferential resources are fewer and his rhetoric is deeply shaped by and adapted for the audience he addresses. He speaks to the educated public with the voice of human reason, and therefore some of the resources he may have desired to draw upon were not available to him.

Newman emphatically denies that religious truth and liberal knowledge are incompatible. Just as he argues in the early sections of the *Idea of a University* that theology is a necessary component of a university education because religion forms a central dimension of the subject matter of knowledge, so too he thinks that liberal knowledge in itself is not the highest form of knowledge, nor is it the highest human good. What is highest and best within the possible sphere of human knowing is direct experiential knowledge of God. This creates a tension that runs throughout *The Idea of a University*. Newman finds himself obliged to say that some of the most important truths are not truths taught within a liberal education. For example, there is a tension between Newman's exaltations of man's 'imperial intellect' and his vehement pronouncements on the omnipotence of God and the legitimacy of the teaching authority of the Catholic Church.[22] The tensions remain unresolved, but identifying these tensions provides much material for reflection. Here is the locus of one of the great shifts in how the wider public views higher education today, as we move to an increased secularisation of

[21] G. E. M. Anscombe, *Human Life, Action and Ethics: Essays by G.E.M. Anscombe*, ed. M. Geach and L. Gormally, Charlottesville, Imprint Academic, 2005, p. 65.

[22] See Ker, *op. cit.*, pp. 384-385.

knowledge and lower our moral expectations for graduates of the university system. What is taught and who teaches it have shifted steadily away from the demands of grace and virtue. In consequence, the place occupied by Catholic theology within Newman's scheme could easily be filled by a blander secular discipline like religious studies. And this is, in fact, exactly what has happened at many universities. We believe that Newman is committed to the norms of education demanded by the Catholic tradition, but *The Idea of a University* is constrained by its argumentative context.[23]

In Discourse VI of *The Idea of a University*, Newman brings out the contrast between the perfective illumination of the intellect, which for want of a better word he calls *philosophy*, and what he refers to as *mere knowledge*. At an intuitive level, we recognise that there is a difference between a person who knows many facts within a disciple and a person who understands a discipline. It is with this in mind that Newman criticises the prevailing state of education of his time.

The commonly held notion that a university education consists in the acquisition of knowledge contains an element of truth, but is not an adequate conception of what a good university education should be. To use two of Newman's own examples, consider how someone achieves mental enlargement through experiencing foreign lands and by viewing the stars through a telescope. There is an enlargement of the mind that goes beyond the mere accumulation of facts. For it is likely that the student already knew, prior to looking through the telescope, that the moon had such-and-such topographical features. But when the moon is seen, a flood of ideas and associations come to mind that situate those facts in a way that organises them and makes them meaningful. Again, to say that someone understands a culture is to say more than that the person knows about the culture. Understanding requires comparison, systemisation, and synthesis of facts, experiences, and ideas, leading to an appreciation of how these all fit together within the holistic fabric of what one knows. Synthetic understanding of this sort, which clearly goes beyond mere knowledge, seeks a coherent understanding of the totality of creation and its Creator so far as is possible for the human intellect. This is philosophy, or, as we describe it in chapter 1, understanding requires know-why.

---

[23] As Newman writes, 'I have no intention, in anything I shall say, of bringing into the argument the authority of the Church, or any authority at all; but I shall consider the question [of university education] simply on the grounds of human reason and human wisdom.' (Introductory)

But this is precisely what Newman thinks is missing in his time. He excoriates those who would reduce education to rote learning. While a good memory, well-furnished with facts and experiences, is beneficial, this does not provide an adequate substitute for the philosophical understanding required for true intellectual cultivation. In fact, an over-focus on the development of the memory can lead to an impairment of the critical and evaluative faculties. Pragmatically, Newman criticises pedagogical methods that emphasise passive, mechanical imbibing of facts, as such methods inevitably result in poor learning.

Newman moderates the traditional elitism associated with liberal education in significant ways. He is explicitly open to universal education of all classes of society. He espouses making scientific and literary works both affordable and widely available. He acknowledges that a broad acquaintance with various branches of knowledge is useful, and is even a necessary condition of intellectual cultivation. Finally, he allows that it is often desirable for a liberal education to be supplemented with an in-depth knowledge of particular disciplines.

Newman: Text

Newman: The Idea of a University
(Abridged)

Discourse 5. Knowledge its Own End

A university may be considered with reference either to its Students or to its Studies; and the principle, that all Knowledge is a whole and the separate Sciences parts of one, which I have hitherto been using in behalf of its studies, is equally important when we direct our attention to its students. Now then I turn to the students, and shall consider the education which, by virtue of this principle, a University will give them; and thus I shall be introduced, Gentlemen, to the second question, which I proposed to discuss, viz., whether and in what sense its teaching, viewed relatively to the taught, carries the attribute of Utility along with it.

1. I have said that all branches of knowledge are connected together, because the subject-matter of knowledge is intimately united in itself, as being the acts and the work of the Creator. Hence it is that the Sciences, into which our knowledge may be said to be cast, have multiplied bearings one on another, and an internal sympathy, and admit, or rather demand, comparison and adjustment. They complete, correct, balance each other. This consideration, if well-founded, must be taken into account, not only as regards the attainment of truth, which is their common end, but as regards the influence which they exercise upon those whose education consists in the study of them. I have said already, that to give undue prominence to one is to be unjust to another; to neglect or supersede these is to divert those from their proper object. It is to unsettle the boundary lines between science and science, to disturb their action, to

destroy the harmony which binds them together. Such a proceeding will have a corresponding effect when introduced into a place of education. There is no science but tells a different tale, when viewed as a portion of a whole, from what it is likely to suggest when taken by itself, without the safeguard, as I may call it, of others.

Let me make use of an illustration. In the combination of colours, very different effects are produced by a difference in their selection and juxta-position; red, green, and white, change their shades, according to the contrast to which they are submitted. And, in like manner, the drift and meaning of a branch of knowledge varies with the company in which it is introduced to the student. If his reading is confined simply to one subject, however such division of labour may favour the advancement of a particular pursuit, a point into which I do not here enter, certainly it has a tendency to contract his mind. If it is incorporated with others, it depends on those others as to the kind of influence which it exerts upon him. Thus the Classics, which in England are the means of refining the taste, have in France sub-served the spread of revolutionary and deistical doctrines. In Meta-physics, again, Butler's Analogy of Religion, which has had so much to do with the conversion to the Catholic faith of members of the University of Oxford, appeared to Pitt and others, who had received a different training, to operate only in the direction of infidelity. And so again, Watson, Bishop of Llandaff, as I think he tells us in the nar-rative of his life, felt the science of Mathematics to indispose the mind to religious belief, while others see in its investigations the best parallel, and thereby defence, of the Christian Mysteries. In like manner, I suppose, Arcesilas would not have handled logic as Aris-totle, nor Aristotle have criticised poets as Plato; yet reasoning and poetry are subject to scientific rules.

It is a great point then to enlarge the range of studies which a Uni-versity professes, even for the sake of the students; and, though they cannot pursue every subject which is open to them, they will be the gainers by living among those and under those who represent the whole circle. This I conceive to be the advantage of a seat of universal learning, considered as a place of education. An assemblage of learned men, zealous for their own sciences, and rivals of each other, are brought, by familiar intercourse and for the sake of intellectual peace, to adjust together the claims and relations of their respective subjects of investigation. They learn to respect, to consult, to aid each other. Thus is created a pure and clear atmosphere of thought, which the student also breathes, though in his own case he only pursues a few sciences out of the multitude. He profits by an intellectual tradition, which is independent of particular teachers, which guides him in his choice of subjects, and duly interprets for him those which he chooses. He apprehends the great outlines of knowledge, the principles on which it rests, the scale of its parts, its lights and its shades, its great points and its little, as he otherwise cannot apprehend them. Hence it is that his education is called 'Liberal.' A habit of mind is formed which lasts through life, of which the attributes are, freedom, equitableness, calmness, moderation, and wisdom; or what in a former Discourse I have ventured to call a philosophical habit. This then I would assign as the special fruit of the education furnished at a University, as contrasted with other places of teaching or modes of teaching. This is the main purpose of a University in its treatment of its students.

And now the question is asked me, What is the *use* of it? and my answer will constitute the main subject of the Discourses which are to follow.

2.   Cautious and practical thinkers, I say, will ask of me, what, after all, is the gain of this Philosophy, of which I make such account, and from which I promise so much. Even supposing it to enable us to exercise the degree of trust exactly due to every science respectively, and to estimate precisely the value of every truth which is anywhere to be found, how are we better for this master view of things, which I have been extolling? Does it not reverse the principle of the division of labour? will practical objects be obtained better or worse by its cultivation? to what then does it lead? where does it end? what does it do? how does it profit? what does it promise? Particular sciences are respectively the basis of definite arts, which carry on to results tangible and beneficial the truths which are the subjects of the knowledge attained; what is the Art of this science of sciences? what is the fruit of such a Philosophy? what are we proposing to effect, what inducements do we hold out to the Catholic community, when we set about the enterprise of founding a University?

I am asked what is the end of University Education, and of the Liberal or Philosophical Knowledge which I conceive it to impart: I answer, that what I have already said has been sufficient to show that it has a very tangible, real, and sufficient end, though the end cannot be divided from that knowledge itself. Knowledge is capable of being its own end. Such is the constitution of the human mind, that any kind of knowledge, if it be really such, is its own reward.

And if this is true of all knowledge, it is true also of that special Philosophy, which I have made to consist in a comprehensive view of truth in all its branches, of the relations of science to science, of their mutual bearings, and their respective values. What the worth of such an acquirement is, compared with other objects which we seek, — wealth or power or honour or the conveniences and comforts of life, I do not profess here to discuss; but I would maintain, and mean to show, that it is an object, in its own nature so really and undeniably good, as to be the compensation of a great deal of thought in the compassing, and a great deal of trouble in the attaining.

Now, when I say that Knowledge is, not merely a means to something beyond it, or the preliminary of certain arts into which it naturally resolves, but an end sufficient to rest in and to pursue for its own sake, surely I am uttering no paradox, for I am stating what is both intelligible in itself, and has ever been the common judgment of philosophers and the ordinary feeling of mankind. I am saying what at least the public opinion of this day ought to be slow to deny, considering how much we have heard of late years, in opposition to Religion, of entertaining, curious, and various knowledge. I am but saying what whole volumes have been written to illustrate, viz., by a 'selection from the records of Philosophy, Literature, and Art, in all ages and countries, of a body of examples, to show how the most unpropitious circumstances have been unable to conquer an ardent desire for the acquisition of knowledge.' That further advantages accrue to us and redound to others by its possession, over and above what it is in itself, I am very far indeed from denying; but, independent of these, we are satisfying a direct need of our nature in its very acquisition; and, whereas our nature, unlike that of the inferior creation, does not at once reach its perfection, but depends, in order to it, on a number of external aids and appliances, Knowledge, as one of the principal of these, is valuable for what its very presence in us does for us after the manner of a habit, even though it be turned to no further account, nor subserve any direct end.

3.   Hence it is that Cicero, in enumerating the various heads of mental excellence, lays down the pursuit of Knowledge for its own sake, as the first of them. 'This pertains most of all to human nature,' he says, 'for we are all of us drawn to the pursuit of Knowledge; in which to excel we consider excellent, whereas to mistake, to err, to be

ignorant, to be deceived, is both an evil and a disgrace.' [1] And he considers Knowledge the very first object to which we are attracted, after the supply of our physical wants. After the calls and duties of our animal existence, as they may be termed, as regards ourselves, our family, and our neighbours, follows, he tells us, 'the search after truth. Accordingly, as soon as we escape from the pressure of necessary cares, forthwith we desire to see, to hear, and to learn; and consider the knowledge of what is hidden or is wonderful a condition of our happiness.'

This passage, though it is but one of many similar passages in a multitude of authors, I take for the very reason that it is so familiarly known to us; and I wish you to observe, Gentlemen, how distinctly it separates the pursuit of Knowledge from those ulterior objects to which certainly it can be made to conduce, and which are, I suppose, solely contemplated by the persons who would ask of me the use of a University or Liberal Education. So far from dreaming of the cultivation of Knowledge directly and mainly in order to our physical comfort and enjoyment, for the sake of life and person, of health, of the conjugal and family union, of the social tie and civil security, the great Orator implies, that it is only after our physical and political needs are supplied, and when we are 'free from necessary duties and cares,' that we are in a condition for 'desiring to see, to hear, and to learn.' Nor does he contemplate in the least degree the reflex or subsequent action of Knowledge, when acquired, upon those material goods which we set out by securing before we seek it; on the contrary, he expressly denies its bearing upon social life altogether, strange as such a procedure is to those who live after the rise of the Baconian philosophy, and he cautions us against such a cultivation of it as will interfere with our duties to our fellow-creatures. 'All these methods,' he says, 'are engaged in the investigation of truth; by the pursuit of which to be carried off from public occupations is a transgression of duty. For the praise of virtue lies altogether in action; yet intermissions often occur, and then we recur to such pursuits; not to say that the incessant activity of the mind is vigorous enough to carry us on in the pursuit of knowledge, even without any exertion of our own.' The idea of benefiting society by means of 'the pursuit of science and knowledge' did not enter at all into the motives which he would assign for their cultivation.

This was the ground of the opposition which the elder Cato made to the introduction of Greek Philosophy among his countrymen,

---

[1]   Cicero, *Offic. init.*

when Carneades and his companions, on occasion of their embassy, were charming the Roman youth with their eloquent expositions of it. The fit representative of a practical people, Cato estimated every thing by what it produced; whereas the Pursuit of Knowledge promised nothing beyond Knowledge itself. He despised that refinement or enlargement of mind of which he had no experience.

4.   Things, which can bear to be cut off from every thing else and yet persist in living, must have life in themselves; pursuits, which issue in nothing, and still maintain their ground for ages, which are regarded as admirable, though they have not as yet proved themselves to be useful, must have their sufficient end in themselves, whatever it turn out to be. And we are brought to the same conclusion by considering the force of the epithet, by which the knowledge under consideration is popularly designated. It is common to speak of '*liberal* knowledge,' of the '*liberal* arts and studies,' and of a '*liberal* education,' as the especial characteristic or property of a University and of a gentleman; what is really meant by the word? Now, first, in its grammatical sense it is opposed to *servile*; and by 'servile work' is understood, as our catechisms inform us, bodily labour, mechanical employment, and the like, in which the mind has little or no part. Parallel to such servile works are those arts, if they deserve the name, of which the poet speaks, [Aristotle, *Nich. Eth.* VI] which owe their origin and their method to hazard, not to skill; as, for instance, the practice and operations of an empiric. As far as this contrast may be considered as a guide into the meaning of the word, liberal education and liberal pursuits are exercises of mind, of reason, of reflection.

But we want something more for its explanation, for there are bodily exercises which are liberal, and mental exercises which are not so. For instance, in ancient times the practitioners in medicine were commonly slaves; yet it was an art as intellectual in its nature, in spite of the pretence, fraud, and quackery with which it might then, as now, be debased, as it was heavenly in its aim. And so in like manner, we contrast a liberal education with a commercial education or a professional; yet no one can deny that commerce and the professions afford scope for the highest and most diversified powers of mind. There is then a great variety of intellectual exercises, which are not technically called 'liberal;' on the other hand, I say, there are exercises of the body which do receive that appellation. Such, for instance, was the palæstra, in ancient times; such the Olympic games, in which strength and dexterity of body as well as of mind gained the prize. In Xenophon we read of the young Persian nobility being taught to ride on horseback and to speak the truth; both being among the accomplishments of a gentleman. War, too, however rough a profession, has ever been accounted liberal, unless in cases when it becomes heroic, which would introduce us to another subject.

Now comparing these instances together, we shall have no difficulty in determining the principle of this apparent variation in the application of the term which I am examining. Manly games, or games of skill, or military prowess, though bodily, are, it seems, accounted liberal; on the other hand, what is merely professional, though highly intellectual, nay, though liberal in comparison of trade and manual labour, is not simply called liberal, and mercantile occupations are not liberal at all. Why this distinction? because that alone is liberal knowledge, which stands on its own pretensions, which is independent of sequel, expects no complement, refuses to be *informed* (as it is called) by any end, or absorbed into any art, in order duly to present itself to our contemplation. The most ordinary pursuits have this specific character, if they are self-sufficient and complete; the highest lose it, when they minister to something beyond them. It is absurd to balance, in point of worth and importance, a treatise on reducing fractures with a game of cricket or a fox-chase; yet of the two the bodily exercise has that quality which we call 'liberal,' and the intellectual has it not. And so of the learned professions altogether, considered merely as professions; although one of them be the most popularly beneficial, and another the most politically important, and the third the most intimately divine of all human pursuits, yet the very greatness of their end, the health of the body, or of the commonwealth, or of the soul, diminishes, not increases, their claim to the appellation 'liberal,' and that still more, if they are cut down to the strict exigencies of that end. If, for instance, Theology, instead of being cultivated as a contemplation, be limited to the purposes of the pulpit or be represented by the catechism, it loses, — not its usefulness, not its divine character, not its meritoriousness (rather it gains a claim upon these titles by such charitable condescension), — but it does lose the particular attribute which I am illustrating; just as a face worn by tears and fasting loses its beauty, or a labourer's hand loses its delicateness; — for Theology thus exercised is not simple knowledge, but rather is an art or a business making use of Theology. And thus it appears that even what is supernatural need not be liberal, nor need a hero be a gentleman, for the plain reason that one idea is not another idea. And in like manner the Baconian Philosophy, by using its physical sciences in the service of man, does thereby transfer them from the order of Liberal Pursuits to, I do not say the inferior, but the distinct class of the Useful. And, to take a different instance, hence again, as is evident, whenever personal gain is the motive, still more distinctive an effect has it upon the character of a given pursuit; thus racing, which was a liberal exercise in Greece, forfeits its rank in times like these, so far as it is made the occasion of gambling.

All that I have been now saying is summed up in a few characteristic words of the great Philosopher. 'Of possessions,' he says, 'those rather are useful, which bear fruit; those *liberal, which tend to enjoyment*. By fruitful, I mean, which yield revenue; by enjoyable, where *nothing accrues of consequence beyond the using*.' [Aristotle, *Rhet.* I.5]

5.   Do not suppose, that in thus appealing to the ancients, I am throwing back the world two thousand years, and fettering Philosophy with the reasonings of paganism. While the world lasts, will Aristotle's doctrine on these matters last, for he is the oracle of nature and of truth. While we are men, we cannot help, to a great extent, being Aristotelians, for the great Master does but analyse the thoughts, feelings, views, and opinions of human kind. He has told us the meaning of our own words and ideas, before we were born. In many subject-matters, to think correctly, is to think like Aristotle; and we are his disciples whether we will or no, though we may not know it. Now, as to the particular instance before us, the word 'liberal' as applied to Knowledge and Education, expresses a specific idea, which ever has been, and ever will be, while the nature of man is the same, just as the idea of the Beautiful is specific, or of the Sublime, or of the Ridiculous, or of the Sordid. It is in the world now, it was in the world then; and, as in the case of the dogmas of faith, it is illustrated by a continuous historical tradition, and never was out of the world, from the time it came into it. There have indeed been differences of opinion from time to time, as to what pursuits and what arts came under that idea, but such differences are but an additional evidence of its reality. That idea must have a substance in it, which has maintained its ground amid these conflicts and changes, which has ever served as a standard to measure things withal, which has passed from mind to mind unchanged, when there was so much to colour, so much to influence any notion or thought whatever, which

was not founded in our very nature. Were it a mere generalisation, it would have varied with the subjects from which it was generalised; but though its subjects vary with the age, it varies not itself. The palæstra may seem a liberal exercise to Lycurgus, and illiberal to Seneca; coach-driving and prize-fighting may be recognised in Elis, and be condemned in England; music may be despicable in the eyes of certain moderns, and be in the highest place with Aristotle and Plato, — (and the case is the same in the particular application of the idea of Beauty, or of Goodness, or of Moral Virtue, there is a difference of tastes, a difference of judgments) — still these variations imply, instead of discrediting, the archetypal idea, which is but a previous hypothesis or condition, by means of which issue is joined between contending opinions, and without which there would be nothing to dispute about.

I consider, then, that I am chargeable with no paradox, when I speak of a Knowledge which is its own end, when I call it liberal knowledge, or a gentleman's knowledge, when I educate for it, and make it the scope of a University. And still less am I incurring such a charge, when I make this acquisition consist, not in Knowledge in a vague and ordinary sense, but in that Knowledge which I have especially called Philosophy or, in an extended sense of the word, Science; for whatever claims Knowledge has to be considered as a good, these it has in a higher degree when it is viewed not vaguely, not popularly, but precisely and transcendently as Philosophy. Knowledge, I say, is then especially liberal, or sufficient for itself, apart from every external and ulterior object, when and so far as it is philosophical, and this I proceed to show.

6.   Now bear with me, Gentlemen, if what I am about to say, has at first sight a fanciful appearance. Philosophy, then, or Science, is related to Knowledge in this way: — Knowledge is called by the name of Science or Philosophy, when it is acted upon, informed, or if I may use a strong figure, impregnated by Reason. Reason is the principle of that intrinsic fecundity of Knowledge, which, to those who possess it, is its especial value, and which dispenses with the necessity of their looking abroad for any end to rest upon external to itself. Knowledge, indeed, when thus exalted into a scientific form, is also power; not only is it excellent in itself, but whatever such excellence may be, it is something more, it has a result beyond itself. Doubtless; but that is a further consideration, with which I am not concerned. I only say that, prior to its being a power, it is a good; that

it is, not only an instrument, but an end. I know well it may resolve itself into an art, and terminate in a mechanical process, and in tangible fruit; but it also may fall back upon that Reason which informs it, and resolve itself into Philosophy. In one case it is called Useful Knowledge, in the other Liberal. The same person may cultivate it in both ways at once; but this again is a matter foreign to my subject; here I do but say that there are two ways of using Knowledge, and in matter of fact those who use it in one way are not likely to use it in the other, or at least in a very limited measure. You see, then, here are two methods of Education; the end of the one is to be philosophical, of the other to be mechanical; the one rises towards general ideas, the other is exhausted upon what is particular and external. Let me not be thought to deny the necessity, or to decry the benefit, of such attention to what is particular and practical, as belongs to the useful or mechanical arts; life could not go on without them; we owe our daily welfare to them; their exercise is the duty of the many, and we owe to the many a debt of gratitude for fulfilling that duty. I only say that Knowledge, in proportion as it tends more and more to be particular, ceases to be Knowledge. It is a question whether Knowledge can in any proper sense be predicated of the brute creation; without pretending to metaphysical exactness of phraseology, which would be unsuitable to an occasion like this, I say, it seems to me improper to call that passive sensation, or perception of things, which brutes seem to possess, by the name of Knowledge. When I speak of Knowledge, I mean something intellectual, something which grasps what it perceives through the senses; something which takes a view of things; which sees more than the senses convey; which reasons upon what it sees, and while it sees; which invests it with an idea. It expresses itself, not in a mere enunciation, but by an enthymeme: it is of the nature of science from the first, and in this consists its dignity. The principle of real dignity in Knowledge, its worth, its desirableness, considered irrespectively of its results, is this germ within it of a scientific or a philosophical process. This is how it comes to be an end in itself; this is why it admits of being called Liberal. Not to know the relative disposition of things is the state of slaves or children; to have mapped out the Universe is the boast, or at least the ambition, of Philosophy.

Moreover, such knowledge is not a mere extrinsic or accidental advantage, which is ours to-day and another's to-morrow, which may be got up from a book, and easily forgotten again, which we can command or communicate at our pleasure, which we can borrow for the occasion, carry about in our hand, and take into the market; it is an acquired illumination, it is a habit, a personal possession, and an inward endowment. And this is the reason, why it is more correct, as well as more usual, to speak of a University as a place of education, than of instruction, though, when knowledge is concerned, instruction would at first sight have seemed the more appropriate word. We are instructed, for instance, in manual exercises, in the fine and useful arts, in trades, and in ways of business; for these are methods, which have little or no effect upon the mind itself, are contained in rules committed to memory, to tradition, or to use, and bear upon an end external to themselves. But education is a higher word; it implies an action upon our mental nature, and the formation of a character; it is something individual and permanent, and is commonly spoken of in connexion with religion and virtue. When, then, we speak of the communication of Knowledge as being Education, we thereby really imply that that Knowledge is a state or condition of mind; and since cultivation of mind is surely worth seeking for its own sake, we are thus brought once more to the conclusion, which the word 'Liberal' and the word 'Philosophy' have already suggested, that there is a Knowledge, which is desirable, though nothing come of it, as being of itself a treasure, and a sufficient remuneration of years of labour.

7.   This, then, is the answer which I am prepared to give to the question with which I opened this Discourse. Before going on to speak of the object of the Church in taking up Philosophy, and the uses to which she puts it, I am prepared to maintain that Philosophy is its own end, and, as I conceive, I have now begun the proof of it. I am prepared to maintain that there is a knowledge worth possessing for what it is, and not merely for what it does; and what minutes remain to me to-day I shall devote to the removal of some portion of the indistinctness and confusion with which the subject may in some minds be surrounded.

It may be objected then, that, when we profess to seek Knowledge for some end or other beyond itself, whatever it be, we speak intelligibly; but that, whatever men may have said, however obstinately the idea may have kept its ground from age to age, still it is simply unmeaning to say that we seek Knowledge for its own sake, and for nothing else; for that it ever leads to something beyond itself, which therefore is its end, and the cause why it is desirable;—moreover, that this end is twofold, either of this world or of the next; that all knowledge is cultivated either for secular objects or for eternal; that if it is directed to secular objects, it is called Useful Knowledge, if to eternal, Religious or Christian Knowledge; — in consequence, that if, as I have allowed, this Liberal Knowledge does not benefit the body or estate, it ought to benefit the soul; but if the fact be really so, that it is neither a physical or a secular good on the one hand, nor a moral good on the other, it cannot be a good at all, and is not worth the trouble which is necessary for its acquisition.

And then I may be reminded that the professors of this Liberal or Philosophical Knowledge have themselves, in every age, recognised this exposition of the matter, and have submitted to the issue in which it terminates; for they have ever been attempting to make men virtuous; or, if not, at least have assumed that refinement of mind was virtue, and that they themselves were the virtuous portion of mankind. This they have professed on the one hand; and on the other, they have utterly failed in their professions, so as ever to make themselves a proverb among men, and a laughing-stock both to the grave and the dissipated portion of mankind, in consequence of them. Thus they have furnished against themselves both the ground and the means of their own exposure, without any trouble at all to any one else. In a word, from the time that Athens was the University of the world, what has Philosophy taught men, but to promise without practising, and to aspire without attaining? What has the deep and lofty thought of its disciples ended in but eloquent words? Nay, what has its teaching ever meditated, when it was boldest in its remedies for human ill, beyond charming us to sleep by its lessons, that we might feel nothing at all? like some melodious air, or rather like those strong and transporting perfumes, which at first spread their sweetness over every thing they touch, but in a little while do but offend in proportion as they once pleased us. Did Philosophy support Cicero under the disfavour of the fickle populace, or nerve Seneca to oppose an imperial tyrant? It abandoned Brutus, as he sorrowfully confessed, in his greatest need, and it forced Cato, as his panegyrist strangely boasts, into the false position of defying heaven. How few can be counted among its professors, who, like Polemo, were thereby converted from a profligate course, or like Anaxagoras, thought the world well lost in exchange for its possession? The philosopher in Rasselas taught a superhuman doctrine, and then succumbed without an effort to a trial of human affection.

'He discoursed,' we are told, 'with great energy on the government of the passions. His look was venerable, his action graceful, his pronunciation clear, and his diction elegant. He showed, with great strength of sentiment and variety of illustration, that human nature is degraded and debased, when the lower faculties predominate over the higher. He communicated the various precepts given, from time to time, for the conquest of passion, and displayed the happiness of those who had obtained the important victory, after which man is no longer the slave of fear, nor the fool of hope … He enumerated many examples of heroes immoveable by pain or pleasure, who looked with indifference on those modes or accidents to which the vulgar give the names of good and evil.'

Rasselas in a few days found the philosopher in a room half darkened, with his eyes misty, and his face pale. 'Sir,' said he, 'you have come at a time when all human friendship is useless; what I suffer cannot be remedied, what I have lost cannot be supplied. My daughter, my only daughter, from whose tenderness I expected all the comforts of my age, died last night of a fever.' 'Sir,' said the prince, 'mortality is an event by which a wise man can never be surprised; we know that death is always near, and it should therefore always be expected.' 'Young man,' answered the philosopher, 'you speak like one who has never felt the pangs of separation.' 'Have you, then, forgot the precept,' said Rasselas, 'which you so powerfully enforced? … consider that external things are naturally variable, but truth and reason are always the same.' 'What comfort,' said the mourner, 'can truth and reason afford me? Of what effect are they now, but to tell me that my daughter will not be restored?'

8.   Better, far better, to make no professions, you will say, than to cheat others with what we are not, and to scandalise them with what we are. The sensualist, or the man of the world, at any rate is not the victim of fine words, but pursues a reality and gains it. The Philosophy of Utility, you will say, Gentlemen, has at least done its work; and I grant it, — it aimed low, but it has fulfilled its aim. If that man of great intellect who has been its Prophet in the conduct of life played false to his own professions, he was not bound by his philosophy to be true to his friend or faithful in his trust. Moral virtue was not the line in which he undertook to instruct men; and though, as the poet calls him, he were the 'meanest' of mankind, he was so in what may be called his private capacity and without any prejudice to the theory of induction. He had a right to be so, if he chose, for any thing that the Idols of the den or the theatre had to say to the contrary. His mission was the increase of physical enjoyment and social comfort; and most wonderfully, most awfully has he fulfilled his conception and

his design. Almost day by day have we fresh and fresh shoots, and buds, and blossoms, which are to ripen into fruit, on that magical tree of Knowledge which he planted, and to which none of us perhaps, except the very poor, but owes, if not his present life, at least his daily food, his health, and general well-being. He was the divinely provided minister of temporal benefits to all of us so great, that whatever I am forced to think of him as a man, I have not the heart, from mere gratitude, to speak of him severely. And, in spite of the tendencies of his philosophy, which are, as we see at this day, to depreciate, or to trample on Theology, he has himself, in his writings, gone out of his way, as if with a prophetic misgiving of those tendencies, to insist on it as the instrument of that beneficent Father, who, when He came on earth in visible form, took on Him first and most prominently the office of assuaging the bodily wounds of human nature. And truly, like the old mediciner in the tale, 'he sat diligently at his work, and hummed, with cheerful countenance, a pious song;' and then in turn 'went out singing into the meadows so gaily, that those who had seen him from afar might well have thought it was a youth gathering flowers for his beloved, instead of an old physician gathering healing herbs in the morning dew.' [Fouqué, 'Unknown Patient']

Alas, that men, in the action of life or in their heart of hearts, are not what they seem to be in their moments of excitement, or in their trances or intoxications of genius,—so good, so noble, so serene! Alas, that Bacon too in his own way should after all be but the fellow of those heathen philosophers who in their disadvantages had some excuse for their inconsistency, and who surprise us rather in what they did say than in what they did not do! Alas, that he too, like Socrates or Seneca, must be stripped of his holy-day coat, which looks so fair, and should be but a mockery amid his most majestic gravity of phrase; and, for all his vast abilities, should, in the littleness of his own moral being, but typify the intellectual narrowness of his school! However, granting all this, heroism after all was not his philosophy:—I cannot deny he has abundantly achieved what he proposed. His is simply a Method whereby bodily discomforts and temporal wants are to be most effectually removed from the greatest number; and already, before it has shown any signs of exhaustion, the gifts of nature, in their most artificial shapes and luxurious profusion and diversity, from all quarters of the earth, are, it is undeniable, by its means brought even to our doors, and we rejoice in them.

9. Useful Knowledge then, I grant, has done its work; and Liberal Knowledge as certainly has not done its work, — that is, supposing, as the objectors assume, its direct end, like Religious Knowledge, is to make men better; but this I will not for an instant allow, and, unless I allow it, those objectors have said nothing to the purpose. I admit, rather I maintain, what they have been urging, for I consider Knowledge to have its end in itself. For all its friends, or its enemies, may say, I insist upon it, that it is as real a mistake to burden it with virtue or religion as with the mechanical arts. Its direct business is not to steel the soul against temptation or to console it in affliction, any more than to set the loom in motion, or to direct the steam carriage; be it ever so much the means or the condition of both material and moral advancement, still, taken by and in itself, it as little mends our hearts as it improves our temporal circumstances. And if its eulogists claim for it such a power, they commit the very same kind of encroachment on a province not their own as the political economist who should maintain that his science educated him for casuistry or diplomacy. Knowledge is one thing, virtue is another; good sense is not conscience, refinement is not humility, nor is largeness and justness of view faith. Philosophy, however enlightened, however profound, gives no command over the passions, no influential motives, no vivifying principles. Liberal Education makes not the Christian, not the Catholic, but the gentleman. It is well to be a gentleman, it is well to have a cultivated intellect, a delicate taste, a candid, equitable, dispassionate mind, a noble and courteous bearing in the conduct of life; — these are the connatural qualities of a large knowledge; they are the objects of a University; I am advocating, I shall illustrate and insist upon them; but still, I repeat, they are no guarantee for sanctity or even for conscientiousness, they may attach to the man of the world, to the profligate, to the heartless, — pleasant, alas, and attractive as he shows when decked out in them. Taken by themselves, they do but seem to be what they are not; they look like virtue at a distance, but they are detected by close observers, and on the long run; and hence it is that they are popularly accused of pretence and hypocrisy, not, I repeat, from their own fault, but because their professors and their admirers persist in taking them for what they are not, and are officious in arrogating for them a praise to which they have no claim. Quarry the granite rock with razors, or moor the vessel with a thread of silk; then may you hope with such keen and delicate instruments as human knowledge

and human reason to contend against those giants, the passion and the pride of man.

Surely we are not driven to theories of this kind, in order to vindicate the value and dignity of Liberal Knowledge. Surely the real grounds on which its pretensions rest are not so very subtle or abstruse, so very strange or improbable. Surely it is very intelligible to say, and that is what I say here, that Liberal Education, viewed in itself, is simply the cultivation of the intellect, as such, and its object is nothing more or less than intellectual excellence. Every thing has its own perfection, be it higher or lower in the scale of things; and the perfection of one is not the perfection of another. Things animate, inanimate, visible, invisible, all are good in their kind, and have a *best* of themselves, which is an object of pursuit. Why do you take such pains with your garden or your park? You see to your walks and turf and shrubberies; to your trees and drives; not as if you meant to make an orchard of the one, or corn or pasture land of the other, but because there is a special beauty in all that is goodly in wood, water, plain, and slope, brought all together by art into one shape, and grouped into one whole. Your cities are beautiful, your palaces, your public buildings, your territorial mansions, your churches; and their beauty leads to nothing beyond itself. There is a physical beauty and a moral: there is a beauty of person, there is a beauty of our moral being, which is natural virtue; and in like manner there is a beauty, there is a perfection, of the intellect. There is an ideal perfection in these various subject-matters, towards which individual instances are seen to rise, and which are the standards for all instances whatever. The Greek divinities and demigods, as the statuary has moulded them, with their symmetry of figure, and their high forehead and their regular features, are the perfection of physical beauty. The heroes, of whom history tells, Alexander, or Cæsar, or Scipio, or Saladin, are the representatives of that magnanimity or self-mastery which is the greatness of human nature. Christianity too has its heroes, and in the supernatural order, and we call them Saints. The artist puts before him beauty of feature and form; the poet, beauty of mind; the preacher, the beauty of grace: then intellect too, I repeat, has its beauty, and it has those who aim at it. To open the mind, to correct it, to refine it, to enable it to know, and to digest, master, rule, and use its knowledge, to give it power over its own faculties, application, flexibility, method, critical exactness, sagacity, resource, address, eloquent expression, is an object as intelligible (for here we are inquiring, not what the object of a Liberal Education is worth, nor what use the Church makes of it, but what it is in itself), I say, an object as intelligible as the cultivation of virtue, while, at the same time, it is absolutely distinct from it.

10.   This indeed is but a temporal object, and a transitory possession; but so are other things in themselves which we make much of and pursue. The moralist will tell us that man, in all his functions, is but a flower which blossoms and fades, except so far as a higher principle breathes upon him, and makes him and what he is immortal. Body and mind are carried on into an eternal state of being by the gifts of Divine Munificence; but at first they do but fail in a failing world; and if the powers of intellect decay, the powers of the body have decayed before them, and, as an Hospital or an Almshouse, though its end be ephemeral, may be sanctified to the service of religion, so surely may a University, even were it nothing more than I have as yet described it. We attain to heaven by using this world well, though it is to pass away; we perfect our nature, not by undoing it, but by adding to it what is more than nature, and directing it towards aims higher than its own.

Discourse 6. Knowledge Viewed in Relation to Learning

1.   It were well if the English, like the Greek language, possessed some definite word to express, simply and generally, intellectual proficiency or perfection, such as 'health,' as used with reference to the animal frame, and 'virtue,' with reference to our moral nature. I am not able to find such a term;—talent, ability, genius, belong distinctly to the raw material, which is the subject-matter, not to that excellence which is the result of exercise and training. When we turn, indeed, to the particular kinds of intellectual perfection, words are forthcoming for our purpose, as, for instance, judgment, taste, and skill; yet even these belong, for the most part, to powers or habits bearing upon practice or upon art, and not to any perfect condition of the intellect, considered in itself. Wisdom, again, is certainly a more comprehensive word than any other, but it has a direct relation to conduct, and to human life. Knowledge, indeed, and Science express purely intellectual ideas, but still not a state or quality of the intellect; for knowledge, in its ordinary sense, is but one of its circumstances, denoting a possession or a habit; and science has been appropriated to the subject-matter of the intellect, instead of belonging in English, as it ought to do, to the intellect itself. The consequence is that, on an occasion like this, many words are necessary, in

order, first, to bring out and convey what surely is no difficult idea in itself, — that of the cultivation of the intellect as an end; next, in order to recommend what surely is no unreasonable object; and lastly, to describe and make the mind realise the particular perfection in which that object consists. Every one knows practically what are the constituents of health or of virtue; and every one recognises health and virtue as ends to be pursued; it is otherwise with intellectual excellence, and this must be my excuse, if I seem to any one to be bestowing a good deal of labour on a preliminary matter.

In default of a recognised term, I have called the perfection or virtue of the intellect by the name of philosophy, philosophical knowledge, enlargement of mind, or illumination; terms which are not uncommonly given to it by writers of this day: but, whatever name we bestow on it, it is, I believe, as a matter of history, the business of a University to make this intellectual culture its direct scope, or to employ itself in the education of the intellect, — just as the work of a Hospital lies in healing the sick or wounded, of a Riding or Fencing School, or of a Gymnasium, in exercising the limbs, of an Almshouse, in aiding and solacing the old, of an Orphanage, in protecting innocence, of a Penitentiary, in restoring the guilty. I say, a University, taken in its bare idea, and before we view it as an instrument of the Church, has this object and this mission; it contemplates neither moral impression nor mechanical production; it professes to exercise the mind neither in art nor in duty; its function is intellectual culture; here it may leave its scholars, and it has done its work when it has done as much as this. It educates the intellect to reason well in all matters, to reach out towards truth, and to grasp it.

2.   This, I said in my foregoing Discourse, was the object of a University, viewed in itself, and apart from the Catholic Church, or from the State, or from any other power which may use it; and I illustrated this in various ways. I said that the intellect must have an excellence of its own, for there was nothing which had not its specific good; that the word 'educate' would not be used of intellectual culture, as it is used, had not the intellect had an end of its own; that, had it not such an end, there would be no meaning in calling certain intellectual exercises 'liberal,' in contrast with 'useful,' as is commonly done; that the very notion of a philosophical temper implied it, for it threw us back upon research and system as ends in themselves, distinct from effects and works of any kind; that a philosophical scheme of knowledge, or system of sciences, could not, from the nature of the

case, issue in any one definite art or pursuit, as its end; and that, on the other hand, the discovery and contemplation of truth, to which research and systematising led, were surely sufficient ends, though nothing beyond them were added, and that they had ever been accounted sufficient by mankind.

Here then I take up the subject; and, having determined that the cultivation of the intellect is an end distinct and sufficient in itself, and that, so far as words go it is an enlargement or illumination, I proceed to inquire what this mental breadth, or power, or light, or philosophy consists in. A Hospital heals a broken limb or cures a fever: what does an Institution effect, which professes the health, not of the body, not of the soul, but of the intellect? What is this good, which in former times, as well as our own, has been found worth the notice, the appropriation, of the Catholic Church?

I have then to investigate, in the Discourses which follow, those qualities and characteristics of the intellect in which its cultivation issues or rather consists; and, with a view of assisting myself in this undertaking, I shall recur to certain questions which have already been touched upon. These questions are three: viz. the relation of intellectual culture, first, to *mere* knowledge; secondly, to *professional* knowledge; and thirdly, to *religious* knowledge. In other words, are *acquirements* and *attainments* the scope of a University Education? or *expertness in particular arts and pursuits*? or *moral and religious proficiency*? or something besides these three? These questions I shall examine in succession, with the purpose I have mentioned; and I hope to be excused, if, in this anxious undertaking, I am led to repeat what, either in these Discourses or elsewhere, I have already put upon paper. And first, of *Mere Knowledge*, or Learning, and its connexion with intellectual illumination or Philosophy.

3.   I suppose the *primâ-facie* view which the public at large would take of a University, considering it as a place of Education, is nothing more or less than a place for acquiring a great deal of knowledge on a great many subjects. Memory is one of the first developed of the mental faculties; a boy's business when he goes to school is to learn, that is, to store up things in his memory. For some years his intellect is little more than an instrument for taking in facts, or a receptacle for storing them; he welcomes them as fast as they come to him; he lives on what is without; he has his eyes ever about him; he has a lively susceptibility of impressions; he imbibes information of every kind; and little does he make his own in a true sense of the word, living

rather upon his neighbours all around him. He has opinions, religious, political, and literary, and, for a boy, is very positive in them and sure about them; but he gets them from his schoolfellows, or his masters, or his parents, as the case may be. Such as he is in his other relations, such also is he in his school exercises; his mind is observant, sharp, ready, retentive; he is almost passive in the acquisition of knowledge. I say this in no disparagement of the idea of a clever boy. Geography, chronology, history, language, natural history, he heaps up the matter of these studies as treasures for a future day. It is the seven years of plenty with him: he gathers in by handfuls, like the Egyptians, without counting; and though, as time goes on, there is exercise for his argumentative powers in the Elements of Mathematics, and for his taste in the Poets and Orators, still, while at school, or at least, till quite the last years of his time, he acquires, and little more; and when he is leaving for the University, he is mainly the creature of foreign influences and circumstances, and made up of accidents, homogeneous or not, as the case may be. Moreover, the moral habits, which are a boy's praise, encourage and assist this result; that is, diligence, assiduity, regularity, despatch, persevering application; for these are the direct conditions of acquisition, and naturally lead to it. Acquirements, again, are emphatically producible, and at a moment; they are a something to show, both for master and scholar; an audience, even though ignorant themselves of the subjects of an examination, can comprehend when questions are answered and when they are not. Here again is a reason why mental culture is in the minds of men identified with the acquisition of knowledge.

The same notion possesses the public mind, when it passes on from the thought of a school to that of a University: and with the best of reasons so far as this, that there is no true culture without acquirements, and that philosophy presupposes knowledge. It requires a great deal of reading, or a wide range of information, to warrant us in putting forth our opinions on any serious subject; and without such learning the most original mind may be able indeed to dazzle, to amuse, to refute, to perplex, but not to come to any useful result or any trustworthy conclusion. There are indeed persons who profess a different view of the matter, and even act upon it. Every now and then you will find a person of vigorous or fertile mind, who relies upon his own resources, despises all former authors, and gives the world, with the utmost fearlessness, his views upon religion, or history, or any other popular subject. And his works may sell for a while; he may get a name in his day; but this will be all. His readers are sure to find on the long run that his doctrines are mere theories, and not the expression of facts, that they are chaff instead of bread, and then his popularity drops as suddenly as it rose.

Knowledge then is the indispensable condition of expansion of mind, and the instrument of attaining to it; this cannot be denied, it is ever to be insisted on; I begin with it as a first principle; however, the very truth of it carries men too far, and confirms to them the notion that it is the whole of the matter. A narrow mind is thought to be that which contains little knowledge; and an enlarged mind, that which holds a great deal; and what seems to put the matter beyond dispute is, the fact of the great number of studies which are pursued in a University, by its very profession. Lectures are given on every kind of subject; examinations are held; prizes awarded. There are moral, metaphysical, physical Professors; Professors of languages, of history, of mathematics, of experimental science. Lists of questions are published, wonderful for their range and depth, variety and difficulty; treatises are written, which carry upon their very face the evidence of extensive reading or multifarious information; what then is wanting for mental culture to a person of large reading and scientific attainments? what is grasp of mind but acquirement? where shall philosophical repose be found, but in the consciousness and enjoyment of large intellectual possessions?

And yet this notion is, I conceive, a mistake, and my present business is to show that it is one, and that the end of a Liberal Education is not mere knowledge, or knowledge considered in its *matter*; and I shall best attain my object, by actually setting down some cases, which will be generally granted to be instances of the process of enlightenment or enlargement of mind, and others which are not, and thus, by the comparison, you will be able to judge for yourselves, Gentlemen, whether Knowledge, that is, acquirement, is after all the real principle of the enlargement, or whether that principle is not rather something beyond it.

4. For instance, let a person, whose experience has hitherto been confined to the more calm and unpretending scenery of these islands, whether here or in England, go for the first time into parts where physical nature puts on her wilder and more awful forms, whether at home or abroad, as into mountainous districts; or let one, who has ever lived in a quiet village, go for the first time to a great metropolis, — then I suppose he will have a sensation which perhaps

he never had before. He has a feeling not in addition or increase of former feelings, but of something different in its nature. He will perhaps be borne forward, and find for a time that he has lost his bearings. He has made a certain progress, and he has a consciousness of mental enlargement; he does not stand where he did, he has a new centre, and a range of thoughts to which he was before a stranger.
Again, the view of the heavens which the telescope opens upon us, if allowed to fill and possess the mind, may almost whirl it round and make it dizzy. It brings in a flood of ideas, and is rightly called an intellectual enlargement, whatever is meant by the term.

And so again, the sight of beasts of prey and other foreign animals, their strangeness, the originality (if I may use the term) of their forms and gestures and habits and their variety and independence of each other, throw us out of ourselves into another creation, and as if under another Creator, if I may so express the temptation which may come on the mind. We seem to have new faculties, or a new exercise for our faculties, by this addition to our knowledge; like a prisoner, who, having been accustomed to wear manacles or fetters, suddenly finds his arms and legs free.

Hence Physical Science generally, in all its departments, as bringing before us the exuberant riches and resources, yet the orderly course, of the Universe, elevates and excites the student, and at first, I may say, almost takes away his breath, while in time it exercises a tranquilising influence upon him.

Again, the study of history is said to enlarge and enlighten the mind, and why? because, as I conceive, it gives it a power of judging of passing events, and of all events, and a conscious superiority over them, which before it did not possess.

And in like manner, what is called seeing the world, entering into active life, going into society, travelling, gaining acquaintance with the various classes of the community, coming into contact with the principles and modes of thought of various parties, interests, and races, their views, aims, habits and manners, their religious creeds and forms of worship, — gaining experience how various yet how alike men are, how low-minded, how bad, how opposed, yet how confident in their opinions; all this exerts a perceptible influence upon the mind, which it is impossible to mistake, be it good or be it bad, and is popularly called its enlargement.

And then again, the first time the mind comes across the arguments and speculations of unbelievers, and feels what a novel light they cast upon what he has hitherto accounted sacred; and still more, if it gives in to them and embraces them, and throws off as so much prejudice what it has hitherto held, and, as if waking from a dream, begins to realise to its imagination that there is now no such thing as law and the transgression of law, that sin is a phantom, and punishment a bugbear, that it is free to sin, free to enjoy the world and the flesh; and still further, when it does enjoy them, and reflects that it may think and hold just what it will, that 'the world is all before it where to choose,' and what system to build up as its own private persuasion; when this torrent of wilful thoughts rushes over and inundates it, who will deny that the fruit of the tree of knowledge, or what the mind takes for knowledge, has made it one of the gods, with a sense of expansion and elevation, — an intoxication in reality, still, so far as the subjective state of the mind goes, an illumination? Hence the fanaticism of individuals or nations, who suddenly cast off their Maker. Their eyes are opened; and, like the judgment-stricken king in the Tragedy, they see two suns, and a magic universe, out of which they look back upon their former state of faith and innocence with a sort of contempt and indignation, as if they were then but fools, and the dupes of imposture.

On the other hand, Religion has its own enlargement, and an enlargement, not of tumult, but of peace. It is often remarked of uneducated persons, who have hitherto thought little of the unseen world, that, on their turning to God, looking into themselves, regulating their hearts, reforming their conduct, and meditating on death and judgment, heaven and hell, they seem to become, in point of intellect, different beings from what they were. Before, they took things as they came, and thought no more of one thing than another. But now every event has a meaning; they have their own estimate of whatever happens to them; they are mindful of times and seasons, and compare the present with the past; and the world, no longer dull, monotonous, unprofitable, and hopeless, is a various and complicated drama, with parts and an object, and an awful moral.

5.   Now from these instances, to which many more might be added, it is plain, first, that the communication of knowledge certainly is either a condition or the means of that sense of enlargement or enlightenment, of which at this day we hear so much in certain quarters: this cannot be denied; but next, it is equally plain, that such communication is not the whole of the process. The enlargement consists, not merely in the passive reception into the mind of a number of ideas hitherto unknown to it, but in the mind's energetic and

simultaneous action upon and towards and among those new ideas, which are rushing in upon it. It is the action of a formative power, reducing to order and meaning the matter of our acquirements; it is a making the objects of our knowledge subjectively our own, or, to use a familiar word, it is a digestion of what we receive, into the substance of our previous state of thought; and without this no enlargement is said to follow. There is no enlargement, unless there be a comparison of ideas one with another, as they come before the mind, and a systematising of them. We feel our minds to be growing and expanding *then*, when we not only learn, but refer what we learn to what we know already. It is not the mere addition to our knowledge that is the illumination; but the locomotion, the movement onwards, of that mental centre, to which both what we know, and what we are learning, the accumulating mass of our acquirements, gravitates. And therefore a truly great intellect, and recognised to be such by the common opinion of mankind, such as the intellect of Aristotle, or of St. Thomas, or of Newton, or of Goethe, (I purposely take instances within and without the Catholic pale, when I would speak of the intellect as such,) is one which takes a connected view of old and new, past and present, far and near, and which has an insight into the influence of all these one on another; without which there is no whole, and no centre. It possesses the knowledge, not only of things, but also of their mutual and true relations; knowledge, not merely considered as acquirement, but as philosophy.

Accordingly, when this analytical, distributive, harmonising process is away, the mind experiences no enlargement, and is not reckoned as enlightened or comprehensive, whatever it may add to its knowledge. For instance, a great memory, as I have already said, does not make a philosopher, any more than a dictionary can be called a grammar. There are men who embrace in their minds a vast multitude of ideas, but with little sensibility about their real relations towards each other. These may be antiquarians, annalists, naturalists; they may be learned in the law; they may be versed in statistics; they are most useful in their own place; I should shrink from speaking disrespectfully of them; still, there is nothing in such attainments to guarantee the absence of narrowness of mind. If they are nothing more than well-read men, or men of information, they have not what specially deserves the name of culture of mind, or fulfils the type of Liberal Education.

In like manner, we sometimes fall in with persons who have seen much of the world, and of the men who, in their day, have played a conspicuous part in it, but who generalise nothing, and have no observation, in the true sense of the word. They abound in information in detail, curious and entertaining, about men and things; and, having lived under the influence of no very clear or settled principles, religious or political, they speak of every one and every thing, only as so many phenomena, which are complete in themselves, and lead to nothing, not discussing them, or teaching any truth, or instructing the hearer, but simply talking. No one would say that these persons, well informed as they are, had attained to any great culture of intellect or to philosophy.

The case is the same still more strikingly where the persons in question are beyond dispute men of inferior powers and deficient education. Perhaps they have been much in foreign countries, and they receive, in a passive, otiose, unfruitful way, the various facts which are forced upon them there. Seafaring men, for example, range from one end of the earth to the other; but the multiplicity of external objects, which they have encountered, forms no symmetrical and consistent picture upon their imagination; they see the tapestry of human life, as it were on the wrong side, and it tells no story. They sleep, and they rise up, and they find themselves, now in Europe, now in Asia; they see visions of great cities and wild regions; they are in the marts of commerce, or amid the islands of the South; they gaze on Pompey's Pillar, or on the Andes; and nothing which meets them carries them forward or backward, to any idea beyond itself. Nothing has a drift or relation; nothing has a history or a promise. Every thing stands by itself, and comes and goes in its turn, like the shifting scenes of a show, which leave the spectator where he was. Perhaps you are near such a man on a particular occasion, and expect him to be shocked or perplexed at something which occurs; but one thing is much the same to him as another, or, if he is perplexed, it is as not knowing what to say, whether it is right to admire, or to ridicule, or to disapprove, while conscious that some expression of opinion is expected from him; for in fact he has no standard of judgment at all, and no landmarks to guide him to a conclusion. Such is mere acquisition, and, I repeat, no one would dream of calling it philosophy.

6.   Instances, such as these, confirm, by the contrast, the conclusion I have already drawn from those which preceded them. That only is true enlargement of mind which is the power of viewing many things at once as one whole, of referring them severally to their true

place in the universal system, of understanding their respective values, and determining their mutual dependence. Thus is that form of Universal Knowledge, of which I have on a former occasion spoken, set up in the individual intellect, and constitutes its perfection. Possessed of this real illumination, the mind never views any part of the extended subject-matter of Knowledge without recollecting that it is but a part, or without the associations which spring from this recollection. It makes every thing in some sort lead to every thing else; it would communicate the image of the whole to every separate portion, till that whole becomes in imagination like a spirit, every where pervading and penetrating its component parts, and giving them one definite meaning. Just as our bodily organs, when mentioned, recall their function in the body, as the word 'creation' suggests the Creator, and 'subjects' a sovereign, so, in the mind of the Philosopher, as we are abstractedly conceiving of him, the elements of the physical and moral world, sciences, arts, pursuits, ranks, offices, events, opinions, individualities, are all viewed as one, with correlative functions, and as gradually by successive combinations converging, one and all, to the true centre.

To have even a portion of this illuminative reason and true philosophy is the highest state to which nature can aspire, in the way of intellect; it puts the mind above the influences of chance and necessity, above anxiety, suspense, unsettlement, and superstition, which is the lot of the many. Men, whose minds are possessed with some one object, take exaggerated views of its importance, are feverish in the pursuit of it, make it the measure of things which are utterly foreign to it, and are startled and despond if it happens to fail them. They are ever in alarm or in transport. Those on the other hand who have no object or principle whatever to hold by, lose their way, every step they take. They are thrown out, and do not know what to think or say, at every fresh juncture; they have no view of persons, or occurrences, or facts, which come suddenly upon them, and they hang upon the opinion of others, for want of internal resources. But the intellect, which has been disciplined to the perfection of its powers, which knows, and thinks while it knows, which has learned to leaven the dense mass of facts and events with the elastic force of reason, such an intellect cannot be partial, cannot be exclusive, cannot be impetuous, cannot be at a loss, cannot but be patient, collected, and majestically calm, because it discerns the end in every beginning, the origin in every end, the law in every interruption, the limit in each delay; because it ever knows where it stands, and how its path lies from one point to another. It is the *tetragônos* of the Peripatetic, and has the 'nil admirari' of the Stoic,—

> Felix qui potuit rerum cognoscere causas,
> Atque metus omnes, et inexorabile fatum
> Subjecit pedibus, strepitumque Acherontis avari.

There are men who, when in difficulties, originate at the moment vast ideas or dazzling projects; who, under the influence of excitement, are able to cast a light, almost as if from inspiration, on a subject or course of action which comes before them; who have a sudden presence of mind equal to any emergency, rising with the occasion, and an undaunted magnanimous bearing, and an energy and keenness which is but made intense by opposition. This is genius, this is heroism; it is the exhibition of a natural gift, which no culture can teach, at which no Institution can aim; here, on the contrary, we are concerned, not with mere nature, but with training and teaching. That perfection of the Intellect, which is the result of Education, and its *beau ideal*, to be imparted to individuals in their respective measures, is the clear, calm, accurate vision and comprehension of all things, as far as the finite mind can embrace them, each in its place, and with its own characteristics upon it. It is almost prophetic from its knowledge of history; it is almost heart-searching from its knowledge of human nature; it has almost supernatural charity from its freedom from littleness and prejudice; it has almost the repose of faith, because nothing can startle it; it has almost the beauty and harmony of heavenly contemplation, so intimate is it with the eternal order of things and the music of the spheres.

7.   And now, if I may take for granted that the true and adequate end of intellectual training and of a University is not Learning or Acquirement, but rather, is Thought or Reason exercised upon Knowledge, or what may be called Philosophy, I shall be in a position to explain the various mistakes which at the present day beset the subject of University Education.

I say then, if we would improve the intellect, first of all, we must ascend; we cannot gain real knowledge on a level; we must generalise, we must reduce to method, we must have a grasp of principles, and group and shape our acquisitions by means of them. It matters not whether our field of operation be wide or limited; in every case, to command it, is to mount above it. Who has not felt the irritation of mind and impatience created by a deep, rich country, visited for the first time, with winding lanes, and high hedges, and green steeps, and tangled woods, and every thing smiling indeed, but in a maze? The same feeling comes upon us in a strange city, when we have no map of its streets. Hence you hear of practised travellers, when they first come into a place, mounting some high hill or church tower, by way of reconnoitring its neighbourhood. In like manner, you must be above your knowledge, not under it, or it will oppress you; and the more you have of it, the greater will be the load. The learning of a Salmasius or a Burman, unless you are its master, will be your tyrant. 'Imperat aut servit;' if you can wield it with a strong arm, it is a great weapon; otherwise,

> Vis consili expers
> Mole ruit suâ.

You will be overwhelmed, like Tarpeia, by the heavy wealth which you have exacted from tributary generations.

Instances abound; there are authors who are as pointless as they are inexhaustible in their literary resources. They measure knowledge by bulk, as it lies in the rude block, without symmetry, without design. How many commentators are there on the Classics, how many on Holy Scripture, from whom we rise up, wondering at the learning which has passed before us, and wondering why it passed! How many writers are there of Ecclesiastical History, such as Mosheim or Du Pin, who, breaking up their subject into details, destroy its life, and defraud us of the whole by their anxiety about the parts! The Sermons, again, of the English Divines in the seventeenth century, how often are they mere repertories of miscellaneous and officious learning! Of course Catholics also may read without thinking; and in their case, equally as with Protestants, it holds good, that such knowledge is unworthy of the name, knowledge which they have not thought through, and thought out. Such readers are only possessed by their knowledge, not possessed of it; nay, in matter of fact they are often even carried away by it, without any volition of their own. Recollect, the Memory can tyrannise, as well as the Imagination. Derangement, I believe, has been considered as a loss of control over the sequence of ideas. The mind, once set in motion, is henceforth deprived of the power of initiation, and becomes the victim of a train of associations, one thought suggesting another, in the way of cause and effect, as if by a mechanical process, or some physical necessity. No one, who has had experience of men of studious habits, but must recognise the existence of a parallel phenomenon in the case of those who have over-stimulated the Memory. In such persons Reason acts almost as feebly and as impotently as in the madman; once fairly started on any subject whatever, they have no power of self-control; they passively endure the succession of impulses which are evolved out of the original exciting cause; they are passed on from one idea to another and go steadily forward, plodding along one line of thought in spite of the amplest concessions of the hearer, or wandering from it in endless digression in spite of his remonstrances. Now, if, as is very certain, no one would envy the madman the glow and originality of his conceptions, why must we extol the cultivation of that intellect, which is the prey, not indeed of barren fancies but of barren facts, of random intrusions from without, though not of morbid imaginations from within? And in thus speaking, I am not denying that a strong and ready memory is in itself a real treasure; I am not disparaging a well-stored mind, though it be nothing besides, provided it be sober, any more than I would despise a bookseller's shop: — it is of great value to others, even when not so to the owner. Nor am I banishing, far from it, the possessors of deep and multifarious learning from my ideal University; they adorn it in the eyes of men; I do but say that they constitute no type of the results at which it aims; that it is no great gain to the intellect to have enlarged the memory at the expense of faculties which are indisputably higher.

8.   Nor indeed am I supposing that there is any great danger, at least in this day, of over-education; the danger is on the other side. I will tell you, Gentlemen, what has been the practical error of the last twenty years, — not to load the memory of the student with a mass of undigested knowledge, but to force upon him so much that he has rejected all. It has been the error of distracting and enfeebling the mind by an unmeaning profusion of subjects; of implying that a smattering in a dozen branches of study is not shallowness, which it really is, but enlargement, which it is not; of considering an acquaintance with the learned names of things and persons, and the possession of clever duodecimos, and attendance on eloquent lecturers, and membership with scientific institutions, and the sight of the experiments of a platform and the specimens of a museum, that all this was not dissipation of mind, but progress. All things now are to be learned at once, not first one thing, then another, not one well, but many badly. Learning is to be without exertion, without attention, without toil; without grounding, without advance, without finishing. There is to be nothing individual in it; and this, forsooth, is the wonder of the age. What the steam engine does with matter, the

printing press is to do with mind; it is to act mechanically, and the population is to be passively, almost unconsciously enlightened, by the mere multiplication and dissemination of volumes. Whether it be the school boy, or the school girl, or the youth at college, or the mechanic in the town, or the politician in the senate, all have been the victims in one way or other of this most preposterous and pernicious of delusions. Wise men have lifted up their voices in vain; and at length, lest their own institutions should be outshone and should disappear in the folly of the hour, they have been obliged, as far as they could with a good conscience, to humour a spirit which they could not withstand, and make temporising concessions at which they could not but inwardly smile.

It must not be supposed that, because I so speak, therefore I have some sort of fear of the education of the people: on the contrary, the more education they have, the better, so that it is really education. Nor am I an enemy to the cheap publication of scientific and literary works, which is now in vogue: on the contrary, I consider it a great advantage, convenience, and gain; that is, to those to whom education has given a capacity for using them. Further, I consider such innocent recreations as science and literature are able to furnish will be a very fit occupation of the thoughts and the leisure of young persons, and may be made the means of keeping them from bad employments and bad companions. Moreover, as to that superficial acquaintance with chemistry, and geology, and astronomy, and political economy, and modern history, and biography, and other branches of knowledge, which periodical literature and occasional lectures and scientific institutions diffuse through the community, I think it a graceful accomplishment, and a suitable, nay, in this day a necessary accomplishment, in the case of educated men. Nor, lastly, am I disparaging or discouraging the thorough acquisition of any one of these studies, or denying that, as far as it goes, such thorough acquisition is a real education of the mind. All I say is, call things by their right names, and do not confuse together ideas which are essentially different. A thorough knowledge of one science and a superficial acquaintance with many, are not the same thing; a smattering of a hundred things or a memory for detail, is not a philosophical or comprehensive view. Recreations are not education; accomplishments are not education. Do not say, the people must be educated, when, after all, you only mean, amused, refreshed, soothed, put into good spirits and good humour, or kept from vicious excesses. I do not say that such amusements, such occupations of mind, are not a great gain; but they are not education. You may as well call drawing and fencing education, as a general knowledge of botany or conchology. Stuffing birds or playing stringed instruments is an elegant pastime, and a resource to the idle, but it is not education; it does not form or cultivate the intellect. Education is a high word; it is the preparation for knowledge, and it is the imparting of knowledge in proportion to that preparation. We require intellectual eyes to know withal, as bodily eyes for sight. We need both objects and organs intellectual; we cannot gain them without setting about it; we cannot gain them in our sleep, or by hap-hazard. The best telescope does not dispense with eyes; the printing press or the lecture room will assist us greatly, but we must be true to ourselves, we must be parties in the work. A University is, according to the usual designation, an Alma Mater, knowing her children one by one, not a foundry, or a mint, or a treadmill.

9.   I protest to you, Gentlemen, that if I had to choose between a so-called University, which dispensed with residence and tutorial superintendence, and gave its degrees to any person who passed an examination in a wide range of subjects, and a University which had no professors or examinations at all, but merely brought a number of young men together for three or four years, and then sent them away as the University of Oxford is said to have done some sixty years since, if I were asked which of these two methods was the better discipline of the intellect,—mind, I do not say which is *morally* the better, for it is plain that compulsory study must be a good and idleness an intolerable mischief,—but if I must determine which of the two courses was the more successful in training, moulding, enlarging the mind, which sent out men the more fitted for their secular duties, which produced better public men, men of the world, men whose names would descend to posterity, I have no hesitation in giving the preference to that University which did nothing, over that which exacted of its members an acquaintance with every science under the sun. And, paradox as this may seem, still if results be the test of systems, the influence of the public schools and colleges of England, in the course of the last century, at least will bear out one side of the contrast as I have drawn it. What would come, on the other hand, of the ideal systems of education which have fascinated the imagination of this age, could they ever take effect, and whether they would not produce a generation frivolous, narrow-minded, and resourceless, intellectually considered, is a fair subject for

debate; but so far is certain, that the Universities and scholastic establishments, to which I refer, and which did little more than bring together first boys and then youths in large numbers, these institutions, with miserable deformities on the side of morals, with a hollow profession of Christianity, and a heathen code of ethics, — I say, at least they can boast of a succession of heroes and statesmen, of literary men and philosophers, of men conspicuous for great natural virtues, for habits of business, for knowledge of life, for practical judgment, for cultivated tastes, for accomplishments, who have made England what it is, — able to subdue the earth, able to domineer over Catholics.

How is this to be explained? I suppose as follows: When a multitude of young men, keen, open-hearted, sympathetic, and observant, as young men are, come together and freely mix with each other, they are sure to learn one from another, even if there be no one to teach them; the conversation of all is a series of lectures to each, and they gain for themselves new ideas and views, fresh matter of thought, and distinct principles for judging and acting, day by day. An infant has to learn the meaning of the information which its senses convey to it, and this seems to be its employment. It fancies all that the eye presents to it to be close to it, till it actually learns the contrary, and thus by practice does it ascertain the relations and uses of those first elements of knowledge which are necessary for its animal existence. A parallel teaching is necessary for our social being, and it is secured by a large school or a college; and this effect may be fairly called in its own department an enlargement of mind. It is seeing the world on a small field with little trouble; for the pupils or students come from very different places, and with widely different notions, and there is much to generalise, much to adjust, much to eliminate, there are inter-relations to be defined, and conventional rules to be established, in the process, by which the whole assemblage is moulded together, and gains one tone and one character.

Let it be clearly understood, I repeat it, that I am not taking into account moral or religious considerations; I am but saying that that youthful community will constitute a whole, it will embody a specific idea, it will represent a doctrine, it will administer a code of conduct, and it will furnish principles of thought and action. It will give birth to a living teaching, which in course of time will take the shape of a self-perpetuating tradition, or a *genius loci*, as it is sometimes called; which haunts the home where it has been born, and which imbues and forms, more or less, and one by one, every individual who is successively brought under its shadow. Thus it is that, independent of direct instruction on the part of Superiors, there is a sort of self-education in the academic institutions of Protestant England; a characteristic tone of thought, a recognised standard of judgment is found in them, which, as developed in the individual who is submitted to it, becomes a twofold source of strength to him, both from the distinct stamp it impresses on his mind, and from the bond of union which it creates between him and others, — effects which are shared by the authorities of the place, for they themselves have been educated in it, and at all times are exposed to the influence of its ethical atmosphere. Here then is a real teaching, whatever be its standards and principles, true or false; and it at least tends towards cultivation of the intellect; it at least recognises that knowledge is something more than a sort of passive reception of scraps and details; it is a something, and it does a something, which never will issue from the most strenuous efforts of a set of teachers, with no mutual sympathies and no intercommunion, of a set of examiners with no opinions which they dare profess, and with no common principles, who are teaching or questioning a set of youths who do not know them, and do not know each other, on a large number of subjects, different in kind, and connected by no wide philosophy, three times a week, or three times a year, or once in three years, in chill lecture-rooms or on a pompous anniversary.

10. Nay, self-education in any shape, in the most restricted sense, is preferable to a system of teaching which, professing so much, really does so little for the mind. Shut your College gates against the votary of knowledge, throw him back upon the searchings and the efforts of his own mind; he will gain by being spared an entrance into your Babel. Few indeed there are who can dispense with the stimulus and support of instructors, or will do any thing at all, if left to themselves. And fewer still (though such great minds are to be found), who will not, from such unassisted attempts, contract a self-reliance and a self-esteem, which are not only moral evils, but serious hindrances to the attainment of truth. And next to none, perhaps, or none, who will not be reminded from time to time of the disadvantage under which they lie, by their imperfect grounding, by the breaks, deficiencies, and irregularities of their knowledge, by the eccentricity of opinion and the confusion of principle which they exhibit. They will be too often ignorant of what every one knows and takes for granted, of that multitude of small truths which fall upon the mind like dust,

impalpable and ever accumulating; they may be unable to converse, they may argue perversely, they may pride themselves on their worst paradoxes or their grossest truisms, they may be full of their own mode of viewing things, unwilling to be put out of their way, slow to enter into the minds of others;—but, with these and whatever other liabilities upon their heads, they are likely to have more thought, more mind, more philosophy, more true enlargement, than those earnest but ill-used persons, who are forced to load their minds with a score of subjects against an examination, who have too much on their hands to indulge themselves in thinking or investigation, who devour premiss and conclusion together with indiscriminate greediness, who hold whole sciences on faith, and commit demonstrations to memory, and who too often, as might be expected, when their period of education is passed, throw up all they have learned in disgust, having gained nothing really by their anxious labours, except perhaps the habit of application.

Yet such is the better specimen of the fruit of that ambitious system which has of late years been making way among us: for its result on ordinary minds, and on the common run of students, is less satisfactory still; they leave their place of education simply dissipated and relaxed by the multiplicity of subjects, which they have never really mastered, and so shallow as not even to know their shallowness. How much better, I say, is it for the active and thoughtful intellect, where such is to be found, to eschew the College and the University altogether, than to submit to a drudgery so ignoble, a mockery so contumelious! How much more profitable for the independent mind, after the mere rudiments of education, to range through a library at random, taking down books as they meet him, and pursuing the trains of thought which his mother wit suggests! How much healthier to wander into the fields, and there with the exiled Prince to find 'tongues in the trees, books in the running brooks!' How much more genuine an education is that of the poor boy in the Poem [Crabbe, 'Tales of the Hall']—a Poem, whether in conception or in execution, one of the most touching in our language—who, not in the wide world, but ranging day by day around his widowed mother's home, 'a dexterous gleaner' in a narrow field, and with only such slender outfit

as the village school and books a few Supplied,

contrived from the beach, and the quay, and the fisher's boat, and the inn's fireside, and the tradesman's shop, and the shepherd's walk, and the smuggler's hut, and the mossy moor, and the screaming gulls, and the restless waves, to fashion for himself a philosophy and a poetry of his own!

But in a large subject, I am exceeding my necessary limits. Gentlemen, I must conclude abruptly; and postpone any summing up of my argument, should that be necessary, to another day.

Mill: Commentary

John Stuart Mill

Groomed from the very beginning of his life to become a politically radical 'utilitarian messiah',[1] John Stuart Mill was the recipient of one of the most extraordinary educations on record. By the age of three he was learning Greek, and was already reading fluently in both Greek and English by the time he turned four. By the age of eight he had digested several Platonic dialogues and had read a staggering number of classical authors: Herodotus, Xenophon, Diogenes Laertius, Isocrates, Lucian, and, in a bow to his tender years, Aesop. The quantity and quality of authors in English is equally extraordinary, including histories by Hume, Gibbon, Hooke, and Plutarch, various works in politics, and a smattering of light novels such as *Robinson Crusoe*, the *Arabian Nights*, and *Don Quixote*.

Mill started learning Latin at eight, and over the next few years added to his extensive list Virgil, Horace, Phaedrus, Livy, Sallust, Ovid, Cicero, Terence, and Lucretius. His mathematical education was not neglected, and by the age of 12 he had mastered algebra, geometry, and differential calculus. He also had a passion for reading works in experimental science, and made his way through several advanced works in chemistry and experimental physics.[2]

Mill was also engaged in various political and social causes. He wrote extensively for several radical periodicals such as the *Westminster Review* (which he edited for a number of years) and wrote widely for the popular press. It is amazing to note that all of Mill's

---

[1]   This particularly apt expression is from the editor's introduction to Mill's *Autobiography*, ed. J. M. Robson, London, Penguin Books, 1989, p. 4.

[2]   These details are gathered from Mill's *Autobiography*. The list of books and authors mentioned here is far from complete; for a survey that attempts to identify everything Mill read up until the age of 16, see his *Collected Works*, vol. 1, Toronto, University of Toronto Press, 1981, Appendix B.

major contributions were made in what was essentially his spare time, since he served for more than 30 years as a senior officer of the British East India Company, overseeing all correspondence and non-military policy implementation for British India. It might be said, with only slight exaggeration, that Mill governed India at a distance while carrying on his various political, philosophical, and scientific researches. Upon the dissolution of the East India Company, Mill retired to an even more active public life, and served as a member of parliament from 1865 to 1868.

It is unsurprising that a life lived at such pace and pitch would bring its share of personal challenges. By his own assessment the watershed event in Mill's intellectual development was a mental crisis that he experienced beginning in 1826.[3] Depression overwhelmed the young Mill when he suddenly realised that the utilitarian causes for which he had worked with such assiduity were meaningless to him.[4] He felt no emotional attachment to the projects and causes which had heretofore given shape to every aspect of his existence.

Mill attributes his crisis to an educational regime which emphasised impersonal analysis to the detriment of the cultivation of the sentiments. To motivate a person to care, it is first necessary to teach them how to feel. For Mill, schooling in the sentiments took the form of an extensive reading of the poet Wordsworth, and by dint of such reading Mill gradually emerged from his depression by 1828. This insight, echoes of which occur within the *Inaugural Address* selected below, became a central pillar of Mill's educational philosophy. He expresses the point with characteristic eloquence:

> I, for the first time, gave its proper place, among the prime necessities of human well-being, to the internal culture of the individual. I ceased to attach almost exclusive importance to the ordering of outward circumstances, and the training of the human being for speculation and for action. I had now learnt by

[3]   Mill devotes an entire chapter in his *Autobiography* documenting his falling into and eventual emergence from depression. See *ibid.*, ch. 5.

[4]   In his own words: 'Suppose that all your objects in life were realised; that all the changes in institutions and opinions which you are looking forward to, could be completely effected at this very instant: would this be a great joy and happiness to you? And an irrepressible self-consciousness distinctly answered, 'No!' At this my heart sank within me: the whole foundation on which my life was constructed fell down. All my happiness was to have been found in the continual pursuit of this end. The end had ceased to charm, and how could there ever again be any interest in the means? I seem to have nothing left to live for.' (*Ibid.*, p. 112.)

experience that the passive susceptibilities needed to be cultivated as well as the active capacities, and required to be nour-
ished and enriched as well as guided....The cultivation of the
feelings became one of the cardinal points in my ethical and
philosophical creed.[5]

Mill made significant contributions to numerous disciplines. His
System of Logic[6] contains one of the fullest treatments of inductive
logic to date, and supplies an empiricist account of how it is possible
to learn through experience without the aid of any innate or infused
ideas. (Mill therefore occupies an extreme position opposed to
Augustine on the question of how learning occurs, since Augustine
defends the notion of innate and infused ideas. Aquinas and
Newman occupy intermediate positions since they think that there
are principles of understanding innate to us given our natures as
human beings created by God. However, they both accept that the
content of our knowing is built on empirical experience.) Mill's contributions to ethics and social philosophy include his classic essays
On Liberty, *Utilitarianism*, and *Considerations on Representative Government*.[7] Among other prominent social causes, Mill was an aboli-
tionist and one of the earliest and most influential voices in favour of
women's rights, advocating full gender equality in all political,
legal, social, and domestic relations. (These latter views are argued
at length in *The Subjection of Women*,[8] and the political context is perhaps best exemplified in *On Liberty*.)

One of the characteristic concerns of Mill is embedded in the social
conditions of his time and is directly related to his social agenda and
his utilitarian perspective. More than any of our other authors, Mill
is keenly aware of the changing economic forces that impact the
material conditions of education and this plays a central role in the
position he takes in his *Inaugural Address*. Thus, in the social sciences,
particularly worthy of mention is Mill's *Principles of Political Economy*. Synoptic in its coverage, this became the standard work in eco-

---

[5]   *Ibid.*, p. 118.

[6]   J.S. Mill, *System of Logic, Ratiocinative and Inductive*, Charleston, Nabu Press, 2010.

[7]   Here we use the following convenient editions of these texts: *On Liberty*, Buffalo,
      Prometheus Books, 1986; *Utilitarianism*, Buffalo, Prometheus Books, 1987;
      Considerations on Representative Government, Rockville, Serenity Publishers, 2008.
      (The Prometheus edition of this last should be avoided as a significant amount of
      text has been omitted.)

[8]   J. S. Mill, *The Subjection of Women*, Buffalo, Prometheus Books, 1986.

nomics for more than a generation and is acknowledged as the definitive culmination of classical economics.[9]

The lasting contribution of the *Principles of Political Economy* is that, contrary to preceding economists, Mill identified the proper focus of economics with the laws of economic production, not the laws of economic distribution. According to Mill, production is governed by laws that operate in a scientifically regular way whereas how any society distributes its goods is determined entirely at the discretion of human free choice.[10] This move had profound implications for the way economics developed as a science. One upshot of the shift of perspective is that, post Mill, economists have largely considered themselves exempt from examining the normative dimensions of their discipline. It became the economist's job to chart out the most efficient path to allow consumers to realise their pre-given desires. This led to an intense focus on private goods and a somewhat grudging acceptance of public goods. Other sorts of economic goods, which might conceivably have an explicitly normative dimension insofar as their provision was expected to involve a critique of prevailing levels of consumer desire, are *a priori* excluded from economic analysis.[11] In short, it might be argued that Mill did for the science of economics what Newman did for university education: drain it of its explicit ethical content.[12]

The major forces dominating the debates on educational theory and practice in the 19th century, as we have seen in our discussion of Newman, were the antagonisms between traditional elites and more egalitarian social activists. The former defended an exclusive liberal (versus manual or servile) education based upon the Greek and Roman classics, and more broadly literature, while the egalitarians advocated a utilitarian approach oriented toward broad social reform. In terms of education, the mainstream utilitarian approach

---

[9] Classical economics is that style of economic analysis and presentation prior to the introduction of explanatory graphs and mathematical analysis which became common with the work of Alfred Marshall. See Marshall, *Principles of Economics*, Amherst, Prometheus Press, 1997.

[10] Mill was explicit about the distinction: see *Principles of Political Economy*, Amherst, Prometheus Books, 2004, Book II, Ch. 1.

[11] A clear example of economic goods of this type are *merit goods*. For discussion see *An Anthology Regarding Merit Goods: The Unfinished Ethical Revolution in Economic Theory*, ed. W. Ver Eecke, Indiana, Purdue University Press, 2007.

[12] R. L. Heilbroner, in *The Worldly Philosophers*, New York, Simon and Schuster, 1961, pp. 107-109, correctly identifies the momentous impact of Mill's new focus on the laws of production, but misconstrues the ethical implications of this shift.

was concerned with providing an immediately useful pragmatic education focused upon the sciences and mechanical arts, and saw little use for the conservative focus on the liberal arts.[13] In this debate Mill adopts a middle position. He rejects as a false dichotomy the exclusive claims to teaching either the classical curriculum or the modern scientific-oriented one. Instead, he advocates a more efficient teaching method that does away with the time-consuming composition of verses in dead languages. This would, he claims, open up sufficient time within the curriculum to teach both.

There is one other broad feature of Mill's educational philosophy that deserves a brief comment. Mill, unlike all our other authors, is an agnostic. Thus the debates that exercised so much of Newman's reflections on the role of theology in the university are scarcely addressed by Mill. It is his general position that religious matters should be the concern of the private, not public, domain, except that he will allow a place for the descriptive study of religion in the university. By an ironic twist of fate, this is what Newman's programme led to in practice as well.

There can be little doubt that the most pervasive influence on Mill's philosophy of education was utilitarianism, though, as we shall see, Mill's version of utilitarianism deviates in certain important respects from its classic statement in Jeremy Bentham. Mill describes *utilitarianism* thus: 'The creed which accepts as the foundation of morals *utility*, or the *greatest happiness principle*, holds that actions are right in proportion as they tend to promote happiness, wrong as they tend to promote the reverse of happiness. By 'happiness' is intended pleasure, and the absence of pain; by 'unhappiness', pain, and the privation of pleasure.'[14]

Mill is clear that motives and intentions do not count when we assess ethical appropriateness. As he puts it: 'the motive has nothing to do with the morality of the action, though much with the worth of the agent.'[15] In taking this view, Mill departs from the moral schemas presented by Augustine, Aquinas, and Newman who take motivation to be central to moral evaluation.

In Bentham's version of utilitarianism, all pleasures and pains are considered to be homogenous. According to this model, one could in

[13] For observations on Mill's specific educational milieu, see E. Anderson, 'John Stuart Mill: Democracy as Sentimental Education', *Philosophers on Education*, ed. A. O. Rorty, London, Routledge, 1998, p. 335.

[14] J. S. Mill, *Utilitarianism*, Buffalo, Prometheus Books, 1987, pp. 16-17.

[15] *Ibid.*, p. 29.

principle scientifically measure the pleasure afforded by different actions by studying human physiology. Indeed, Bentham proposed a 'hedonic calculus' — a quasi-scientific procedure for determining amounts of pleasure and pain. This position has the attractive feature of holding out hope that we may one day discover through scientific advancement those actions that lead to the maximisation of human happiness, and so we might place ethics on a firm scientific footing.[16]

Mill's account of pleasure departs from this model in that he admits the existence of higher and lower pleasures that are not only heterogeneous but incommensurable.[17] Higher pleasures, which are often intellectual in nature and embody ideals constitutive of human dignity, such as sympathy and autonomy, trump any quantity of qualitatively baser pleasures. In distinguishing higher and lower pleasures Mill interestingly undercuts one of the central platforms of Bentham's utilitarianism. Bentham had thought the pleasure of the intellectual aesthete counts equally with that of the lady who drinks gin. In denying this, Mill allows for a dimension of elitism in his thinking which squares well with the notion of self-cultivation elaborated in the *Inaugural Address*.

To determine which pleasures are higher and which lower, the procedure Mill advocates is to survey those individuals who have experienced both sorts of pleasure. 'It is better to be a human being dissatisfied than a pig satisfied; better to be Socrates dissatisfied than a fool satisfied. And if the fool, or the pig, are of a different opinion, it is because they only know their own side of the question. The other party to the comparison knows both sides.'[18]

While there is much that is attractive in Mill's view, in accepting the existence of incommensurable pleasures he has deprived utilitarianism of any obvious scientific foundation because the subjective dimension of the procedure for weighing respective pleasures

---

[16] For a well-known objection to this understanding of utilitarianism, see R. Nozick's thought experiment involving the 'experience machine' in *Anarchy, State, and Utopia*, New York, Basic Books, 1974, pp. 42–45.

[17] In *Utilitarianism* Mill writes that 'It is quite compatible with the principle of utility to recognise the fact, that some *kinds* of pleasure are more desirable and more valuable than others. It would be absurd that while, in estimating all other things, quality is considered as well as quantity, the estimation of pleasures should be supposed to depend on quantity alone.' *Ibid.*, p. 18.

[18] *Ibid.*, p. 20. There are many objections to this position. For instance, there may be value to an integrated life that is chaste, and it would be odd to say that only those who have lost their chastity are in a position to judge its relative superiority.

undercuts the possibility of Bentham's hedonic calculus. What is more, the existence of incommensurable pleasures creates conceptual difficulties for those social sciences, economics in particular, that rely upon utilitarian calculations to express consumer preferences for various goods on the same scale. How many ice cream cones are worth either learning to play the piano or coming to appreciate poetry? What basket of goods should we prefer to maximise the happiness of the greatest number?

The connection between Mill's utilitarianism and his ambitions for educational reform are clear. He writes: 'Next to selfishness, the principal cause which makes life unsatisfactory is want of mental cultivation.' [19] The capacity of education to open up students to the higher pleasures of the intellect and, in doing so, groom an intellectual elite capable of fostering and carrying through appropriate social reforms, is a defining note of Mill's educational agenda. It may be noted that there is an implicit tension in Mill's advocacy of broadly egalitarian social and educational reform and his staunch elitism and commitment to the traditional liberal arts framework. This tension can partly be overcome by observing that Mill is an egalitarian with respect to the capacities all human beings have available for cultivation, but he is an elitist with respect to the individual capacities within a person to be actualised. [20]

While Mill in the literary form of the *Inaugural Address* is not explicitly committed to the dialectical model adopted by Augustine and Aquinas, he is nonetheless deeply concerned with bringing out the powers latent in learners and with the critical and evaluative dimensions of understanding, teaching, and learning. The value of dialectic and Socratic-style education is discussed at length in various works by Mill,[21] though it does not occupy as explicit a role in the *Inaugural Address*; however the assumption of full freedom of intel-

---

[19] *Ibid.*, p. 24. He adds: 'A cultivated mind (I do not mean that of a philosopher, but any mind to which the fountains of knowledge have been opened and which has been taught, in any tolerable degree, to exercise its faculties) finds sources of inexhaustible interest in all that surrounds it; in the objects of nature, the achievements of art, the imaginations of poetry, the incidents of history, the ways of mankind, past and present, and their prospects in the future....Now there is absolutely no reason in the nature of things why an amount of mental culture sufficient to give an intelligent interest in these objects of contemplation, should not be the inheritance of everyone born in a civilised country.' *Ibid.*, pp. 24-25.

[20] See also E. Anderson, *op. cit.*

[21] See e.g. *Autobiography*, pp. 38-39, and *On Liberty*, *passim*.

lectual investigation, discussion, collaborative learning, and self-discovery are certainly presumed.

Understanding the *Inaugural Address*

The occasion of the *Inaugural Address* was Mill's election by the students of the University of St Andrews to the office of Lord Rector in 1866. This is remarkable given that Mill himself had never graduated or for that matter formally attended any university. He delivered his lecture on 1 February 1867 over the course of three hours.[22]

It is prudent to acknowledge that there may be some difficulty involved in interpreting Mill's *Inaugural Address*, since, as a committed utilitarian, he was primarily concerned with producing useful effects and only secondarily with the public articulation of abstract truth.[23] Nonetheless, in his own assessment of the *Address* in his *Autobiography*, Mill summarises his contribution in these words:

> The position I took up, vindicating the high educational value alike of the old classic and the new scientific studies, on even stronger grounds than are urged by most of their advocates, and insisting that it is only the stupid inefficiency of the usual teaching which makes those studies be regarded as competitors instead of allies, was, I think, calculated, not only to aid and stimulate the improvement which has happily commenced in the national institutions for higher education, but to diffuse juster ideas than we often find even in highly educated men on the conditions of the highest mental cultivation.[24]

As Mill sees it, he makes two key contributions. First, Mill elevates technical and scientific education to the status of university subjects. There is, in Mill, a typically utilitarian hierarchy of scientific and technical subjects, such that certain disciplines are privileged to the degree that they are made precise by mathematics. The social sciences, including economics, are inferior to more precise subjects like

---

[22] Apart from Mill's *Autobiography*, on the details of his life we have consulted in particular R. Reeves, *John Stuart Mill: Victorian Firebrand*, London, Atlantic Books, 2008, and N. Capaldi, *John Stuart Mill: A Biography*, Cambridge, Cambridge University Press, 2004.

[23] Consider this revealing passage from his *Autobiography*: 'I was not only as ardent as ever for democratic institutions, but earnestly hoped that … anti-property doctrines might spread widely among the poorer classes; not that I thought those doctrines true, or desired that they should be acted on, but in order that the higher classes might be made to see that they had more to fear from the poor when uneducated, than when educated.' *Op. cit.*, pp. 136-137

[24] *Autobiography*, p. 225.

physics; and social sciences should explicitly adopt the methodologies of the positive sciences.[25]

Mill's second key contribution, which is easy for us to overlook, is the central role he accords to aesthetic education and the role of the fine arts. As a result of the rigours of his own education and the mental crisis he experienced, Mill insists on the value and necessity of educating the sentiments as a counterweight to the exclusive development of analytic intellectual capacities. The heart must be schooled as much as the mind, for education promotes the autonomy of holistic individuals in keeping with the Romantic conception of personal self-actualisation.[26]

Mill conceives of education in broad terms as the process by which a person is shaped as an individual. The university as an institution has as its goal the production of cultivated individuals. Cultivation extends over the entire range of personal formation from family life through schooling and into society at large, in which individuals are expected to take an active part. One fundamental arena in personal formation is the university.

A university for Mill is not supposed to be a place of professional education because the worth of civilisation does not principally depend on professional education, and because professional education is needed only by a minority. Rather, the university should elicit mental habits that direct the use of professional and scientific knowledge. It ought to systematise and unify knowledge. It does so by imparting a general and liberal education, *general* because it is both literary (including the classical languages) and scientific; and *liberal* because aimed at strengthening, exalting, purifying, and beautifying human nature. The cultivation of habits supportive of these goals entails rejecting the notion that education is primarily rote memorisation. Rather, education is essentially critical and reflective. Mill, like Newman, embraces the universal and unifying role of the university. There is no limit to the variety of subjects one may learn, but one must guard against studying a particular subject to the exclusion of others as this will tend to narrow and pervert the mind.

Mill contends that we should combine a minute knowledge of one subject with a general knowledge of many subjects. To have a general knowledge of a subject is to know thoroughly only its leading truths. It is this combination of depth and breath that leads to an

[25] As Mill writes: 'I already regarded the methods of physical science as the proper models for political.' *Ibid.,* p. 132.

[26] See Capaldi, *op. cit.,* pp. 252-254, 361-362, and especially 329-330.

enlightened public, capable of appreciating experts and leaders and of distinguishing them from charlatans and demagogues. In forming such judgments we do well to mark the dividing line between what we know accurately and what we do not.

Mill thus thinks that a university education need not address every subject in depth or even every subject. Some subjects, including geography and history, are better learnt independently (though philosophy of history should be taught). Others, especially modern languages, are more readily acquired in a different environment, by spending time in foreign countries. He does think the university should require a mastery of Latin and Greek. Interestingly, this is not primarily because the languages of Greece and Rome constitute the patrimony of Western culture, and in studying them we better understand ourselves (as Newman thought); rather, reading Latin and Greek literature, for Mill, puts us in contact with cultures radically alien to our own.

Mastery of Latin and Greek is needed for many reasons. First, the tendency to mistake words for things (echoing a concern raised by Augustine) is often corrected by translating one language to another. Translation strips idiomatic expressions of their power to deceive. Second, without knowing the language of a people, we never really know their thoughts, their feelings, or their character. Hence, such knowledge is needed to correct our opinions. Mill implicitly acknowledges the homogeneity of modern European culture, and so the study of Latin and Greek is valuable precisely because it puts us in contact with rich cultures possessed of thoughts and assumptions different from the modern European. Third, no modern language is as formally valuable as Latin and Greek because these have the most regular and complicated structures. Their grammar is expressive of logic and thus grounds analysis of the thinking process. Fourth, works in Latin and Greek provide a rich store of experience of human nature and conduct, and thus wisdom. Fifth, their literature is, for socio-cultural reasons, aesthetically superior and lays an admirable model for ethical and philosophical culture. The extant works of ancient authors typically have something important to communicate and they do so with admirable concision.

Partly because of the great advances made in the sciences in the 19th century, including the social sciences, Mill, perhaps more than our other three authors, is sensitive to the role that empirical science plays in advancing wider society. Scientific instruction is important because we should be conversant with the laws of nature—in other words, the properties of the things which we have to work with, work among, and work upon. Moreover, unless an elementary knowledge of scientific truths is diffused among the public, we would not recognise legitimate authorities and be able to evaluate appropriate practices. Mill thinks scientific instruction is especially valuable because it involves the training and disciplining of the mind. It is, in Mill's opinion, chiefly in regard to our contemporary expertise in empirical reasoning that modern society displays its advantages over the ancients. The study of the sciences thus inculcates habits of mind that are truth-directed and which are unlikely to develop without explicit cultivation, thus rendering the public vulnerable to superstitions.

Truth can be discovered by observation, experimentation, and reasoning, and this is best displayed within the physical sciences. In this regard, Mill points to astronomy and physics as exemplifying the discovery of truth by reasoning and direct observation. Experimental sciences, such as chemistry, provide models for gathering and weighing evidence.

However, it is chiefly from mathematics we come to understand that there is a road to truth by means of abstract reasoning. Our first studies in geometry teach us two invaluable lessons. First, we are enjoined to clearly express all the premises from which we intend to reason. Second, we learn to make each logical step clear, separate, and secure. The success of applied mathematics in the empirical sciences demonstrates the universe's intelligible structure and our capacity to understand it.

Unlike our other three authors, Mill thinks that the social sciences are integral to the university curriculum. Again he emphasises the habits of mind produced by their study. For example, the study of political science requires the union of induction and deduction, and appeals to an abstract understanding of human nature that is in some sense *a priori*.

Empirical sciences, mathematics, and the social sciences provide instances of the application of good reasoning. The art and science of good reasoning is logic. Logic has two parts: ratiocinative (that is, deductive) and inductive logic. Deduction keeps us right in reasoning from premises, and induction guides us to draw appropriate conclusions from observations. Logic, even if confined to the theory of names, propositions, and the syllogism, is of the utmost intellectual value. It enables us to guard against fallacy, is straightforward, and may be learnt quickly. Without logic there is no sure guide to truth, even in the experimental sciences, for without logic we could not distinguish reliable methods from poor ones. Logic gives form to our truth-seeking virtues and is the means by which they are operationalised.

Other less-developed sciences should be taught as part of a general university education. Physiology, the understanding of the true conditions of health and disease, deserves to be taught because of its potential utility. As a discipline, physiology sheds light upon and is informed by the disciplines it borders. Mill points to its relation to psychology and the range of questions which emerge from their conjunction, as they open up to metaphysics, bringing in questions such as whether the will is free or determined by physical causes. It is a part of liberal education to know that such deeper controversies exist, and, in a general way, what has been said on them. Mill also sees the study of metaphysics as providing the training ground and impetus for those keener intellects who will push forward speculation within the various disciplines. It is interesting to note that despite Mill's egalitarian propensities he remains in some ways elitist in his view of intellectual potential. He thinks that intellectual elites are necessary to leaven society at large and that the university is the primary locus of cultivation for these elites.[27]

The university should also teach ethics and politics. For Mill these disciplines have value in that they train students in the interpretation and qualitative assessment of facts and stretch the mind to discover associations. Mill is very concerned that subjects like ethics and the philosophy of history should not be delivered as if students were empty vessels waiting to be filled, nor as comprising ready-made truths to be imbibed without critical reflection. The key facts of these disciplines should already be familiar to the student from prior training or private study. At the university level the full active powers of the student must be brought to bear in interpreting and evaluating the facts and theories presented. He remains ada-

[27] As Mill puts it rather bluntly in his *Autobiography*: 'the mass of mankind…must, from the necessity of the case, accept most of their opinions on political and social matters, as they do on physical, from the authority of those who have bestowed more study on those subjects than they generally have it in their power to do.' *Op. cit.*, p. 162. Such elitist language is common in Mill's writings. For instance, he also claims that a 'change of character must take place both in the uncultivated herd who now compose the labouring masses, and in the immense majority of their employers.' *Ibid.*, 176. In his professional capacity as a senior bureaucrat of the British East India Company, Mill the professed radical democrat and author of *On Liberty* was a firm and ardent imperialist.

mant that what matters most in education is cultivating an aptitude for uncovering the meaning of facts, not the facts themselves.

The study of ethics, politics, and the philosophy of history directly relate to the duties of active citizenship. For Mill, politics should include study of political economy, or as we would call it today, economics. These subjects open to the study of jurisprudence and the study of law in its formulation and application more generally. Mill's cosmopolitanism is evident in his suggestion that international law should be taught in all universities. He conceives of international law as codifying the norms governing civilised communities, and thus knowledge of such rules of conduct and the sentiments that give rise to them are essential for informed democratic citizenship.

Like Newman, Mill thinks that neither inculcation of morality nor religious formation are the particular provenance of university education. These are more appropriately connected with our social teachers, primarily the family and broader community. The university teacher, however, should act as a moral exemplar, prompting the students to emulate those habits of refined and elevated sentiment manifested in his or her conduct.

Mill seems to tolerate university-level education in religion. This might be partially explained by the specific occasion of his lecture, for the Church of Scotland was not established in Scottish higher education in the formal sense that the Church of England was in English universities. Mill's preference for religious education in universities is akin to what we would now call religious studies, in which religions are studied not in respect to their truth but rather with regard to their chief doctrines and sociological features set out in a descriptive manner. At all costs the study of religion should, according to Mill, not be confessional. The university must be open to diversity of religious opinion and practice, including freethinking.

Mill's own life experience convinced him of the importance of educating the sentiments because such education is required for the development of a rounded personality. So, inquiry into the nature of Beauty, study of the fine arts, and general aesthetic education should be part of the university curriculum. The university thus has an indirect and supporting role to play in moral education, insofar as it can, by calling forth sympathetic responses along aesthetic lines, provide matter for the development of the morally significant sentiments. Mill takes up a position articulated also by Augustine, Aquinas, and Newman, in holding that cultivation of the whole student must involve not just knowing truth and virtue, but in coming to love them. While Mill, as an agnostic, lacks a developed doctrine of sin, he replaces it with an education in the Arts, for the high standards of execution in artistic production teach us never to be satisfied with our own imperfections. Beauty bears the mark of perfection.

A university education that addresses the critical, analytic, and sentimental faculties of the student will bring forth a richer and more varied interest in the value of life itself and will pay social dividends. This restless striving for improvement of self and society captures the dynamic personal and social dialectic of the *Inaugural Address*, and displays much of the faith in progress characteristic of the Victorian age. Education is a life-long pursuit, never complete, never an object of complacency. As Mill writes: 'A pupil from whom nothing is ever demanded which he cannot do, never does all he can.'[28]

---

[28] *Autobiography*, p. 45.

CHAPTER 5.2

Mill: Text

Mill: Inaugural Address Delivered To The University Of St Andrews

IN COMPLYING WITH THE CUSTOM which prescribes that the person whom you have called by your suffrages to the honorary presidency of your University should embody in an Address a few thoughts on the subjects which most nearly concern a seat of liberal education; let me begin by saying, that this usage appears to me highly commendable. Education, in its larger sense, is one of the most inexhaustible of all topics. Though there is hardly any subject on which so much has been written, by so many of the wisest men, it is as fresh to those who come to it with a fresh mind, a mind not hopelessly filled full with other people's conclusions, as it was to the first explorers of it: and notwithstanding the great mass of excellent things which have been said respecting it, no thoughtful person finds any lack of things both great and small still waiting to be said, or waiting to be developed and followed out to their consequences. Education, moreover, is one of the subjects which most essentially require to be considered by various minds, and from a variety of points of view. For, of all many-sided subjects, it is the one which has the greatest number of sides. Not only does it include whatever we do for ourselves, and whatever is done for us by others, for the express purpose of bringing us somewhat nearer to the perfection of our nature; it does more: in its largest acceptation, it comprehends even the indirect effects produced on character and on the human faculties, by things of which the direct purposes are quite different; by laws, by forms of government, by the industrial arts, by modes of social life; nay even by physical facts not dependent on human will; by climate, soil, and local position. Whatever helps to shape the human being; to make the individual what he is, or hinder him from

being what he is not — is part of his education. And a very bad education it often is; requiring all that can be done by cultivated intelligence and will, to counteract its tendencies. To take an obvious
instance; the niggardliness of Nature in some places, by engrossing
the whole energies of the human being in the mere preservation of
life, and her over-bounty in others, affording a sort of brutish subsis-
tence on too easy terms, with hardly any exertion of the human faculties, are both hostile to the spontaneous growth and development
of the mind; and it is at those two extremes of the scale that we find
human societies in the state of most unmitigated savagery. I shall
confine myself, however, to education in the narrower sense; the culture which each generation purposely gives to those who are to be its
successors, in order to qualify them for at least keeping up, and if
possible for raising, the level of improvement which has been
attained. Nearly all here present are daily occupied either in receiving or in giving this sort of education: and the part of it which most
concerns you at present is that in which you are yourselves
engaged — the stage of education which is the appointed business of
a national University.

The proper function of an University in national education is tolerably well understood. At least there is a tolerably general agreement
about what an University is not. It is not a place of professional education. Universities are not intended to teach the knowledge
required to fit men for some special mode of gaining their livelihood.
Their object is not to make skilful lawyers, or physicians, or engi-
neers, but capable and cultivated human beings. It is very right that
there should be public facilities for the study of professions. It is well
that there should be Schools of Law, and of Medicine, and it would
be well if there were schools of engineering, and the industrial arts.
The countries which have such institutions are greatly the better for
them; and there is something to be said for having them in the same
localities, and under the same general superintendence, as the establishments devoted to education properly so called. But these things
are no part of what every generation owes to the next, as that on
which its civilisation and worth will principally depend. They are
needed only by a comparatively few, who are under the strongest
private inducements to acquire them by their own efforts; and even
those few do not require them until after their education, in the ordinary sense, has been completed. Whether those whose speciality
they are, will learn them as a branch of intelligence or as a mere
trade, and whether, having learnt them, they will make a wise and

conscientious use of them or the reverse, depends less on the manner in which they are taught their profession, than upon what sort of minds they bring to it—what kind of intelligence, and of conscience, the general system of education has developed in them. Men are men before they are lawyers, or physicians, or merchants, or manufacturers; and if you make them capable and sensible men, they will make themselves capable and sensible lawyers or physicians. What professional men should carry away with them from an University, is not professional knowledge, but that which should direct the use of their professional knowledge, and bring the light of general culture to illuminate the technicalities of a special pursuit. Men may be competent lawyers without general education, but it depends on general education to make them philosophic lawyers—who demand, and are capable of apprehending, principles, instead of merely cramming their memory with details. And so of all other useful pursuits, mechanical included. Education makes a man a more intelligent shoemaker, if that be his occupation, but not by teaching him how to make shoes; it does so by the mental exercise it gives, and the habits it impresses.

This, then, is what a mathematician would call the higher limit of University education: its province ends where education, ceasing to be general, branches off into departments adapted to the individual's destination in life. The lower limit is more difficult to define. An University is not concerned with elementary instruction: the pupil is supposed to have acquired that before coming here. But where does elementary instruction end, and the higher studies begin? Some have given a very wide extension to the idea of elementary instruction. According to them, it is not the office of an University to give instruction in single branches of knowledge from the commencement. What the pupil should be taught here (they think), is to methodise his knowledge: to look at every separate part of it in its relation to the other parts, and to the whole; combining the partial glimpses which he has obtained of the field of human knowledge at different points, into a general map, if I may so speak, of the entire region; observing how all knowledge is connected, how we ascend to one branch by means of another, how the higher modifies the lower, and the lower helps us to understand the higher; how every existing reality is a compound of many properties, of which each science or distinct mode of study reveals but a small part, but the whole of which must be included to enable us to know it truly as a fact in Nature, and not as a mere abstraction.

This last stage of general education, destined to give the pupil a comprehensive and connected view of the things which he has already learnt separately, includes a philosophic study of the Methods of the sciences; the modes in which the human intellect proceeds from the known to the unknown. We must be taught to generalise our conception of the resources which the human mind possesses for the exploration of nature; to understand how man discovers the real facts of the world, and by what tests he can judge whether he has really found them. And doubtless this is the crown and consummation of a liberal education: but before we restrict an University to this highest department of instruction — before we confine it to teaching, not knowledge, but the philosophy of knowledge — we must be assured that the knowledge itself has been acquired elsewhere. Those who take this view of the function of an University are not wrong in thinking that the schools, as distinguished from the universities, ought to be adequate to teaching every branch of general instruction required by youth, so far as it can be studied apart from the rest. But where are such schools to be found? Since science assumed its modern character, nowhere: and in these islands less even than elsewhere. This ancient kingdom, thanks to its great religious reformers, had the inestimable advantage, denied to its southern sister, of excellent parish schools, which gave, really and not in pretence, a considerable amount of valuable literary instruction to the bulk of the population, two centuries earlier than in any other country. But schools of a still higher description have been, even in Scotland, so few and inadequate, that the Universities have had to perform largely the functions which ought to be performed by schools; receiving students at an early age, and undertaking not only the work for which the schools should have prepared them, but much of the preparation itself. Every Scottish University is not an University only, but a High School, to supply the deficiency of other schools. And if the English Universities do not do the same, it is not because the same need does not exist, but because it is disregarded. Youths come to the Scottish Universities ignorant, and are there taught. The majority of those who come to the English Universities come still more ignorant, and ignorant they go away.

In point of fact, therefore, the office of a Scottish University comprises the whole of a liberal education, from the foundations upwards. And the scheme of your Universities has, almost from the beginning, really aimed at including the whole, both in depth and in breadth. You have not, as the English Universities so long did, confined all the stress of your teaching, all your real effort to teach, within the limits of two subjects, the classical languages and mathematics. You did not wait till the last few years to establish a Natural Science and a Moral Science Tripos. Instruction in both those departments was organised long ago: and your teachers of those subjects have not been nominal professors, who did not lecture: some of the greatest names in physical and in moral science have taught in your Universities, and by their teaching contributed to form some of the most distinguished intellects of the last and present centuries. To comment upon the course of education at the Scottish Universities is to pass in review every essential department of general culture. The best use, then, which I am able to make of the present occasion, is to offer a few remarks on each of those departments, considered in its relation to human cultivation at large: adverting to the nature of the claims which each has to a place in liberal education; in what special manner they each conduce to the improvement of the individual mind and the benefit of the race; and how they all conspire to the common end, the strengthening, exalting, purifying, and beautifying of our common nature, and the fitting out of mankind with the necessary mental implements for the work they have to perform through life.

Let me first say a few words on the great controversy of the present day with regard to the higher education, the difference which most broadly divides educational reformers and conservatives; the vexed question between the ancient languages and the modern sciences and arts; whether general education should be classical—let me use a wider expression, and say literary—or scientific. A dispute as endlessly, and often as fruitlessly agitated as that old controversy which it resembles, made memorable by the names of Swift and Sir William Temple in England and Fontenelle in France—the contest for superiority between the ancients and the moderns. This question, whether we should be taught the classics or the sciences, seems to me, I confess, very like a dispute whether painters should cultivate drawing or colouring, or, to use a more homely illustration, whether a tailor should make coats or trousers. I can only reply by the question, why not both? Can anything deserve the name of a good education which does not include literature and science too? If there were no more to be said than that scientific education teaches us to think, and literary education to express our thoughts, do we not require both? and is not any one a poor, maimed, lopsided fragment of humanity who is deficient in either? We are not obliged to ask ourselves whether it is more important to know the languages or the sciences. Short as life is, and shorter still as we make it by the time we waste on things which are neither business, nor meditation, nor pleasure, we are not so badly off that our scholars need be ignorant of the laws and properties of the world they live in, or our scientific men destitute of poetic feeling and artistic cultivation. I am amazed at the limited conception which many educational reformers have formed to themselves of a human being's power of acquisition. The study of science, they truly say, is indispensable: our present education neglects it: there is truth in this too, though it is not all truth: and they think it impossible to find room for the studies which they desire to encourage, but by turning out, at least from general education, those which are now chiefly cultivated. How absurd, they say, that the whole of boyhood should be taken up in acquiring an imperfect knowledge of two dead languages. Absurd indeed: but is the human mind's capacity to learn, measured by that of Eton and Westminster to teach? I should prefer to see these reformers pointing their attacks against the shameful inefficiency of the schools, public and private, which pretend to teach these two languages and do not. I should like to hear them denounce the wretched methods of teaching, and the criminal idleness and supineness, which waste the entire boyhood of the pupils without really giving to most of them more than a smattering, if even that, of the only kind of knowledge which is even pretended to be cared for. Let us try what conscientious and intelligent teaching can do, before we presume to decide what cannot be done.

Scotland has on the whole, in this respect, been considerably more fortunate than England. Scotch youths have never found it impossible to leave school or the university having learnt somewhat of other things besides Greek and Latin; and why? Because Greek and Latin have been better taught. A beginning of classical instruction has all along been made in the common schools: and the common schools of Scotland, like her Universities, have never been the mere shams that the English Universities were during the last century, and the greater part of the English classical schools still are. The only tolerable Latin grammars for school purposes that I know of, which had been produced in these islands until very lately, were written by Scotchmen. Reason, indeed, is beginning to find its way by gradual infiltration even into English schools, and to maintain a contest, though as yet a very unequal one, against routine. A few practical reformers of school tuition, of whom Arnold was the most eminent, have made a beginning of amendment in many things: but reforms, worthy of the name, are always slow, and reform even of governments and churches is not so slow as that of schools, for there is the great preliminary difficulty of fashioning the instruments: of teaching the teachers. If all the improvements in the mode of teaching languages which are already sanctioned by experience, were adopted into our classical schools, we should soon cease to hear of Latin and Greek as studies which must engross the school years, and render impossible any other acquirements. If a boy learnt Greek and Latin on the same principle on which a mere child learns with such ease and rapidity any modern language, namely, by acquiring some familiarity with the vocabulary by practice and repetition, before being troubled with grammatical rules — those rules being acquired with tenfold greater facility when the cases to which they apply are already familiar to the mind; an average schoolboy, long before the age at which schooling terminates, would be able to read fluently and with intelligent interest any ordinary Latin or Greek author in prose or verse, would have a competent knowledge of the grammatical structure of both languages, and have had time besides for an ample amount of scientific instruction. I might go much further; but I am as unwilling to speak out all that I think practicable in this matter, as George Stephenson was about railways, when he calculated the average speed of a train at ten miles an hour, because if he had estimated it higher, the practical men would have turned a deaf ear to him, as that most unsafe character in their estimation, an enthusiast and a visionary. The results have shewn, in that case, who was the real practical man. What the results would shew in the other case, I will not attempt to anticipate. But I will say confidently, that if the two classical languages were properly taught, there would be no need whatever for ejecting them from the school course, in order to have sufficient time for everything else that need be included therein.

Let me say a few words more on this strangely limited estimate of what it is possible for human beings to learn, resting on a tacit assumption that they are already as efficiently taught as they ever can be. So narrow a conception not only vitiates our idea of education, but actually, if we receive it, darkens our anticipations as to the future progress of mankind. For if the inexorable conditions of human life make it useless for one man to attempt to know more than one thing, what is to become of the human intellect as facts accumulate? In every generation, and now more rapidly than ever, the things which it is necessary that somebody should know are more and more multiplied. Every department of knowledge becomes so loaded with details, that one who endeavours to know it with minute accuracy, must confine himself to a smaller and smaller portion of the whole extent: every science and art must be cut up into subdivisions, until each man's portion, the district which he thoroughly knows, bears about the same ratio to the whole range of useful knowledge that the art of putting on a pin's head does to the field of human industry. Now, if in order to know that little completely, it is necessary to remain wholly ignorant of all the rest, what will soon be the worth of a man, for any human purpose except his own infinitesimal fraction of human wants and requirements? His state will be even worse than that of simple ignorance. Experience proves that there is no one study or pursuit, which, practised to the exclusion of all others, does not narrow and pervert the mind; breeding in it a class of prejudices special to that pursuit, besides a general prejudice, common to all narrow specialities, against large views, from an incapacity to take in and appreciate the grounds of them. We should have to expect that human nature would be more and more dwarfed, and unfitted for great things, by its very proficiency in small ones. But matters are not so bad with us: there is no ground for so dreary an anticipation. It is not the utmost limit of human acquirement to know only one thing, but to combine a minute knowledge of one or a few things with a general knowledge of many things. By a general knowledge I do not mean a few vague impressions. An eminent man, one of whose writings is part of the course of this University, Archbishop Whately, has well discriminated between a general knowledge and a superficial knowledge. To have a general knowledge of a subject is to know only its leading truths, but to know these not superficially but thoroughly, so as to have a true conception of the subject in its great features; leaving the minor details to those who require them for the purposes of their special pursuit. There is no incompatibility between knowing a wide range of subjects up to this point, and some one subject with the completeness required by those who make it their principal occupation. It is this combination which gives an enlightened public: a body of cultivated intellects, each taught by its attainments in its own province what real knowledge is, and knowing enough of other subjects to be able to discern who are those that know them better. The amount of knowledge is not to be lightly estimated, which qualifies us for judging to whom we may have recourse for more. The elements of the more important studies being widely diffused, those who have reached the higher summits find a public capable of appreciating their superiority, and prepared to follow their lead. It is thus too that minds are formed capable of guiding and improving public opinion on the greater concerns of practical life. Government and civil society are the most complicated of all subjects accessible to the human mind: and he who would deal competently with them as a thinker, and not as a blind follower of a party, requires not only a general knowledge of the leading facts of life, both moral and material, but an understanding exercised and disciplined in the principles and rules of sound thinking, up to a point which neither the experience of life, nor any one science or branch of knowledge, affords. Let us understand, then, that it should be our aim in learning, not merely to know the one thing which is to be our principal occupation, as well as it can be known, but to do this and also to know something of all the great subjects of human interest: taking care to know that something accurately; marking well the dividing line between what we know accurately and what we do not: and remembering that our object should be to obtain a true view of nature and life in their broad outline, and that it is idle to throw away time upon the details of anything which is to form no part of the occupation of our practical energies.

It by no means follows, however, that every useful branch of general, as distinct from professional, knowledge, should be included in the curriculum of school or university studies. There are things which are better learnt out of school, or when the school years, and even those usually passed in a Scottish university, are over. I do not agree with those reformers who would give a regular and prominent place in the school or university course to modern languages. This is not because I attach small importance to the knowledge of them. No one can in our age be esteemed a well-instructed person who is not familiar with at least the French language, so as to read French books with ease; and there is great use in cultivating a familiarity with German. But living languages are so much more easily acquired by intercourse with those who use them in daily life; a few months in the country itself, if properly employed, go so much farther than as many years of school lessons; that it is really waste of time for those to whom that easier mode is attainable, to labour at them with no help but that of books and masters: and it will in time be made attainable, through international schools and colleges, to many more than at present. Universities do enough to facilitate the study of modern languages, if they give a mastery over that ancient language which is the foundation of most of them, and the possession of which makes it easier to learn four or five of the continental languages than it is to learn one of them without it. Again, it has always seemed to me a great absurdity that history and geography should be taught in schools; except in elementary schools for the children of the labouring classes, whose subsequent access to books is limited. Who ever really learnt history and geography except by private reading? and what an utter failure a system of education must be, if it has not given the pupil a sufficient taste for reading to seek for himself those most attractive and easily intelligible of all kinds of knowledge? Besides, such history and geography as can be taught in schools exercise none of the faculties of the intelligence except the memory. An University is indeed the place where the student should be introduced to the Philosophy of History; where Professors who not merely know the facts but have exercised their minds on them, should initiate him into the causes and explanation, so far as within our reach, of the past life of mankind in its principal features. Historical criticism also—the tests of historical truth—are a subject to which his attention may well be drawn in this stage of his education. But of the mere facts of history, as commonly accepted, what educated youth of any mental activity does not learn as much as is necessary, if he is simply turned loose into an historical library? What he needs on this, and on most other matters of common information, is not that he should be taught it in boyhood, but that abundance of books should be accessible to him.

The only languages, then, and the only literature, to which I would allow a place in the ordinary curriculum, are those of the Greeks and Romans; and to these I would preserve the position in it which they at present occupy. That position is justified, by the great value, in education, of knowing well some other cultivated language and literature than one's own, and by the peculiar value of those particular languages and literatures.

There is one purely intellectual benefit from a knowledge of languages, which I am specially desirous to dwell on. Those who have seriously reflected on the causes of human error, have been deeply impressed with the tendency of mankind to mistake words for things. Without entering into the metaphysics of the subject, we know how common it is to use words glibly and with apparent propriety, and to accept them confidently when used by others, without ever having had any distinct conception of the things denoted by them. To quote again from Archbishop Whately, it is the habit of mankind to mistake familiarity for accurate knowledge. As we seldom think of asking the meaning of what we see every day, so when our ears are used to the sound of a word or a phrase, we do not suspect that it conveys no clear idea to our minds, and that we should have the utmost difficulty in defining it, or expressing, in any other words, what we think we understand by it. Now it is obvious in what manner this bad habit tends to be corrected by the practice of translating with accuracy from one language to another, and hunting out the meanings expressed in a vocabulary with which we have not grown familiar by early and constant use. I hardly know any greater proof of the extraordinary genius of the Greeks, than that they were able to make such brilliant achievements in abstract thought, knowing, as they generally did, no language but their own. But the Greeks did not escape the effects of this deficiency. Their greatest intellects, those who laid the foundation of philosophy and of all our intellectual culture, Plato and Aristotle, are continually led away by words; mistaking the accidents of language for real relations in nature, and supposing that things which have the same name in the Greek tongue must be the same in their own essence. There is a well-known saying of Hobbes, the far-reaching significance of which you will more and more appreciate in proportion to the growth of your own intellect: 'Words are the counters of wise men, but the money of fools.' With the wise man a word stands for the fact which it represents; to the fool it is itself the fact. To carry on Hobbes' metaphor, the counter is far more likely to be taken for merely what it is, by those who are in the habit of using many different kinds of counters. But besides the advantage of possessing another cultivated language, there is a further consideration equally important. Without knowing the language of a people, we never really know their thoughts, their feelings, and their type of character: and unless we do possess this knowledge, of some other people than ourselves, we remain, to the hour of our death, with our intellects only half expanded. Look at a youth who has never been out of his family circle: he never dreams of any other opinions or ways of thinking than those he has been bred up in; or, if he has heard of any such, attributes them to some moral defect, or inferiority of nature or education. If his family are Tory, he cannot conceive the possibility of being a Liberal; if Liberal, of being a Tory. What the notions and habits of a single family are to a boy who has had no intercourse beyond it, the notions and habits of his own country are to him who is ignorant of every other. Those notions and habits are to him human nature itself; whatever varies from them is an unaccountable aberration which he cannot mentally realise: the idea that any other ways can be right, or as near an approach to right as some of his own, is inconceivable to him. This does not merely close his eyes to the many things which every country still has to learn from others: it hinders every country from reaching the improvement which it could otherwise attain by itself. We are not likely to correct any of our opinions or mend any of our ways, unless we begin by conceiving that they are capable of amendment: but merely to know that foreigners think differently from ourselves, without understanding why they do so, or what they really do think, does but confirm us in our self-conceit, and connect our national vanity with the preservation of our own peculiarities. Improvement consists in bringing our opinions into nearer agreement with facts; and we shall not be likely to do this while we look at facts only through glasses coloured by those very opinions. But since we cannot divest ourselves of preconceived notions, there is no known means of eliminating their influence but by frequently using the differently coloured glasses of other people: and those of other nations, as the most different, are the best. But if it is so useful, on this account, to know the language and literature of any other cultivated and civilised people, the most valuable of all to us in this respect are the languages and literature of the ancients. No nations of modern and civilised Europe are so unlike one another, as the Greeks and Romans are unlike all of us; yet without being, as some remote Orientals are, so totally dissimilar, that the labour of a life is required to enable us to understand them. Were this the only gain to be derived from a knowledge of the ancients, it would already place the study of them in a high rank among enlightening and liberalising pursuits. It is of no use saying that we may know them through modern writings. We may know something of them in that way; which is much better than knowing nothing. But modern books do not teach us ancient thought; they teach us some modern writer's notion of ancient thought. Modern books do not shew us the Greeks and Romans: they tell us some modern writer's opinions about the Greeks and Romans. Translations are scarcely better. When we want really to know what a person thinks or says, we seek it at first hand from himself. We do not trust to another person's impression of his meaning, given in another person's words; we refer to his own. Much more is it necessary to do so when his words are in one language, and those of his reporter in another. Modern phraseology never conveys the exact meaning of a Greek writer; it cannot do so, except by a diffuse explanatory circumlocution which no translator dares use. We must be able, in a certain degree, to think in Greek, if we would represent to ourselves how a Greek thought: and this not only in the abstruse region of metaphysics, but about the political, religious, and even domestic concerns of life. I will mention a further aspect of this question, which, though I have not the merit of originating it, I do not remember to have seen noticed in any book. There is no part of our knowledge which it is more useful to obtain at first hand—to go to the fountain head for—than our knowledge of history. Yet this, in most cases, we hardly ever do. Our conception of the past is not drawn from its own records, but from books written about it, containing not the facts, but a view of the facts which has shaped itself in the mind of somebody of our own or a very recent time. Such books are very instructive and valuable; they help us to understand history, to interpret history, to draw just conclusions from it; at the worst, they set us the example of trying to do all this; but they are not themselves history. The knowledge they give is upon trust, and even when they have done their best, it is not only incomplete but partial, because confined to what a few modern writers have seen in the materials, and have thought worth picking out from among them. How little we learn of our own ancestors from Hume, or Hallam, or Macaulay, compared with what we know if we add to what these tell us, even a little reading of cotemporary authors and documents! The most recent historians are so well aware of this, that they fill their pages with extracts from the original materials, feeling that these extracts are the real history, and their comments and thread of narrative are only helps towards understanding it. Now it is part of the great worth to us of our Greek and Latin studies, that in them we do read history in the original sources. We are in actual contact with cotemporary minds; we are not dependent on hearsay; we have something by which we can test and check the representations and theories of modern historians. It may be asked, why then not study the original materials of modern history? I answer, it is highly desirable to do so; and let me remark by the way, that even this requires a dead language; nearly all the documents prior to the Reformation, and many subsequent to it, being written in Latin. But the exploration of these documents, though a most useful pursuit, cannot be a branch of education. Not to speak of their vast extent, and the fragmentary nature of each, the strongest reason is, that in learning the spirit of our own past ages, until a comparatively recent period, from cotemporary writers, we learn hardly anything else. Those authors, with a few exceptions, are little worth reading on their own account. While, in studying the great writers of antiquity, we are not only learning to understand the ancient mind, but laying in a stock of wise thought and observation, still valuable to ourselves; and at the same time making ourselves familiar with a number of the most perfect and finished literary compositions which the human mind has produced—compositions which, from the altered conditions of human life, are likely to be seldom paralleled, in their sustained excellence, by the times to come.

Even as mere languages, no modern European language is so valuable a discipline to the intellect as those of Greece and Rome, on account of their regular and complicated structure. Consider for a moment what grammar is. It is the most elementary part of logic. It is the beginning of the analysis of the thinking process. The principles and rules of grammar are the means by which the forms of language are made to correspond with the universal forms of thought. The distinctions between the various parts of speech, between the cases of nouns, the moods and tenses of verbs, the functions of particles, are distinctions in thought, not merely in words. Single nouns and verbs express objects and events, many of which can be cognised by the senses: but the modes of putting nouns and verbs together, express the relations of objects and events, which can be cognised only by the intellect; and each different mode corresponds to a different relation. The structure of every sentence is a lesson in logic. The various rules of syntax oblige us to distinguish between the subject and predicate of a proposition, between the agent, the action, and the thing acted upon; to mark when an idea is intended to modify or qualify, or merely to unite with, some other idea; what assertions are categorical, what only conditional; whether the intention is to express similarity or contrast, to make a plurality of assertions conjunctively or disjunctively; what portions of a sentence, though grammatically complete within themselves, are mere members or subordinate parts of the assertion made by the entire sentence. Such things form the subject-matter of universal grammar; and the languages which teach it best are those which have the most definite rules, and which provide distinct forms for the greatest number of distinctions in thought, so that if we fail to attend precisely and accurately to any of these, we cannot avoid committing a solecism in language. In these qualities the classical languages have an incomparable superiority over every modern language, and over all languages, dead or living, which have a literature worth being generally studied.

But the superiority of the literature itself, for purposes of education, is still more marked and decisive. Even in the substantial value of the matter of which it is the vehicle, it is very far from having been superseded. The discoveries of the ancients in science have been greatly surpassed, and as much of them as is still valuable loses nothing by being incorporated in modern treatises: but what does not so well admit of being transferred bodily, and has been very imperfectly carried off even piecemeal, is the treasure which they accumulated of what may be called the wisdom of life: the rich store of experience of human nature and conduct, which the acute and observing minds of those ages, aided in their observations by the greater simplicity of manners and life, consigned to their writings, and most of which retains all its value. The speeches in Thucydides; the *Rhetoric, Ethics,* and *Politics* of Aristotle; the Dialogues of Plato; the Orations of Demosthenes; the *Satires,* and especially the *Epistles* of Horace; all the writings of Tacitus; the great work of Quintilian, a repertory of the best thoughts of the ancient world on all subjects connected with education; and, in a less formal manner, all that is left to us of the ancient historians, orators, philosophers, and even dramatists, are replete with remarks and maxims of singular good sense and penetration, applicable both to political and to private life: and the actual truths we find in them are even surpassed in value by the encouragement and help they give us in the pursuit of truth. Human invention has never produced anything so valuable, in the way both of stimulation and of discipline to the inquiring intellect, as the dialectics of the ancients, of which many of the works of Aristotle illustrate the theory, and those of Plato exhibit the practice. No modern writings come near to these, in teaching, both by precept and example, the way to investigate truth, on those subjects, so vastly important to us, which remain matters of controversy, from the difficulty or impossibility of bringing them to a directly experimental test. To question all things; never to turn away from any difficulty; to accept no doctrine either from ourselves or from other people without a rigid scrutiny by negative criticism, letting no fallacy, or incoherence, or confusion of thought, slip by unperceived; above all, to insist upon having the meaning of a word clearly understood before using it, and the meaning of a proposition before assenting to it; these are the lessons we learn from the ancient dialecticians. With all this vigorous management of the negative element, they inspire no scepticism about the reality of truth, or indifference to its pursuit. The noblest enthusiasm, both for the search after truth and for applying it to its highest uses, pervades these writers, Aristotle no less than Plato, though Plato has incomparably the greater power of imparting those feelings to others. In cultivating, therefore, the ancient languages as our best literary education, we are all the while laying an admirable foundation for ethical and philosophical culture. In purely literary excellence — in perfection of form — the pre-eminence of the ancients is not disputed. In every department which they attempted, and they attempted almost all, their composition, like their sculpture, has been to the greatest modern artists an example, to be looked up to with hopeless admiration, but of inappreciable value as a light on high, guiding their own endeavours. In prose and in poetry, in epic, lyric, or dramatic, as in historical, philosophical, and oratorical art, the pinnacle on which they stand is equally eminent. I am now speaking of the form, the artistic perfection of treatment: for, as regards substance, I consider modern poetry to be superior to ancient, in the same manner, though in a less degree, as modern science: it enters deeper into nature. The feelings of the modern mind are more various, more complex and manifold, than those of the ancients ever were. The modern mind is, what the ancient mind was not, brooding and self-conscious; and its meditative self-consciousness has discovered depths in the human soul which the Greeks and Romans did not dream of, and would not have understood. But what they had got to express, they expressed in a manner which few even of the greatest moderns have seriously attempted to rival. It must be remembered that they had more time, and that they wrote chiefly for a select class, possessed of leisure. To us who write in a hurry for people who read in a hurry, the attempt to give an equal degree of finish would be loss of time. But to be familiar with perfect models is not the less important to us because the element in which we work precludes even the effort to equal them. They shew us at least what excellence is, and make us desire it, and strive to get as near to it as is within our reach. And this is the value to us of the ancient writers, all the more emphatically, because their excellence does not admit of being copied, or directly imitated. It does not consist in a trick which can be learnt, but in the perfect adaptation of means to ends. The secret of the style of the great Greek and Roman authors, is that it is the perfection of good sense. In the first place, they never use a word without a meaning, or a word which adds nothing to the meaning. They always (to begin with) had a meaning; they knew what they wanted to say; and their whole purpose was to say it with the highest degree of exactness and completeness, and bring it home to the mind with the greatest possible clearness and vividness. It never entered into their thoughts to conceive of a piece of writing as beautiful in itself, abstractedly from what it had to express: its beauty must all be subservient to the most perfect expression of the sense. The *curiosa felicitas* which their critics ascribed in a pre-eminent degree to Horace, expresses the standard at which they all aimed. Their style is exactly described by Swift's definition, 'the right words in the right places.' Look at an oration of Demosthenes; there is nothing in it which calls attention to itself as style at all, it is only after a close examination we perceive that every word is what it should be, and where it should be, to lead the hearer smoothly and imperceptibly into the state of mind which the orator wishes to produce. The perfection of the workmanship is only visible in the total absence of any blemish or fault, and of anything which checks the flow of thought and feeling, anything which even momentarily distracts the mind from the main purpose. But then (as has been well said) it was not the object of Demosthenes to make the Athenians cry out 'What a splendid speaker!' but to make them say 'Let us march against Philip!' It was only in the decline of ancient literature that ornament began to be cultivated merely as ornament. In the time of its maturity, not the merest epithet was put in because it was thought beautiful in itself; nor even for a merely descriptive purpose, for epithets purely descriptive were one of the corruptions of style which abound in Lucan, for example: the word had no business there unless it brought out some feature which was wanted, and helped to place the object in the light which the purpose of the composition required. These conditions being complied with, then indeed the intrinsic beauty of the means used was a source of additional effect, of which it behoved them to avail themselves, like rhythm and melody of versification. But these great writers knew that ornament for the sake of ornament, ornament which attracts attention to itself, and shines by its own beauties, only does so by calling off the mind from the main object, and thus not only interferes with the higher purpose of human discourse, which ought, and generally professes, to have some matter to communicate, apart from the mere excitement of the moment, but also spoils the perfection of the composition as a piece of fine art, by destroying the unity of effect. This, then, is the first great lesson in composition to be learnt from the classical authors. The second is, not to be prolix. In a single paragraph, Thucydides can give a clear and vivid representation of a battle, such as a reader who has once taken it into his mind can seldom forget. The most powerful and affecting piece of narrative perhaps in all historical literature, is the account of the Sicilian catastrophe in his seventh book, yet how few pages does it fill! The ancients were concise, because of the extreme pains they took with their compositions; almost all moderns are prolix, because they do not. The great ancients could express a thought so perfectly in a few words or sentences, that they did not need to add any more: the moderns, because they cannot bring it out clearly and completely at once, return again and again, heaping sentence upon sentence, each adding a little more elucidation, in hopes that though no single sentence expresses the full meaning, the whole together may give a sufficient notion of it. In this respect I am afraid we are growing worse instead of better, for want of time and patience, and from the necessity we are in of addressing almost all writings to a busy and imperfectly prepared public. The demands of modern life are such—the work to be done, the mass to be worked upon, are so vast, that those who have anything particular to say—who have, as the phrase goes, any message to deliver—cannot afford to devote their time to the production of masterpieces. But they would do far worse than they do, if there had never been masterpieces, or if they had never known them. Early familiarity with the perfect, makes our most imperfect production far less bad than it otherwise would be. To have a high standard of excellence often makes the whole difference of rendering our work good when it would otherwise be mediocre.

For all these reasons I think it important to retain these two languages and literatures in the place they occupy, as a part of liberal education, that is, of the education of all who are not obliged by their circumstances to discontinue their scholastic studies at a very early age. But the same reasons which vindicate the place of classical studies in general education, shew also the proper limitation of them. They should be carried as far as is sufficient to enable the pupil, in after life, to read the great works of ancient literature with ease. Those who have leisure and inclination to make scholarship, or ancient history, or general philology, their pursuit, of course require much more, but there is no room for more in general education. The laborious idleness in which the school-time is wasted away in the English classical schools deserves the severest reprehension. To what purpose should the most precious years of early life be irreparably squandered in learning to write bad Latin and Greek verses? I do not see that we are much the better even for those who end by writing good ones. I am often tempted to ask the favourites of nature and fortune, whether all the serious and important work of the world is done, that their time and energy can be spared for these *nugae difficiles*? I am not blind to the utility of composing in a language, as a means of learning it accurately. I hardly know any other means equally effectual. But why should not prose composition suffice? What need is there of original composition at all? if that can be called original which unfortunate schoolboys, without any thoughts to express, hammer out on compulsion from mere memory, acquiring the pernicious habit which a teacher should consider it one of his first duties to repress, that of merely stringing together borrowed phrases? The exercise in composition, most suitable to the requirements of learners, is that most valuable one, of retranslating from translated passages of a good author: and to this might be added, what still exists in many Continental places of education, occasional practice in talking Latin. There would be something to be said for the time spent in the manufacture of verses, if such practice were necessary for the enjoyment of ancient poetry; though it would be better to lose that enjoyment than to purchase it at so extravagant a price. But the beauties of a great poet would be a far poorer thing than they are, if they only impressed us through a knowledge of the technicalities of his art. The poet needed those technicalities: they are not necessary to us. They are essential for criticising a poem, but not for enjoying it. All that is wanted is sufficient familiarity with the language, for its meaning to reach us without any sense of effort, and clothed with the associations on which the poet counted for producing his effect. Whoever has this familiarity, and a practised ear, can have as keen a relish of the music of Virgil and Horace, as of Gray, or Burns, or Shelley, though he know not the metrical rules of a common Sapphic or Alcaic. I do not say that these rules ought not to be taught, but I would have a class apart for them, and would make the appropriate exercises an optional, not a compulsory part of the school teaching.

Much more might be said respecting classical instruction, and literary cultivation in general, as a part of liberal education. But it is time to speak of the uses of scientific instruction: or rather its indispensable necessity, for it is recommended by every consideration which pleads for any high order of intellectual education at all.

The most obvious part of the value of scientific instruction, the mere information that it gives, speaks for itself. We are born into a world which we have not made; a world whose phenomena take place according to fixed laws, of which we do not bring any knowledge into the world with us. In such a world we are appointed to live, and in it all our work is to be done. Our whole working power depends on knowing the laws of the world — in other words, the properties of the things which we have to work with, and to work among, and to work upon. We may and do rely, for the greater part of this knowledge, on the few who in each department make its acquisition their main business in life. But unless an elementary knowledge of scientific truths is diffused among the public, they never know what is certain and what is not, or who are entitled to speak with authority and who are not: and they either have no faith at all in the testimony of science, or are the ready dupes of charlatans and impostors. They alternate between ignorant distrust, and blind, often misplaced, confidence. Besides, who is there who would not wish to understand the meaning of the common physical facts that take place under his eye? Who would not wish to know why a pump raises water, why a lever moves heavy weights, why it is hot at the tropics and cold at the poles, why the moon is sometimes dark and sometimes bright, what is the cause of the tides? Do we not feel that he who is totally ignorant of these things, let him be ever so skilled in a special profession, is not an educated man but an ignoramus? It is surely no small part of education to put us in intelligent possession of the most important and most universally interesting facts of the universe, so that the world which surrounds us may not be a sealed book to us, uninteresting because unintelligible. This, however, is but the simplest and most obvious part of the utility of science, and the part which, if neglected in youth, may be the most easily made up for afterwards. It is more important to understand the value of scientific instruction as a training and disciplining process, to fit the intellect for the proper work of a human being. Facts are the materials of our knowledge, but the mind itself is the instrument: and it is easier to acquire facts, than to judge what they prove, and how, through the facts which we know, to get to those which we want to know.

The most incessant occupation of the human intellect throughout life is the ascertainment of truth. We are always needing to know what is actually true about something or other. It is not given to us all to discover great general truths that are a light to all men and to future generations; though with a better general education the number of those who could do so would be far greater than it is. But we all require the ability to judge between the conflicting opinions which are offered to us as vital truths; to choose what doctrines we will receive in the matter of religion, for example; to judge whether we ought to be Tories, Whigs, or Radicals, or to what length it is our duty to go with each; to form a rational conviction on great questions of legislation and internal policy, and on the manner in which our country should behave to dependencies and to foreign nations. And the need we have of knowing how to discriminate truth, is not confined to the larger truths. All through life it is our most pressing interest to find out the truth about all the matters we are concerned with. If we are farmers we want to find what will truly improve our soil; if merchants, what will truly influence the markets of our commodities; if judges, or jurymen, or advocates, who it was that truly did an unlawful act, or to whom a disputed right truly belongs. Every time we have to make a new resolution or alter an old one, in any situation in life, we shall go wrong unless we know the truth about the facts on which our resolution depends. Now, however different these searches for truth may look, and however unlike they really are in their subject-matter, the methods of getting at truth, and the tests of truth, are in all cases much the same. There are but two roads by which truth can be discovered; observation, and reasoning: observation, of course, including experiment. We all observe, and we all reason, and therefore, more or less successfully, we all ascertain truths: but most of us do it very ill, and could not get on at all were we not able to fall back on others who do it better. If we could not do it in any degree, we should be mere instruments in the hands of those who could: they would be able to reduce us to slavery. Then how shall we best learn to do this? By being shewn the way in which it has already been successfully done. The processes by which truth is attained, reasoning and observation, have been carried to their greatest known perfection in the physical sciences. As classical literature furnishes the most perfect types of the art of expression, so do the physical sciences those of the art of thinking. Mathematics, and its application to astronomy and natural philosophy, are the most complete example of the discovery of truths by reasoning; experimental science, of their discovery by direct observation. In all these cases we know that we can trust the operation, because the conclusions to which it has led have been found true by subsequent trial. It is by the study of these, then, that we may hope to qualify ourselves for distinguishing truth, in cases where there do not exist the same ready means of verification.

In what consists the principal and most characteristic difference between one human intellect and another? In their ability to judge correctly of evidence. Our direct perceptions of truth are so limited; we know so few things by immediate intuition, or, as it used to be called, by simple apprehension — that we depend for almost all our valuable knowledge, on evidence external to itself; and most of us are very unsafe hands at estimating evidence, where an appeal cannot be made to actual eyesight. The intellectual part of our education has nothing more important to do, than to correct or mitigate this almost universal infirmity — this summary and substance of nearly all purely intellectual weakness. To do this with effect needs all the resources which the most perfect system of intellectual training can command. Those resources, as every teacher knows, are but of three kinds: first, models, secondly rules, thirdly, appropriate practice. The models of the art of estimating evidence are furnished by science; the rules are suggested by science, and the study of science is the most fundamental portion of the practice.

Take in the first instance mathematics. It is chiefly from mathematics we realise the fact that there actually is a road to truth by means of reasoning, that anything real, and which will be found true when tried, can be arrived at by a mere operation of the mind. The flagrant abuse of mere reasoning in the days of the schoolmen, when men argued confidently to supposed facts of outward nature without properly establishing their premises, or checking the conclusions by observation, created a prejudice in the modern, and especially in the English mind, against deductive reasoning altogether, as a mode of investigation. The prejudice lasted long, and was upheld by the misunderstood authority of Lord Bacon; until the prodigious applications of mathematics to physical science — to the discovery of the laws of external nature — slowly and tardily restored the reasoning process to the place which belongs to it as a source of real knowledge. Mathematics, pure and applied, are still the great conclusive example of what can be done by reasoning. Mathematics also habituates us to several of the principal precautions for the safety of the process. Our first studies in geometry teach us two invaluable lessons. One is, to lay down at the beginning, in express and clear terms, all the premises from which we intend to reason. The other is, to keep every step in the reasoning distinct and separate from all the other steps, and to make each step safe before proceeding to another; expressly stating to ourselves, at every joint in the reasoning, what new premise we there introduce. It is not necessary that we should do this at all times, in all our reasonings. But we must be always able and ready to do it. If the validity of our argument is denied, or if we doubt it ourselves, that is the way to check it. In this way we are often enabled to detect at once the exact place where paralogism or confusion get in: and after sufficient practice we may be able to keep them out from the beginning. It is to mathematics, again, that we owe our first notion of a connected body of truth; truths which grow out of one another, and hang together so that each implies all the rest; that no one of them can be questioned without contradicting another or others, until in the end it appears that no part of the system can be false unless the whole is so. Pure mathematics first gave us this conception; applied mathematics extends it to the realm of physical nature. Applied mathematics shews us that not only the truths of abstract number and extension, but the external facts of the universe, which we apprehend by our senses, form, at least in a large part of all nature, a web similarly held together. We are able, by reasoning from a few fundamental truths, to explain and predict the phenomena of material objects: and what is still more remarkable, the fundamental truths were themselves found out by reasoning; for they are not such as are obvious to the senses, but had to be inferred by a mathematical process from a mass of minute details, which alone came within the direct reach of human observation. When Newton, in this manner, discovered the laws of the solar system, he created, for all posterity, the true idea of science. He gave the most perfect example we are ever likely to have, of that union of reasoning and observation, which by means of facts that can be directly observed, ascends to laws which govern multitudes of other facts — laws which not only explain and account for what we see, but give us assurance beforehand of much that we do not see, much that we never could have found out by observation, though, having been found out, it is always verified by the result. While mathematics, and the mathematical sciences, supply us with a typical example of the ascertainment of truth by reasoning; those physical sciences which are not mathematical, such as chemistry, and purely experimental physics, shew us in equal perfection the other mode of arriving at certain truth, by observation, in its most accurate form, that of experiment. The value of mathematics in a logical point of view is an old topic with mathematicians, and has even been insisted on so exclusively as to provoke a counter-exaggeration, of which a well-known essay by Sir William Hamilton is an example: but the logical value of experimental science is comparatively a new subject, yet there is no intellectual discipline more important than that which the experimental sciences afford. Their whole occupation consists in doing well, what all of us, during the whole of life, are engaged in doing, for the most part badly. All men do not affect to be reasoners, but all profess, and really attempt, to draw inferences from experience: yet hardly any one, who has not been a student of the physical sciences, sets out with any just idea of what the process of interpreting experience really is. If a fact has occurred once or oftener, and another fact has followed it, people think they have got an experiment, and are well on the road towards shewing that the one fact is the cause of the other. If they did but know the immense amount of precaution necessary to a scientific experiment; with what sedulous care the accompanying circumstances are contrived and varied, so as to exclude every agency but that which is the subject of the experiment—or, when disturbing agencies cannot be excluded, the minute accuracy with which their influence is calculated and allowed for, in order that the residue may contain nothing but what is due to the one agency under examination; if these things were attended to, people would be much less easily satisfied that their opinions have the evidence of experience; many popular notions and generalisations which are in all mouths, would be thought a great deal less certain than they are supposed to be; but we should begin to lay the foundation of really experimental knowledge, on things which are now the subjects of mere vague discussion, where one side finds as much to say and says it as confidently as another, and each person's opinion is less determined by evidence than by his accidental interest or prepossession. In politics, for instance, it is evident to whoever comes to the study from that of the experimental sciences, that no political conclusions of any value for practice can be arrived at by direct experience. Such specific experience as we can have, serves only to verify, and even that insufficiently, the conclusions of reasoning. Take any active force you please in politics, take the liberties of England, or free trade: how should we know that either of these things conduced to prosperity, if we could discern no tendency in the things themselves to produce it? If we had only the evidence of what is called our experience, such prosperity as we enjoy might be owing to a hundred other causes, and might have been obstructed, not promoted, by these. All true political science is, in one sense of the phrase, *à priori*, being deduced from the tendencies of things, tendencies known either through our general experience of human nature, or as the result of an analysis of the course of history, considered as a progressive evolution. It requires, therefore, the union of induction and deduction, and the mind that is equal to it must have been well disciplined in both. But familiarity with scientific experiment at least does the useful service of inspiring a wholesome scepticism about the conclusions which the mere surface of experience suggests.

The study, on the one hand, of mathematics and its applications, on the other, of experimental science, prepares us for the principal business of the intellect, by the practice of it in the most characteristic cases, and by familiarity with the most perfect and successful models of it. But in great things as in small, examples and models are not sufficient: we want rules as well. Familiarity with the correct use of a language in conversation and writing does not make rules of grammar unnecessary; nor does the amplest knowledge of sciences of reasoning and experiment dispense with rules of logic. We may have heard correct reasonings and seen skilful experiments all our lives — we shall not learn by mere imitation to do the like, unless we pay careful attention to how it is done. It is much easier in these abstract matters, than in purely mechanical ones, to mistake bad work for good. To mark out the difference between them is the province of logic. Logic lays down the general principles and laws of the search after truth; the conditions which, whether recognised or not, must actually have been observed if the mind has done its work rightly. Logic is the intellectual complement of mathematics and physics. Those sciences give the practice, of which Logic is the theory. It declares the principles, rules, and precepts, of which they exemplify the observance.

The science of Logic has two parts; ratiocinative and inductive logic. The one helps to keep us right in reasoning from premises, the other in concluding from observation. Ratiocinative logic is much older than inductive, because reasoning in the narrower sense of the word is an easier process than induction, and the science which works by mere reasoning, pure mathematics, had been carried to a considerable height while the sciences of observation were still in the purely empirical period. The principles of ratiocination, therefore, were the earliest understood and systematised, and the logic of ratiocination is even now suitable to an earlier stage in education than that of induction. The principles of induction cannot be properly understood without some previous study of the inductive sciences; but the logic of reasoning, which was already carried to a high degree of perfection by Aristotle, does not absolutely require even a knowledge of mathematics, but can be sufficiently exemplified and illustrated from the practice of daily life.

Of Logic I venture to say, even if limited to that of mere ratiocination, the theory of names, propositions, and the syllogism, that there is no part of intellectual education which is of greater value, or whose place can so ill be supplied by anything else. Its uses, it is true, are chiefly negative; its function is, not so much to teach us to go right, as to keep us from going wrong. But in the operations of the intellect it is so much easier to go wrong than right, it is so utterly impossible for even the most vigorous mind to keep itself in the path but by maintaining a vigilant watch against all deviations, and noting all the byways by which it is possible to go astray — that the chief difference between one reasoner and another consists in their less or greater liability to be misled. Logic points out all the possible ways in which, starting from true premises, we may draw false conclusions. By its analysis of the reasoning process, and the forms it supplies for stating and setting forth our reasonings, it enables us to guard the points at which a fallacy is in danger of slipping in, or to lay our fingers upon the place where it has slipped in. When I consider how very simple the theory of reasoning is, and how short a time is sufficient for acquiring a thorough knowledge of its principles and rules, and even considerable expertness in applying them, I can find no excuse for omission to study it on the part of any one who aspires to succeed in any intellectual pursuit. Logic is the great disperser of hazy and confused thinking: it clears up the fogs which hide from us our own ignorance, and make us believe that we understand a subject when we do not. We must not be led away by talk about inarticulate giants who do great deeds without knowing how, and see into the most recondite truths without any of the ordinary helps, and without being able to explain to other people how they reach their conclusions, nor consequently to convince any other people of the truth of them. There may be such men, as there are deaf and dumb persons who do clever things, but for all that, speech and hearing are faculties by no means to be dispensed with. If you want to know whether you are thinking rightly, put your thoughts into words. In the very attempt to do this you will find yourselves, consciously or unconsciously, using logical forms. Logic compels us to throw our meaning into distinct propositions, and our reasonings into distinct steps. It makes us conscious of all the implied assumptions on which we are proceeding, and which, if not true, vitiate the entire process. It makes us aware what extent of doctrine we commit ourselves to by any course of reasoning, and obliges us to look the implied premises in the face, and make up our minds whether we can stand to them. It makes our opinions consistent with themselves and with one another, and forces us to think clearly, even when it cannot make us think correctly. It is true that error may be consistent and systematic as well as truth; but this is not the common case. It is no small advantage to see clearly the principles and consequences involved in our opinions, and which we must either accept, or else abandon those opinions. We are much nearer to finding truth when we search for it in broad daylight. Error, pursued rigorously to all that is implied in it, seldom fails to get detected by coming into collision with some known and admitted fact.

You will find abundance of people to tell you that logic is no help to thought, and that people cannot be taught to think by rules. Undoubtedly rules by themselves, without practice, go but a little way in teaching anything. But if the practice of thinking is not improved by rules, I venture to say it is the only difficult thing done by human beings that is not so. A man learns to saw wood principally by practice, but there are rules for doing it, grounded on the nature of the operation, and if he is not taught the rules, he will not saw well until he has discovered them for himself. Wherever there is a right way and a wrong, there must be a difference between them, and it must be possible to find out what the difference is; and when found out and expressed in words, it is a rule for the operation. If any one is inclined to disparage rules, I say to him, try to learn anything which there are rules for, without knowing the rules, and see how you succeed. To those who think lightly of the school logic, I say, take the trouble to learn it. You will easily do so in a few weeks, and you will see whether it is of no use to you in making your mind clear, and keeping you from stumbling in the dark over the most outrageous fallacies. Nobody, I believe, who has really learnt it, and who goes on using his mind, is insensible to its benefits, unless he started with a prejudice, or, like some eminent English and Scottish thinkers of the past century, is under the influence of a reaction against the exaggerated pretensions made by the schoolmen, not so much in behalf of logic as of the reasoning process itself. Still more highly must the use of logic be estimated, if we include in it, as we ought to do, the principles and rules of Induction as well as of Ratiocination. As the one logic guards us against bad deduction, so does the other against bad generalisation, which is a still more universal error. If men easily err in arguing from one general proposition to another, still more easily do they go wrong in interpreting the observations made by themselves and others. There is nothing in which an untrained mind shews itself more hopelessly incapable, than in drawing the proper general conclusions from its own experience. And even trained minds, when all their training is on a special subject, and does not extend to the general principles of induction, are only kept right when there are ready opportunities of verifying their inferences by facts. Able scientific men, when they venture upon subjects in which they have no facts to check them, are often found drawing conclusions or making generalisations from their experimental knowledge, such as any sound theory of induction would shew to be utterly unwarranted. So true is it that practice alone, even of a good kind, is not sufficient without principles and rules. Lord Bacon had the great merit of seeing that rules were necessary, and conceiving, to a very considerable extent, their true character. The defects of his conception were such as were inevitable while the inductive sciences were only in the earliest stage of their progress, and the highest efforts of the human mind in that direction had not yet been made. Inadequate as the Baconian view of induction was, and rapidly as the practice outgrew it, it is only within a generation or two that any considerable improvement has been made in the theory; very much through the impulse given by two of the many distinguished men who have adorned the Scottish universities, Dugald Stewart and Brown.

I have given a very incomplete and summary view of the educational benefits derived from instruction in the more perfect sciences, and in the rules for the proper use of the intellectual faculties which the practice of those sciences has suggested. There are other sciences, which are in a more backward state, and tax the whole powers of the mind in its mature years, yet a beginning of which may be beneficially made in university studies, while a tincture of them is valuable even to those who are never likely to proceed further. The first is physiology; the science of the laws of organic and animal life, and especially of the structure and functions of the human body. It would be absurd to pretend that a profound knowledge of this difficult subject can be acquired in youth, or as a part of general education. Yet an acquaintance with its leading truths is one of those acquirements which ought not to be the exclusive property of a particular profession. The value of such knowledge for daily uses has been made familiar to us all by the sanitary discussions of late years. There is hardly one among us who may not, in some position of authority, be required to form an opinion and take part in public action on sanitary subjects. And the importance of understanding the true conditions of health and disease—of knowing how to acquire and preserve that healthy habit of body which the most tedious and costly medical treatment so often fails to restore when once lost, should secure a place in general education for the principal maxims of hygiene, and some of those even of practical medicine. For those who aim at high intellectual cultivation, the study of physiology has still greater recommendations, and is, in the present state of advancement of the higher studies, a real necessity. The practice which it gives in the study of nature is such as no other physical science affords in the same kind, and is the best introduction to the difficult questions of politics and social life. Scientific education, apart from professional objects, is but a preparation for judging rightly of Man, and of his requirements and interests. But to this final pursuit, which has been called *par excellence* the proper study of mankind, physiology is the most serviceable of the sciences, because it is the nearest. Its subject is already Man: the same complex and manifold being, whose properties are not independent of circumstance, and immovable from age to age, like those of the ellipse and hyperbola, or of sulphur and phosphorus, but are infinitely various, indefinitely modifiable by art or accident, graduating by the nicest shades into one another, and reacting upon one another in a thousand ways, so that they are seldom capable of being isolated and observed separately. With the difficulties of the study of a being so constituted, the physiologist, and he alone among scientific enquirers, is already familiar. Take what view we will of man as a spiritual being, one part of his nature is far more like another than either of them is like anything else. In the organic world we study nature under disadvantages very similar to those which affect the study of moral and political phenomena: our means of making experiments are almost as limited, while the extreme complexity of the facts makes the conclusions of general reasoning unusually precarious, on account of the vast number of circumstances that conspire to determine every result. Yet in spite of these obstacles, it is found possible in physiology to arrive at a considerable number of well-ascertained and important truths. This therefore is an excellent school in which to study the means of overcoming similar difficulties elsewhere. It is in physiology too that we are first introduced to some of the conceptions which play the greatest part in the moral and social sciences, but which do not occur at all in those of inorganic nature. As, for instance, the idea of predisposition, and of predisposing causes, as distinguished from exciting causes. The operation of all moral forces is immensely influenced by predisposition: without that element, it is impossible to explain the commonest facts of history and social life. Physiology is also the first science in which we recognise the influence of habit—the tendency of something to happen again merely because it has happened before. From physiology, too, we get our clearest notion of what is meant by development or evolution. The growth of a plant or animal from the first germ is the typical specimen of a phenomenon which rules through the whole course of the history of man and society—increase of function, through expansion and differentiation of structure by internal forces. I cannot enter into the subject at greater length; it is enough if I throw out hints which may be germs of further thought in yourselves. Those who aim at high intellectual achievements may be assured that no part of their time will be less wasted, than that which they employ in becoming familiar with the methods and with the main conceptions of the science of organisation and life.

Physiology, at its upper extremity, touches on Psychology, or the Philosophy of Mind: and without raising any disputed questions about the limits between Matter and Spirit, the nerves and brain are admitted to have so intimate a connexion with the mental operations, that the student of the last cannot dispense with a considerable knowledge of the first. The value of psychology itself need hardly be expatiated upon in a Scottish university; for it has always been there studied with brilliant success. Almost everything which has been contributed from these islands towards its advancement since Locke and Berkeley, has until very lately, and much of it even in the present generation, proceeded from Scottish authors and Scottish professors. Psychology, in truth, is simply the knowledge of the laws of human nature. If there is anything that deserves to be studied by man, it is his own nature and that of his fellow-men: and if it is worth studying at all, it is worth studying scientifically, so as to reach the fundamental laws which underlie and govern all the rest. With regard to the suitableness of this subject for general education, a distinction must be made. There are certain observed laws of our thoughts and of our feelings which rest upon experimental evidence, and, once seized, are a clue to the interpretation of much that we are conscious of in ourselves, and observe in one another. Such, for example, are the laws of association. Psychology, so far as it consists of such laws—I speak of the laws themselves, not of their disputed applications — is as positive and certain a science as chemistry, and fit to be taught as such. When, however, we pass beyond the bounds of these admitted truths, to questions which are still in controversy among the different philosophical schools — how far the higher operations of the mind can be explained by association, how far we must admit other primary principles — what faculties of the mind are simple, what complex, and what is the composition of the latter — above all, when we embark upon the sea of metaphysics properly so called, and enquire, for instance, whether time and space are real existences, as is our spontaneous impression, or forms of our sensitive faculty, as is maintained by Kant, or complex ideas generated by association; whether matter and spirit are conceptions merely relative to our faculties, or facts existing *per se*, and in the latter case, what is the nature and limit of our knowledge of them; whether the will of man is free or determined by causes, and what is the real difference between the two doctrines; matters on which the most thinking men, and those who have given most study to the subjects, are still divided; it is neither to be expected nor desired that those who do not specially devote themselves to the higher departments of speculation should employ much of their time in attempting to get to the bottom of these questions. But it is a part of liberal education to know that such controversies exist, and, in a general way, what has been said on both sides of them. It is instructive to know the failures of the human intellect as well as its successes, its imperfect as well as its perfect attainments; to be aware of the open questions, as well as of those which have been definitively resolved. A very summary view of these disputed matters may suffice for the many; but a system of education is not intended solely for the many: it has to kindle the aspirations and aid the efforts of those who are destined to stand forth as thinkers above the multitude: and for these there is hardly to be found any discipline comparable to that which these metaphysical controversies afford. For they are essentially questions about the estimation of evidence; about the ultimate grounds of belief; the conditions required to justify our most familiar and intimate convictions; and the real meaning and import of words and phrases which we have used from infancy as if we understood all about them, which are even at the foundation of human language, yet of which no one except a metaphysician has rendered to himself a complete account. Whatever philosophical opinions the study of these questions may lead us to adopt, no one ever came out of the discussion of them without increased vigour of understanding, an increased demand for precision of thought and language, and a more careful and exact appreciation of the nature of proof. There never was any sharpener of the intellectual faculties superior to the Berkeleian controversy. There is even now no reading more profitable to students — confining myself to writers in our own language, and notwithstanding that so many of their speculations are already obsolete — than Hobbes and Locke, Reid and Stewart, Hume, Hartley, and Brown: on condition that these great thinkers are not read passively, as masters to be followed, but actively, as supplying materials and incentives to thought. To come to our own contemporaries, he who has mastered Sir William Hamilton and your own lamented Ferrier as distinguished representatives of one of the two great schools of philosophy, and an eminent Professor in a neighbouring University, Professor Bain, probably the greatest living authority in the other, has gained a practice in the most searching methods of philosophic investigation applied to the most arduous subjects, which is no inadequate preparation for any intellectual difficulties that he is ever likely to be called on to resolve.

In this brief outline of a complete scientific education, I have said nothing about direct instruction in that which it is the chief of all the ends of intellectual education to qualify us for — the exercise of thought on the great interests of mankind as moral and social beings — ethics and politics, in the largest sense. These things are not, in the existing state of human knowledge, the subject of a science, generally admitted and accepted. Politics cannot be learnt once for all, from a text-book, or the instructions of a master. What we require to be taught on that subject, is to be our own teachers. It is a subject on which we have no masters to follow; each must explore for himself, and exercise an independent judgment. Scientific politics do not consist in having a set of conclusions ready made, to be applied everywhere indiscriminately, but in setting the mind to work in a scientific spirit to discover in each instance the truths applicable to the given case. And this, at present, scarcely any two persons do in the same way. Education is not entitled, on this subject, to recommend any set of opinions as resting on the authority of established science. But it can supply the student with materials for his own mind, and helps to use them. It can make him acquainted with the best speculations on the subject, taken from different points of view: none of which will be found complete, while each embodies some considerations really relevant, really requiring to be taken into the account. Education may also introduce us to the principal facts which have a direct bearing on the subject, namely the different modes or stages of civilisation that have been found among mankind, and the characteristic properties of each. This is the true purpose of historical studies, as prosecuted in an University. The leading facts of ancient and modern history should be known by the student from his private reading: if that knowledge be wanting, it cannot possibly be supplied here. What a Professor of History has to teach, is the meaning of those facts. His office is to help the student in collecting from history what are the main differences between human beings, and between the institutions of society, at one time or place and at another: in picturing to himself human life and the human conception of life, as they were at the different stages of human development: in distinguishing between what is the same in all ages and what is progressive, and forming some incipient conception of the causes and laws of progress. All these things are as yet very imperfectly understood even by the most philosophic enquirers, and are quite unfit to be taught dogmatically. The object is to lead the student to attend to them; to make him take interest in history not as a mere narrative, but as a chain of causes and effects still unwinding itself before his eyes, and full of momentous consequences to himself and his descendants; the unfolding of a great epic or dramatic action, to terminate in the happiness or misery, the elevation or degradation, of the human race; an unremitting conflict between good and evil powers, of which every act done by any of us, insignificant as we are, forms one of the incidents; a conflict in which even the smallest of us cannot escape from taking part, in which whoever does not help the right side is helping the wrong, and for our share in which, whether it be greater or smaller, and let its actual consequences be visible or in the main invisible, no one of us can escape the responsibility. Though education cannot arm and equip its pupils for this fight with any complete philosophy either of politics or of history, there is much positive instruction that it can give them, having a direct bearing on the duties of citizenship. They should be taught the outlines of the civil and political institutions of their own country, and in a more general way, of the more advanced of the other civilised nations. Those branches of politics, or of the laws of social life, in which there exists a collection of facts or thoughts sufficiently sifted and methodised to form the beginning of a science, should be taught *ex professo*. Among the chief of these is Political Economy; the sources and conditions of wealth and material prosperity for aggregate bodies of human beings. This study approaches nearer to the rank of a science, in the sense in which we apply that name to the physical sciences, than anything else connected with politics yet does. I need not enlarge on the important lessons which it affords for the guidance of life, and for the estimation of laws and institutions, or on the necessity of knowing all that it can teach in order to have true views of the course of human affairs, or form plans for their improvement which will stand actual trial. The same persons who cry down Logic will generally warn you against Political Economy. It is unfeeling, they will tell you. It recognises unpleasant facts. For my part, the most unfeeling thing I know of is the law of gravitation: it breaks the neck of the best and most amiable person without scruple, if he forgets for a single moment to give heed to it. The winds and waves too are very unfeeling. Would you advise those who go to sea to deny the winds and waves — or to make use of them, and find the means of guarding against their dangers? My advice to you is to study the great writers on Political Economy, and hold firmly by whatever in them you find true; and depend upon it that if you are not selfish or hard-hearted already, Political Economy will not make you so. Of no less importance than Political Economy is the study of what is called Jurisprudence; the general principles of law; the social necessities which laws are required to meet; the features common to all systems of law, and the differences between them; the requisites of good legislation, the proper mode of constructing a legal system, and the best constitution of courts of justice and modes of legal procedure. These things are not only the chief part of the business of government, but the vital concern of every citizen; and their improvement affords a wide scope for the energies of any duly prepared mind, ambitious of contributing towards the better condition of the human race. For this, too, admirable helps have been provided by writers of our own or of a very recent time. At the head of them stands Bentham; undoubtedly the greatest master who ever devoted the labour of a life to let in light on the subject of law; and who is the more intelligible to non-professional persons, because, as his way is, he builds up the subject from its foundation in the facts of human life, and shews by careful consideration of ends and means, what law might and ought to be, in deplorable contrast with what it is. Other enlightened jurists have followed with contributions of two kinds, as the type of which I may take two works, equally admirable in their respective lines. Mr. Austin, in his *Lectures on Jurisprudence*, takes for his basis the Roman law, the most elaborately consistent legal system which history has shewn us in actual operation, and that which the greatest number of accomplished minds have employed themselves in harmonising. From this he singles out the principles and distinctions which are of general applicability, and employs the powers and resources of a most precise and analytic mind to give to those principles and distinctions a philosophic basis, grounded in the universal reason of mankind, and not in mere technical convenience. Mr. Maine, in his treatise on *Ancient Law in its relations to Modern Thought,* shews from the history of law, and from what is known of the primitive institutions of mankind, the origin of much that has lasted till now, and has a firm footing both in the laws and in the ideas of modern times; shewing that many of these things never originated in reason, but are relics of the institutions of barbarous society, modified more or less by civilisation, but kept standing by the persistency of ideas which were the offspring of those barbarous institutions, and have survived their parent. The path opened by Mr. Maine has been followed up by others, with additional illustrations of the influence of obsolete ideas on modern institutions, and of obsolete institutions on modern ideas; an action and reaction which perpetuate, in many of the greatest concerns, a mitigated barbarism: things being continually accepted as dictates of nature and necessities of life, which, if we knew all, we should see to have originated in artificial arrangements of society, long since abandoned and condemned.

To these studies I would add International Law; which I decidedly think should be taught in all universities, and should form part of all liberal education. The need of it is far from being limited to diplomatists and lawyers; it extends to every citizen. What is called the Law of Nations is not properly law, but a part of ethics: a set of moral rules, accepted as authoritative by civilised states. It is true that these rules neither are nor ought to be of eternal obligation, but do and must vary more or less from age to age, as the consciences of nations become more enlightened and the exigencies of political society undergo change. But the rules mostly were at their origin, and still are, an application of the maxims of honesty and humanity to the intercourse of states. They were introduced by the moral sentiments of mankind, or by their sense of the general interest, to mitigate the crimes and sufferings of a state of war, and to restrain governments and nations from unjust or dishonest conduct towards one another in time of peace. Since every country stands in numerous and various relations with the other countries of the world, and many, our own among the number, exercise actual authority over some of these, a knowledge of the established rules of international morality is essential to the duty of every nation, and therefore of every person in it who helps to make up the nation, and whose voice and feeling form a part of what is called public opinion. Let not any one pacify his conscience by the delusion that he can do no harm if he takes no part, and forms no opinion. Bad men need nothing more to compass their ends, than that good men should look on and do nothing. He is not a good man who, without a protest, allows wrong to be committed in his name, and with the means which he helps to supply, because he will not trouble himself to use his mind on the subject. It depends on the habit of attending to and looking into public transactions, and on the degree of information and solid judgment respecting them that exists in the community, whether the conduct of the nation as a nation, both within itself and towards others, shall be selfish, corrupt, and tyrannical, or rational and enlightened, just and noble.

Of these more advanced studies, only a small commencement can be made at schools and universities; but even this is of the highest value, by awakening an interest in the subjects, by conquering the first difficulties, and inuring the mind to the kind of exertion which the studies require, by implanting a desire to make further progress, and directing the student to the best tracks and the best helps. So far as these branches of knowledge have been acquired, we have learnt, or been put into the way of learning, our duty, and our work in life. Knowing it, however, is but half the work of education; it still remains, that what we know, we shall be willing and determined to put in practice. Nevertheless, to know the truth is already a great way towards disposing us to act upon it. What we see clearly and apprehend keenly, we have a natural desire to act out. 'To see the best, and yet the worst pursue,' is a possible but not a common state of mind; those who follow the wrong have generally first taken care to be voluntarily ignorant of the right. They have silenced their conscience, but they are not knowingly disobeying it. If you take an average human mind while still young, before the objects it has chosen in life have given it a turn in any bad direction, you will generally find it desiring what is good, right, and for the benefit of all; and if that season is properly used to implant the knowledge and give the training which shall render rectitude of judgment more habitual than sophistry, a serious barrier will have been erected against the inroads of selfishness and falsehood. Still, it is a very imperfect education which trains the intelligence only, but not the will. No one can dispense with an education directed expressly to the moral as well as the intellectual part of his being. Such education, so far as it is direct, is either moral or religious; and these may either be treated as distinct, or as different aspects of the same thing. The subject we are now considering is not education as a whole, but scholastic education, and we must keep in view the inevitable limitations of what schools and universities can do. It is beyond their power to educate morally or religiously. Moral and religious education consist in training the feelings and the daily habits; and these are, in the main, beyond the sphere and inaccessible to the control of public education. It is the home, the family, which gives us the moral or religious education we really receive: and this is completed, and modified, sometimes for the better, often for the worse, by society, and the opinions and feelings with which we are there surrounded. The moral or religious influence which an university can exercise, consists less in any express teaching, than in the pervading tone of the place. Whatever it teaches, it should teach as penetrated by a sense of duty; it should present all knowledge as chiefly a means to worthiness of life, given for the double purpose of making each of us practically useful to his fellow-creatures, and of elevating the character of the species itself; exalting and dignifying our nature. There is nothing which spreads more contagiously from teacher to pupil than elevation of sentiment: often and often have students caught from the living influence of a professor, a contempt for mean and selfish objects, and a noble ambition to leave the world better than they found it, which they have carried with them throughout life. In these respects, teachers of every kind have natural and peculiar means of doing with effect, what every one who mixes with his fellow-beings, or addresses himself to them in any character, should feel bound to do to the extent of his capacity and opportunities. What is special to an university on these subjects belongs chiefly, like the rest of its work, to the intellectual department. An university exists for the purpose of laying open to each succeeding generation, as far as the conditions of the case admit, the accumulated treasure of the thoughts of mankind. As an indispensable part of this, it has to make known to them what mankind at large, their own country, and the best and wisest individual men, have thought on the great subjects of morals and religion. There should be, and there is in most universities, professorial instruction in moral philosophy; but I could wish that this instruction were of a somewhat different type from what is ordinarily met with. I could wish that it were more expository, less polemical, and above all less dogmatic. The learner should be made acquainted with the principal systems of moral philosophy which have existed and been practically operative among mankind, and should hear what there is to be said for each: the Aristotelian, the Epicurean, the Stoic, the Judaic, the Christian in the various modes of its interpretation, which differ almost as much from one another as the teachings of those earlier schools. He should be made familiar with the different standards of right and wrong which have been taken as the basis of ethics: general utility, natural justice, natural rights, a moral sense, principles of practical reason, and the rest. Among all these, it is not so much the teacher's business to take a side, and fight stoutly for some one against the rest, as it is to direct them all towards the establishment and preservation of the rules of conduct most advantageous to mankind. There is not one of these systems which has not its good side; not one from which there is not something to be learnt by the votaries of the others; not one which is not suggested by a keen, though it may not always be a clear, perception of some important truths, which are the prop of the system, and the neglect or undervaluing of which in other systems is their characteristic infirmity. A system which may be as a whole erroneous, is still valuable, until it has forced upon mankind a sufficient attention to the portion of truth which suggested it. The ethical teacher does his part best, when he points out how each system may be strengthened even on its own basis, by taking into more complete account the truths which other systems have realised more fully and made more prominent. I do not mean that he should encourage an essentially skeptical eclecticism. While placing every system in the best aspect it admits of, and endeavouring to draw from all of them the most salutary consequences compatible with their nature, I would by no means debar him from enforcing by his best arguments his own preference for some one of the number. They cannot be all true; though those which are false as theories may contain particular truths, indispensable to the completeness of the true theory. But on this subject, even more than on any of those I have previously mentioned, it is not the teacher's business to impose his own judgment, but to inform and discipline that of his pupil.

And this same clue, if we keep hold of it, will guide us through the labyrinth of conflicting thought into which we enter when we touch the great question of the relation of education to religion. As I have already said, the only really effective religious education is the parental—that of home and childhood. All that social and public education has in its power to do, further than by a general pervading tone of reverence and duty, amounts to little more than the information which it can give; but this is extremely valuable. I shall not enter into the question which has been debated with so much vehemence in the last and present generation, whether religion ought to be taught at all in universities and public schools, seeing that religion is the subject of all others on which men's opinions are most widely at variance. On neither side of this controversy do the disputants seem to me to have sufficiently freed their minds from the old notion of education, that it consists in the dogmatic inculcation from authority, of what the teacher deems true. Why should it be impossible, that information of the greatest value, on subjects connected with religion, should be brought before the student's mind; that he should be made acquainted with so important a part of the national thought, and of the intellectual labours of past generations, as those relating to religion, without being taught dogmatically the doctrines of any church or sect? Christianity being a historical religion, the sort of religious instruction which seems to me most appropriate to an University is the study of ecclesiastical history. If teaching, even on matters of scientific certainty, should aim quite as much at shewing how the results are arrived at, as at teaching the results themselves, far more, then, should this be the case on subjects where there is the widest diversity of opinion among men of equal ability, and who have taken equal pains to arrive at the truth. This diversity should of itself be a warning to a conscientious teacher that he has no right to impose his opinion authoritatively upon a youthful mind. His teaching should not be in the spirit of dogmatism, but in that of enquiry. The pupil should not be addressed as if his religion had been chosen for him, but as one who will have to choose it for himself. The various Churches, established and unestablished, are quite competent to the task which is peculiarly theirs, that of teaching each its own doctrines, as far as necessary, to its own rising generation. The proper business of an University is different: not to tell us from authority what we ought to believe, and make us accept the belief as a duty, but to give us information and training, and help us to form our own belief in a manner worthy of intelligent beings, who seek for truth at all hazards, and demand to know all the difficulties, in order that they may be better qualified to find, or recognise, the most satisfactory mode of resolving them. The vast importance of these questions—the great results as regards the conduct of our lives, which depend upon our choosing one belief or another—are the strongest reasons why we should not trust our judgment when it has been formed in ignorance of the evidence, and why we should not consent to be restricted to a one-sided teaching, which informs us of what a particular teacher or association of teachers receive as true doctrine and sound argument, but of nothing more.

I do not affirm that an University, if it represses free thought and enquiry, must be altogether a failure, for the freest thinkers have often been trained in the most slavish seminaries of learning. The great Christian reformers were taught in Roman Catholic Universities; the sceptical philosophers of France were mostly educated by the Jesuits. The human mind is sometimes impelled all the more violently in one direction, by an over zealous and demonstrative attempt to drag it in the opposite. But this is not what Universities are appointed for—to drive men from them, even into good, by excess of evil. An University ought to be a place of free speculation. The more diligently it does its duty in all other respects, the more certain it is to be that. The old English Universities, in the present generation, are doing better work than they have done within human memory in teaching the ordinary studies of their curriculum; and one of the consequences has been, that whereas they formerly seemed to exist mainly for the repression of independent thought, and the chaining up of the individual intellect and conscience, they are now the great foci of free and manly enquiry, to the higher and professional classes, south of the Tweed. The ruling minds of those ancient seminaries have at last remembered that to place themselves in hostility to the free use of the understanding, is to abdicate their own best privilege, that of guiding it. A modest deference, at least provisional, to the united authority of the specially instructed, is becoming in a youthful and imperfectly formed mind; but when there is no united authority—when the specially instructed are so divided and scattered that almost any opinion can boast of some high authority, and no opinion whatever can claim all; when, therefore, it can never be deemed extremely improbable that one who uses his mind freely may see reason to change his first opinion; then, whatever you do, keep, at all risks, your minds open: do not barter away your freedom of thought. Those of you who are destined for the clerical profession are, no doubt, so far held to a certain number of doctrines, that if they ceased to believe them they would not be justified in remaining in a position in which they would be required to teach insincerely. But use your influence to make those doctrines as few as possible. It is not right that men should be bribed to hold out against conviction—to shut their ears against objections, or, if the objections penetrate, to continue professing full and unfaltering belief when their confidence is already shaken. Neither is it right that if men honestly profess to have changed some of their religious opinions, their honesty should as a matter of course exclude them from taking a part for which they may be admirably qualified, in the spiritual instruction of the nation. The tendency of the age, on both sides of the ancient Border, is towards the relaxation of formularies, and a less rigid construction of articles. This very circumstance, by making the limits of orthodoxy less definite, and obliging every one to draw the line for himself, is an embarrassment to consciences. But I hold entirely with those clergymen who elect to remain in the national church, so long as they are able to accept its articles and confessions in any sense or with any interpretation consistent with common honesty, whether it be the generally received interpretation or not. If all were to desert the church who put a large and liberal construction on its terms of communion, or who would wish to see those terms widened, the national provision for religious teaching and worship would be left utterly to those who take the narrowest, the most literal, and purely textual view of the formularies; who, though by no means necessarily bigots, are under the great disadvantage of having the bigots for their allies, and who, however great their merits may be, and they are often very great, yet if the church is improvable, are not the most likely persons to improve it. Therefore, if it were not an impertinence in me to tender advice in such a matter, I should say, let all who conscientiously can, remain in the church. A church is far more easily improved from within than from without. Almost all the illustrious reformers of religion began by being clergymen: but they did not think that their profession as clergymen was inconsistent with being reformers. They mostly indeed ended their days outside the churches in which they were born; but it was because the churches, in an evil hour for themselves, cast them out. They did not think it any business of theirs to withdraw. They thought they had a better right to remain in the fold, than those had who expelled them.

I have now said what I had to say on the two kinds of education which the system of schools and universities is intended to promote—intellectual education, and moral education: knowledge and the training of the knowing faculty, conscience and that of the moral faculty. These are the two main ingredients of human culture; but they do not exhaust the whole of it. There is a third division, which, if subordinate, and owing allegiance to the two others, is barely inferior to them, and not less needful to the completeness of the human being; I mean the aesthetic branch; the culture which comes through poetry and art, and may be described as the education of the feelings, and the cultivation of the beautiful. This department of things deserves to be regarded in a far more serious light than is the custom of these countries. It is only of late, and chiefly by a superficial imitation of foreigners, that we have begun to use the word Art by itself, and to speak of Art as we speak of Science, or Government, or Religion: we used to talk of the Arts, and more specifically of the Fine Arts: and even by them were vulgarly meant only two forms of art, Painting and Sculpture, the two which as a people we cared least about — which were regarded even by the more cultivated among us as little more than branches of domestic ornamentation, a kind of elegant upholstery. The very words 'Fine Arts' called up a notion of frivolity, of great pains expended on a rather trifling object — on something which differed from the cheaper and commoner arts of producing pretty things, mainly by being more difficult, and by giving fops an opportunity of pluming themselves on caring for it and on being able to talk about it. This estimate extended in no small degree, though not altogether, even to poetry; the queen of arts, but, in Great Britain, hardly included under the name. It cannot exactly be said that poetry was little thought of; we were proud of our Shakespeare and Milton, and in one period at least of our history, that of Queen Anne, it was a high literary distinction to be a poet; but poetry was hardly looked upon in any serious light, or as having much value except as an amusement or excitement, the superiority of which over others principally consisted in being that of a more refined order of minds. Yet the celebrated saying of Fletcher of Saltoun, 'Let who will make the laws of a people if I write their songs,' might have taught us how great an instrument for acting on the human mind we were undervaluing. It would be difficult for anybody to imagine that 'Rule Britannia,' for example, or 'Scots wha hae,' had no permanent influence on the higher region of human character; some of Moore's songs have done more for Ireland than all Grattan's speeches: and songs are far from being the highest or most impressive form of poetry. On these subjects, the mode of thinking and feeling of other countries was not only not intelligible, but not credible, to an average Englishman. To find Art ranking on a complete equality, in theory at least, with Philosophy, Learning, and Science — as holding an equally important place among the agents of civilisation and among the elements of the worth of humanity; to find even painting and sculpture treated as great social powers, and the art of a country as a feature in its character and condition, little inferior in importance to either its religion or its government; all this only did not amaze and puzzle Englishmen, because it was too strange for them to be able to realise it, or, in truth, to believe it possible: and the radical difference of feeling on this matter between the British people and those of France, Germany, and the Continent generally, is one among the causes of that extraordinary inability to understand one another, which exists between England and the rest of Europe, while it does not exist to anything like the same degree between one nation of Continental Europe and another. It may be traced to the two influences which have chiefly shaped the British character since the days of the Stuarts: commercial money-getting business, and religious Puritanism. Business, demanding the whole of the faculties, and whether pursued from duty or the love of gain, regarding as a loss of time whatever does not conduce directly to the end; Puritanism, which looking upon every feeling of human nature, except fear and reverence for God, as a snare, if not as partaking of sin, looked coldly, if not disapprovingly, on the cultivation of the sentiments. Different causes have produced different effects in the Continental nations; among whom it is even now observable that virtue and goodness are generally for the most part an affair of the sentiments, while with us they are almost exclusively an affair of duty. Accordingly, the kind of advantage which we have had over many other countries in point of morals — I am not sure that we are not losing it — has consisted in greater tenderness of conscience. In this we have had on the whole a real superiority, though one principally negative; for conscience is with most men a power chiefly in the way of restraint — a power which acts rather in staying our hands from any great wickedness, than by the direction it gives to the general course of our desires and sentiments. One of the commonest types of character among us is that of a man all whose ambition is self-regarding; who has no higher purpose in life than to enrich or raise in the world himself and his family; who never dreams of making the good of his fellow-creatures or of his country an habitual object, further than giving away, annually or from time to time, certain sums in charity; but who has a conscience sincerely alive to whatever is generally considered wrong, and would scruple to use any very illegitimate means for attaining his self-interested objects. While it will often happen in other countries that men whose feelings and whose active energies point strongly in an unselfish direction, who have the love of their country, of human improvement, of human freedom, even of virtue, in great strength, and of whose thoughts and activity a large share is devoted to disinterested objects, will yet, in the pursuit of these or of any other objects that they strongly desire, permit themselves to do wrong things which the other man, though intrinsically, and taking the whole of his character, farther removed from what a human being ought to be, could not bring himself to commit. It is of no use to debate which of these two states of mind is the best, or rather the least bad. It is quite possible to cultivate the conscience and the sentiments too. Nothing hinders us from so training a man that he will not, even for a disinterested purpose, violate the moral law, and also feeding and encouraging those high feelings, on which we mainly rely for lifting men above low and sordid objects, and giving them a higher conception of what constitutes success in life. If we wish men to practise virtue, it is worth while trying to make them love virtue, and feel it an object in itself, and not a tax paid for leave to pursue other objects. It is worth training them to feel, not only actual wrong or actual meanness, but the absence of noble aims and endeavours, as not merely blameable but also degrading: to have a feeling of the miserable smallness of mere self in the face of this great universe, of the collective mass of our fellow creatures, in the face of past history and of the indefinite future — the poorness and insignificance of human life if it is to be all spent in making things comfortable for ourselves and our kin, and raising ourselves and them a step or two on the social ladder. Thus feeling, we learn to respect ourselves only so far as we feel capable of nobler objects: and if unfortunately those by whom we are surrounded do not share our aspirations, perhaps disapprove the conduct to which we are prompted by them — to sustain ourselves by the ideal sympathy of the great characters in history, or even in fiction, and by the contemplation of an idealised posterity: shall I add, of ideal perfection embodied in a Divine Being? Now, of this elevated tone of mind the great source of inspiration is poetry, and all literature so far as it is poetical and artistic. We may imbibe exalted feelings from Plato, or Demosthenes, or Tacitus, but it is in so far as those great men are not solely philosophers or orators or historians, but poets and artists. Nor is it only loftiness, only the heroic feelings, that are bred by poetic cultivation. Its power is as great in calming the soul as in elevating it — in fostering the milder emotions, as the more exalted. It brings home to us all those aspects of life which take hold of our nature on its unselfish side, and lead us to identify our joy and grief with the good or ill of the system of which we form a part; and all those solemn or pensive feelings, which, without having any direct application to conduct, incline us to take life seriously, and predispose us to the reception of anything which comes before us in the shape of duty. Who does not feel a better man after a course of Dante, or of Wordsworth, or, I will add, of Lucretius or the *Georgics*, or after brooding over Gray's *Elegy*, or Shelley's 'Hymn to Intellectual Beauty'? I have spoken of poetry, but all the other modes of art produce similar effects in their degree. The races and nations whose senses are naturally finer and their sensuous perceptions more exercised than ours, receive the same kind of impressions from painting and sculpture: and many of the more delicately organised among ourselves do the same. All the arts of expression tend to keep alive and in activity the feelings they express. Do you think that the great Italian painters would have filled the place they did in the European mind, would have been universally ranked among the greatest men of their time, if their productions had done nothing for it but to serve as the decoration of a public hall or a private *salon*? Their Nativities and Crucifixions, their glorious Madonnas and Saints, were to their susceptible Southern countrymen the great school not only of devotional, but of all the elevated and all the imaginative feelings. We colder Northerns may approach to a conception of this function of art when we listen to an oratorio of Handel, or give ourselves up to the emotions excited by a Gothic cathedral. Even apart from any specific emotional expression, the mere contemplation of beauty of a high order produces in no small degree this elevating effect on the character. The power of natural scenery addresses itself to the same region of human nature which corresponds to Art. There are few capable of feeling the sublimer order of natural beauty, such as your own Highlands and other mountain regions afford, who are not, at least temporarily, raised by it above the littlenesses of humanity, and made to feel the puerility of the petty objects which set men's interests at variance, contrasted with the nobler pleasures which all might share. To whatever avocations we may be called in life, let us never quash these susceptibilities within us, but carefully seek the opportunities of maintaining them in exercise. The more prosaic our ordinary duties, the more necessary it is to keep up the tone of our minds by frequent visits to that higher region of thought and feeling, in which every work seems dignified in proportion to the ends for which, and the spirit in which, it is done; where we learn, while eagerly seizing every opportunity of exercis-

ing higher faculties and performing higher duties, to regard all useful and honest work as a public function, which may be ennobled by
the mode of performing it—which has not properly any other nobility than what that gives—and which, if ever so humble, is never
mean but when it is meanly done, and when the motives from which
it is done are mean motives. There is, besides, a natural affinity
between goodness and the cultivation of the Beautiful, when it is real
cultivation, and not a mere unguided instinct. He who has learnt
what beauty is, if he be of a virtuous character, will desire to realise it
in his own life—will keep before himself a type of perfect beauty in
human character, to light his attempts at self-culture. There is a true
meaning in the saying of Goethe, though liable to be misunderstood
and perverted, that the Beautiful is greater than the Good; for it
includes the Good, and adds something to it: it is the Good made
perfect, and fitted with all the collateral perfections which make it a
finished and completed thing. Now, this sense of perfection, which
would make us demand from every creation of man the very utmost
that it ought to give, and render us intolerant of the smallest fault in
ourselves or in anything we do, is one of the results of Art cultivation. No other human productions come so near to perfection as
works of pure Art. In all other things, we are, and may reasonably be,
satisfied if the degree of excellence is as great as the object immediately in view seems to us to be worth: but in Art, the perfection is
itself the object. If I were to define Art, I should be inclined to call it,
the endeavour after perfection in execution. If we meet with even a
piece of mechanical work which bears the marks of being done in
this spirit—which is done as if the workman loved it, and tried to
make it as good as possible, though something less good would have
answered the purpose for which it was ostensibly made—we say
that he has worked like an artist. Art, when really cultivated, and not
merely practised empirically, maintains, what it first gave the conception of, an ideal Beauty, to be eternally aimed at, though surpass-
ing what can be actually attained; and by this idea it trains us never
to be completely satisfied with imperfection in what we ourselves do
and are: to idealise, as much as possible, every work we do, and most
of all, our own characters and lives.

  And now, having travelled with you over the whole range of the
materials and training which an University supplies as a preparation
for the higher uses of life, it is almost needless to add any exhortation
to you to profit by the gift. Now is your opportunity for gaining a
degree of insight into subjects larger and far more ennobling than the

minutiae of a business or a profession, and for acquiring a facility of using your minds on all that concerns the higher interests of man, which you will carry with you into the occupations of active life, and which will prevent even the short intervals of time which that may leave you, from being altogether lost for noble purposes. Having once conquered the first difficulties, the only ones of which the irksomeness surpasses the interest; having turned the point beyond which what was once a task becomes a pleasure; in even the busiest after-life, the higher powers of your mind will make progress imperceptibly, by the spontaneous exercise of your thoughts, and by the lessons you will know how to learn from daily experience. So, at least, it will be if in your early studies you have fixed your eyes upon the ultimate end from which those studies take their chief value — that of making you more effective combatants in the great fight which never ceases to rage between Good and Evil, and more equal to coping with the ever new problems which the changing course of human nature and human society present to be resolved. Aims like these commonly retain the footing which they have once established in the mind; and their presence in our thoughts keeps our higher faculties in exercise, and makes us consider the acquirements and powers which we store up at any time of our lives, as a mental capital, to be freely expended in helping forward any mode which presents itself of making mankind in any respect wiser or better, or placing any portion of human affairs on a more sensible and rational footing than its existing one. There is not one of us who may not qualify himself so to improve the average amount of opportunities, as to leave his fellow creatures some little the better for the use he has known how to make of his intellect. To make this little greater, let us strive to keep ourselves acquainted with the best thoughts that are brought forth by the original minds of the age; that we may know what movements stand most in need of our aid, and that, as far as depends on us, the good seed may not fall on a rock, and perish without reaching the soil in which it might have germinated and flourished. You are to be a part of the public who are to welcome, encourage, and help forward the future intellectual benefactors of humanity; and you are, if possible, to furnish your contingent to the number of those benefactors. Nor let any one be discouraged by what may seem, in moments of despondency, the lack of time and of opportunity. Those who know how to employ opportunities will often find that they can create them: and what we achieve depends less on the amount of time we possess, than on the use we make of our time. You and your like are the hope and resource of your country in the coming generation. All great things which that generation is destined to do, have to be done by some like you; several will assuredly be done by persons for whom society has done much less, to whom it has given far less preparation, than those whom I am now addressing. I do not attempt to instigate you by the prospect of direct rewards, either earthly or heavenly; the less we think about being rewarded in either way, the better for us. But there is one reward which will not fail you, and which may be called disinterested, because it is not a consequence, but is inherent in the very fact of deserving it; the deeper and more varied interest you will feel in life: which will give it tenfold its value, and a value which will last to the end. All merely personal objects grow less valuable as we advance in life: this not only endures but increases.

Epilogue

Our four authors — Augustine, Aquinas, Newman, and Mill — share fundamental concerns about the nature of understanding, teaching, and learning. There are marked differences in their approaches and in the social contexts to which they respond. Nonetheless, they share a common commitment to the inter-relatedness of teacher and pupil, and a concern for the selves of those engaged in the processes of understanding, teaching, and learning. Cultivation of the self, understood as an awakening of the powers of the student brought forth with the aid of the teacher, informs the models of human nature defended by all four authors. In Augustine, Aquinas, and Newman, there is the added dimension of a Divine teacher who provides human beings with the natures they possess and the orientation of those natures with respect to which this cultivation must be understood and evaluated. Mill, lacking this overt commitment to the Divine, also discerns a goal-seeking structure underlying human development, a progressive melioristic vision in which he displays unwavering faith.

In chapter 1, we provided a model for thinking about educational theory and practice which brings out much of the thematic unity among our authors. In particular, we stressed the presence of three types of knowing: know-that, know-how, and know-why. All of our authors are implicitly committed to this schema; and by it we hoped to provide a conceptual bridge by means of which those who reflect on educational issues might be able to identify aspects of their own experience that either confirm or disconfirm the theories advanced by our authors. The positive and negative examples of successful and unsuccessful understanding, teaching, and learning that we discussed in chapter 1 are crucial. It is one thing to get the facts right (know-that), another to acquire skills (know-how), and yet another to comprehend the purpose of both of these (know-why). The examples also address the specific norms that constitute good teaching and learning, thus illuminating the existential bases for understanding, self-actualisation, and self-transcendence, and how these might be thwarted.

Our authors are primarily concerned with know-why and, at least in the selections in this volume, do not enter into many of the specific questions that are the meat of much contemporary educational debate. To say that certain subjects belong within a curriculum is useful, but this does not yet determine the proper proportions and balance among those subjects, let alone determine the specific content within disciplines to be covered, nor indeed give guidance on how to adjust for the practical exigencies and material conditions affecting understanding, teaching, and learning. One pragmatic reason for the focus on the higher reaches of education by our authors is that it is at the tips of the branches of the educational tree that we see the greatest differentiation. We also gain a finer appreciation of what sort of trunk and roots are necessary for their support and from which they derive their unity. While much varies in education, key elements remain constant, not the least of which is the human subject and the need for establishing healthy and productive modes of relatedness between teacher, student, and the truths at which they aim.

The analyses of educational theory and practice advanced by our authors open up profound questions concerning the objectives of understanding, teaching, and learning. These questions need to be reformulated anew by each generation since their answers must be informed by the social and material conditions of education. Having engaged our four authors, the reader is in a better position to formulate and strive to answer a series of questions concerning the possibility of education, the nature of the teacher, the nature of the learner, and the processes involved in teaching and learning. There is also the question of what needs to be understood and which methods are most appropriate for its acquisition.

This inevitably leads us to a second series of questions involving more concrete dimensions of the educational project since the material conditions of contemporary life are in many ways different from those of our authors. Augustine's world was one in which Christianity was undergoing consolidation and was situated within a decaying polytheistic Roman culture. Aquinas' world was one in which the Christian norm was confronted with the learning of the Ancient and Medieval Near East. Newman's world embodied Christianity in conflict with itself, as Reformation institutions were re-appropriated and transformed for Catholic use. Mill's world was one in which secularism and science struggled to find a place within a broadly Christian culture.

We now live in a world that is increasingly secularised, globalised, and technologised. As a result we must inquire anew into the methods of education: What is to be taught and how should a curriculum be structured? What are the relationships among religion, reason, and education in various communities? What broad social dimensions of education and educational institutions need to be attended to as these play out in the selection of courses, methods, and objectives? What counts as a successfully educated individual? What counts as a successfully educated public?

Theoretical extrapolations to contemporary issues in education involve taking up further questions. Where do we see the insights of the classic authors in this volume adopted, developed, challenged, or rejected in contemporary educational theory and practice? Significant modern contributors to consult would certainly include John Dewey, Maria Montessori, Ivan Snook, Richard Peters, Paul Hirst, and Israel Scheffler. Indeed, our distinction of the three ways of knowing — know-that, know-how, and know-why — can be used to illuminate where specific thinkers place their emphasis as educators.[1]

Further questions arise because of the increasing levels of professionalisation and institutionalisation of education, teaching, and learning. This opens out issues related to setting qualifications for teachers, accrediting educational institutions, and issues of equity and access to education, including education for special needs. There are also meta-questions concerning the nature of the discipline of educational theory as it has evolved. For instance, how should we distinguish philosophy of education as a field and what

---

[1] Dewey is concerned with know-how, see for example *Experience and Education*, New York, Simon & Schuster, 1997. For debates centring on contested know-that, see *Concepts of Indoctrination*, ed. I. A. Snook, New York, Routledge, 2010. Many educational theorists are preoccupied with know-why. For instance, Montessori relies on assumptions concerning the student's natural desire for understanding; see E. M. Standing, *Maria Montessori: Her Life And Work*, New York, Plume, 1998. For contemporary discussions closer to the account of know-why and self-transformation in our four authors, see Hirst and Peters, *The Logic of Education*, London, Routledge, 1970. For discussion of the relationships among teacher and pupil, know-why, and the moral dimension of education, see the works of I. Scheffler, especially his *Reason and Teaching*, London, Routledge and Kegan Paul, 1973. For a critical discussion of Scheffler's thought, see *Reason and Education*, ed. H. Siegel, Dordrecht, Kluwer, 1997.

ought to be its defining features and central concerns? How can understanding, teaching, and learning operate in a pluralist society wherein basic values and even what counts as being reasonable are contested? What claims may civil society make on the content, methods, and practice of education? Given the trend towards evaluating teaching and learning according to standardised test criteria, is it possible to measure quality in teaching and learning? These questions are only some of the ones that need to be addressed. Augustine, Aquinas, Newman, and Mill have, we believe, provided us with an invaluable framework for further inquiry.

We should not expect to finish the debate on education, nor should we expect a complete account of understanding, teaching, and learning. But we now have an excellent place to start.

Bibliography

Adkins, A. W. H., '"Friendship" and "Self-Sufficiency" in Homer and Aristotle', *The Classical Quarterly* (New Series) 13, 1963.

Anderson, E., 'John Stuart Mill: Democracy as Sentimental Education', in Rorty 1998.

Anscombe, G. E. M., *Human Life, Action and Ethics: Essays by G.E.M. Anscombe*, ed. M. Geach and L. Gormally, Charlottesville, Imprint Academic, 2005.

Augustine, *De Magistro*, in *Patrologia Latina*, vol. 32, ed. J.P. Migne, Paris, 1845.

Augustine, *St. Augustine's Confessions*, trans. W. Watts, Cambridge, Harvard University Press, 1988.

Augustine, *De Genesi imperfecta*, in *On Genesis*, trans. E. Hill, ed. J. E. Rotelle, New York, New City Press, 2002.

Aquinas, *De Magistro*, in Mayer 1929.

Aquinas, Siger of Brabant, and St. Bonaventure, *On the Eternity of the World*, 2nd ed., trans. C. Vollert, L. H. Kendzierski, and P. M. Byrne, Milwaukee, Marquette University Press, 1984.

Aristotle, *The Complete Works of Aristotle, vol. 1 & 2*, ed. J. Barnes, Princeton, Bollingen Press, 1971.

Aristotle's Protrepticus, An Attempt at Reconstruction, I. Düring, Göteborg, Studia graeca et latina Gothoburgensia, 1961; trans. A. H. Chroust, South Bend, University of Notre Dame Press, 1964.

Arnold, M., *Culture and Anarchy*, New Haven, Yale University Press, 1994.

BeDuhn, J., *The Manichaen Body: In Discipline and Ritual*, Baltimore, The Johns Hopkins University Press, 2000.

Bloom, A., *The Closing of the American Mind*, New York, Simon & Schuster, 1987.

Brennan, R. E., *Thomistic Psychology: A Philosophic Analysis of the Nature of Man*, New York, The Macmillan Company, 1941.

Brock, S. L., *Action and Conduct: Thomas Aquinas and the Theory of Action*, Edinburgh, T&T Clark, 1998.

Brown, P., *Augustine of Hippo: A Biography*, Berkeley, University of California Press, 2000.

Bullough, E., 'Psychical Distance as a factor in Art and an Aesthetic Principle', *British Journal of Psychology*, 5, 1912.

Capaldi, N., *John Stuart Mill: A Biography*, Cambridge, Cambridge University Press, 2004.

Chidester, D., 'The Symbolism of Learning in St. Augustine', *The Harvard Theological Review* 76:1, 1983.

Cohen, R.W., 'Evidence to XVIII R.C. *Civil Service, the Employment of University Graduates in Business*', London, 1913.

Copleston, F. C., *Aquinas*, Harmondsworth, Penguin Books, 1955.

Davies, B. (ed.), *Thomas Aquinas: Contemporary Philosophical Perspectives*, Oxford, Oxford University Press, 2002.

Dawkins, R., *The God Delusion*, New York, Houghton Mifflin, 2006.

Derbyshire, D. C. and G. K. Pullum (eds), *Handbook of Amazonian Languages*, vol. 1, Berlin, Mouton de Gruyter, 1986.

Dewey, J., *Experience and Education*, New York, Simon & Schuster, 1997.

Epstein, S. A., *Wage Labor and Guilds in Medieval Europe*, Chapel Hill, University of North Carolina Press, 1991.

Everett, D., 'Piraha' in Derbyshire and Pullum 1986.

Fabro, C., *Participation et Causalité selon S. Tomas d'Aquin*, Louvain, Université Catholique de Louvain, 1961.

Finnis, J., *Aquinas: Moral, Political, and Legal Theory*, Oxford, Oxford University Press, 2004.

Frank, M. C. *et al.*, 'Number as a cognitive technology: Evidence from Pirahã language and cognition', *Cognition* 108, 2008.

Fuller, T. (ed.), *The Voice of Liberal Learning: Michael Oakeshott on Education*, New Haven, Yale University Press, 1989.

Gallagher, D. M. (ed.), *Thomas Aquinas and His Legacy*, Washington D.C., Catholic University of America Press, 1994.

Gilson, E., *The Christian Philosophy of St. Thomas Aquinas*, trans. L. K. Shook, South Bend, University of Notre Dame Press, 1994.

Guthrie, W. K. C., *A History of Greek Philosophy*, Vol. 5, Cambridge, Cambridge University Press, 1978.

Hadot, P., *Philosophy as a Way of Life: Spiritual Exercises from Socrates to Foucault*, ed. A.I. Davidson, trans. M. Chase, Oxford, Blackwell, 1995.

Hardin, G., 'The Tragedy of the Commons', *Science* 162:3859, 1968.

Harrison, S., 'Augustinian Learning', in Rorty 1998.

Hawking, S. and Mlodinow, L., *The Grand Design*, New York, Bantam Books, 2010.

Heilbroner, R. L., *The Worldly Philosophers*, New York, Simon and Schuster, 1961.

Hirst, P. H. and Peters, R. L., *The Logic of Education*, London, Routledge, 1970.

Honderich, T. (ed.), *The Oxford Companion to Philosophy*, Oxford, Oxford University Press, 1995.

Horsey, R., 'The Art of Chicken Sexing', University College London, *UCL Working Papers in Linguistics*, 14, 2002.

Huxley, T. H., *A Liberal Education; And Where To Find It*, Charleston, BiblioBazaar, 2006.

Katkov, G., 'The Pleasant and the Beautiful', *Proceedings of the Aristotelian Society*, XL, 1939-40.

Kenny, A., *Aquinas on Mind*, London, Routledge, 1994.

Ker, I., *John Henry Newman: A Biography*, Oxford, Oxford University Press, 2009.

Kerferd, G. B., *The Sophistic Movement*, Cambridge, Cambridge University Press, 1981.

Knowles, D., *The Evolution of Medieval Thought*, Hong Kong, Longman, 1962.

Kretzmann, N., and E. Stump (eds), *The Cambridge Companion to Aquinas*, Cambridge, Cambridge University Press, 1993.

MacIntyre, A., *The Tasks of Philosophy*, vol. 1, Cambridge, Cambridge University Press, 2006.

'Aquinas's Critique of Education: Against His Own Age, Against Ours,' in Rorty 1998.

Mahoney, E. P., 'Aquinas's Critique of Averroes' Doctrine of the Unity of the Intellect', in Gallagher 1994.

May, J. L., *Cardinal Newman*, New York, The Dial Press, 1930.

Mayer, M. H., *The Philosophy of Teaching of Saint Thomas Aquinas*, New York, Bruce Publishing Co., 1929.

Marrou, H. I., *A History of Education in Antiquity*, New York, Sheed and Ward, 1956.

Marshall, A., *Principles of Economics*, Amherst, Prometheus Press, 1997.

Matthews, G., *The Philosophy of Childhood*, Cambridge, Harvard University Press, 1996.

McInerny, R., *Aquinas Against the Averroists: On There Being Only One Intellect*, West Lafayette, Purdue University Press, 1993.

Mill, J. S., *Inaugural Address Delivered to the University of St Andrews 1867*, in *The Collected Works of John Stuart Mill*, vol. 21, ed. J. M. Robson, intro. S. Collini, Toronto, University of Toronto Press, 1984.

Mill, J. S., *Autobiography*, ed. J. M. Robson, London, Penguin Books, 1989.

Mill, J. S., *The Collected Works of John Stuart Mill*, vol. 1, ed. J. M. Robson and J. Stillinger, intro. Lord Robbins, Toronto, University of Toronto Press, 1981.

Mill, J. S., *System of Logic, Ratiocinative and Inductive*, Charleston, Nabu Press, 2010.

Mill, J. S., *On Liberty*, Buffalo, Prometheus Books, 1986.

Mill, J. S., *Utilitarianism*, Buffalo, Prometheus Books, 1987.

Mill, J. S., *Considerations on Representative Government*, Rockville, Serenity Publishers, 2008.

Mill, J. S., *The Subjection of Women*, Buffalo, Prometheus Books, 1986.

Mill, J. S., *Principles of Political Economy*, Amherst, Prometheus Books, 2004.

Monahan, W. B., *The Psychology of St. Thomas Aquinas*, Worcester, Trinity Press, 1935.

Newman, J. H., *The Idea of a University*, London, Longmans, Green, and Company, 1899.

Newman, J. H., *The Idea of a University*, ed. M. J. Svaglic, South Bend, University of Notre Dame Press, 1982.

Newman, J. H., *Historical Sketches*, London, Longmans, Green and Co., 1899, vol. iii.

Newman, J. H., *Apologia pro vita sua*, ed. I. Ker, London, Penguin Books, 1994.

Newman, J. H., *An Essay in Aid of a Grammar of Assent*, Notre Dame, University of Notre Dame Press, 1979.

Newman, J. H., *Tracts for the Times*, by J. H. Newman, J. Keble, J. B. Pusey, *et al.*, Charleston, Nabu Press, 2010.

Nozick, R., *Anarchy, State, and Utopia*, New York, Basic Books, 1974.

Nussbaum, M. C., *Not For Profit: Why Democracy Needs the Humanities*, Princeton, Princeton University Press, 2010.

Oakeshott, M., *Rationalism in Politics*, ed. T. Fuller, London, Liberty Fund, 1991.

Pasnau, R., *Thomas Aquinas on Human Nature*, Cambridge, Cambridge University Press, 2002.

Pearson, B. A., *Ancient Gnosticism: Traditions And Literature*, Minneapolis, Fortress Press, 2007.

Phillips, D. C., 'Philosophy of Education', *Stanford Encyclopedia of Philosophy* 2008, http://plato.stanford.edu/entries/education-philosophy/.

Plato, *Lysis Symposium Gorgias*, trans. W.R.M. Lamb, Loeb Classical Library, Cambridge, Harvard University Press, 1991.

Priest, G., 'To be and not to be — that is the answer. On Aristotle on the Law of Non-Contradiction.' *Philosophiegeschichte und Logische Analyse* 1, 1998.

Quine, W. V. O., *Word and Object*, Cambridge, Harvard University Press, 1960.

Rashdall, H., *The Universities of Europe in the Middle Ages*, 3 vols., Oxford, Clarendon Press, 1895.

Rawson, E., *Cicero: A Portrait*, London, Duckworth, 2009.

Reeves, R., *John Stuart Mill: Victorian Firebrand*, London, Atlantic Books, 2008.

Rist, J. M., *Augustine: Ancient Thought Baptized*, Cambridge, Cambridge University Press, 2003.

Rorty, A. O. (ed.), *Philosophers on Education: Historical Perspectives*, London and New York, Routledge, 1998.

Sanderson, M., 'Vocational and Liberal Education: a historian's view', *European Journal of Education*, 28:2, 1993.

Scheffler, I., *Reason and Teaching*, London, Routledge and Kegan Paul, 1973.

Schumpeter, J. A., *History of Economic Analysis*, London, Allen & Unwin Ltd, 1954.

Sidgwick, H., 'The Theory of Classical Education', originally published in *Essays on a Liberal Education*, ed. F.W. Farrar, London, Macmillan, 1867.

Siegel, H. (ed.), *Reason and Education*, Dordrecht, Kluwer, 1997.

Smart, J. J. C. and Williams, B., *Utilitarianism: For and Against*, Cambridge, Cambridge University Press, 1973.

Snook, I. A. (ed.), *Concepts of Indoctrination*, New York, Routledge, 2010.

Standing, E. M., *Maria Montessori: Her Life And Work*, New York, Plume, 1998.

Stock, A., 'Chiastic Awareness and Education In Antiquity', *Biblical Theology Bulletin*, 14: 23, 1984.

Strauss, L., 'What is Liberal Education?', in *Liberalism Ancient and Modern*, Ithaca, Cornell University Press, 1968.

Stump, E., *Aquinas*, London, Routledge, 2005.

Torrell, J. P., *Saint Thomas Aquinas: Vol. 1: The Person and His Work*, trans. R. Royal, Washington D.C., Catholic University of America Press, 1996.

Ver Eecke, W. (ed.), *An Anthology Regarding Merit Goods: The Unfinished Ethical Revolution in Economic Theory*, Indiana, Purdue University Press, 2007.

Weisheipl, J., *Friar Thomas D'Aquino: His Life, Thought, and Works*, Oxford, Basil Blackwell, 1974.

Wippel, J. F., *Metaphysical Themes in Thomas Aquinas*, Washington D.C., Catholic University of America Press, 1984.

Index

Lycurgus: 173

Magnus, Albertus: 103, 108
Manichaeism: 47–50, 110
Mediaeval philosophy: 108–111, 122
Methodology of education: 8, 14, 16, 21, 23, 26–30, 36, 39, 108–109, 164, 174, 205, 220, 264–266. See also: Learning, experiential; Pedagogy
Mill, James: 156
Mill, John Stuart: 1–3, 11, 27, 36, 40–42, 44, 115n, 152, 156, 201–214, 263–266
　Education and background of: 201–203
　Habits of mind: 211
　On education as holistic: 205, 208–209, 219–220, 222
　On ethics and politics: 246–252
　On history and geography: 224
　On logic: 239–242
　On mathematics: 235–237
　On physiology: 242–244
　On psychology: 244–245
　On religion: 252–254
　On subjects to be taught in university: 209–214
　On the experimental sciences: 237–239
　On the function of the university: 216–218, 254–255
　On the importance of education in aesthetics: 255–260
　On the use of learning Greek and Latin: 220–221, 224, 226–233
　On the use of learning modern languages: 223–226
　On the use of scientific instruction: 233–235
Montessori, Maria: 265
Morant, Robert: 154
Moses Maimonides: 107

Motivation: See under: Teacher, motivation of

Narratives: 9–10, 14, 33, 247
Nature: 8, 64, 87, 93, 114, 118, 128–129, 134–135, 138–139, 144, 146, 185, 207n, 210–211, 216–218, 223, 230, 236–237, 243
　As teacher: See under: Teacher
　Of humans: 8, 25, 41, 114, 116, 118n, 121, 146, 158–159, 162, 172–173, 177–181, 191, 203, 209–211, 215, 219, 222, 226, 229, 238, 243–244, 249, 251, 257–259, 261, 263
　Of students: 8, 14, 41, 56, 135, 162, 263–264
　Of subjects/disciplines: 17, 23, 30, 174, 236–237, 241, 264
　Of teachers: 10, 12, 14, 122, 149n, 263–264
Needs: 11–13, 33, 123, 218, 224, 235, 249, 264–265
　Actual: 11, 43
　Natural: 8, 168–169
　Perceived: 11, 41
Newman: 1–3, 11, 27–28, 36, 40–42, 44, 151–164, 203–205, 209–210, 213, 263–266
　Education and political background: 151–154
　Liberal education and theology: 153–157, 162–163
　On knowledge as a whole: 165–166, 190–198 *passim*
　On knowledge as acquisition: 183–189, 191, 193
　On liberal education: 153–164. See also: Education, liberal
　On philosophical habits: 158, 160–161, 167
　On philosophical knowledge as its own end: 167–170, 173, 175
　The Idea of a University text: 3, 151n, 152, 155–156, 162–163, 165–199